The Least
of These

The Least of These

Race, Law, and Religion in American Culture

Anthony E. Cook

Routledge
Taylor & Francis Group

NEW YORK AND LONDON

Published in 1997 by
Routledge
Taylor & Francis Group
711 Third Avenue
New York, NY 10017

Published in Great Britain by
Routledge
Taylor & Francis Group
2 Park Sqaure
Milton Park, Abingdon
Oxon OX14 4RN

Routledge is an imprint of the Taylor & Francis Group, an informa business

Copyright © 1997 by Routledge, Inc.

Library of Congress Cataloging-in-Publication Data

Cook, Anthony E., 1960–.
The least of these: race, law, and religion in American culture /
Anthony E. Cook
    p.   cm.
Includes bibliographical references and index.
ISBN 0-415-91646-1 — ISBN 0-415-91647-X (pbk.)
1. Christianity and politics—United States—History—20th century.
2. Liberalism—United States—Philosophy—History—20th century.
3. King, Martin Luther, Jr., 1929–1968. 4. Dewey, John, 1859–1952.
I. Title.
BR115.P7C646   1996
320.51'3'0973—dc20   96-48799
                                                             CIP

Dedicated
to my mother,
For a love that touches me yet,
from heaven

Contents

Introduction

We live in perilous times. The progressive liberal vision has suffered a premature death in American history. Conservative detractors have successfully linked this vision to the problems of big government and the bureaucratic welfare state: to be a progressive liberal is to be a defender of a governmental culture that has grown fat and inefficient, and has become a direct or indirect promoter of cultural decay, political apathy and economic decline. These conservative detractors have sold a significant segment of the American public on this depiction of progressive politics, and, unfortunately, too many traditional liberals have accepted the portrayal as true and thereby they abide, if not promote, conservative solutions.

This book argues for the revival of a progressive vision of American politics based on a different understanding of one of the fundamental tenets of progressive liberalism—that a justly ordered society must protect the interests of and promote opportunities for the least advantaged of its population. The different understanding explored in this work contends that the spiritual foundation of this progressive liberal tenet must be rediscovered and elaborated to fit our times. That spiritual foundation consists of the belief that a Social Compassion for the least advantaged is a window of opportunity for our own spiritual and social development, an opportunity to understand ourselves and others more fully than we do. By cultivating this compassion for others, through the social institutions we construct to order our shared existence, we see more clearly our interdependence, the bonds of humanity on which we might build a common destiny that embraces the highest ideals of a multicultural and multiracial democracy. The commitment to distributive justice, so long a part of the progressive vision, has withered in the heat of a reactionary campaign designed to destroy the slow but noble strides toward democracy. Caricatured as a debased instance of interest-group politics devised to rob a wealthy Peter to pay a less wealthy Paul, the progressive vision has fallen from grace, stripped of its angelic nobility and made to appear as evil incarnate.

My hypothesis is that, having failed to develop a *spiritual* understanding of this progressive liberal tenet and a discourse to communicate its spiritual implications for law and policy, progressive liberals unwittingly created a spiritual void eventually filled by reactionary forces that challenged and reversed progressive gains. Progressives allowed the secular project of institutional transformation to be divorced from any moral obligation and spiritual aspiration, divorced, that is, from a normative vision that might inspire all to realize their highest collective potential. In so doing, conservatives seized the moral high ground as justification for policies that undermined the egalitarian struggles of the last half-century.

The premature death of the progressive liberal vision is attributable, then, to two factors. First, there has been a reluctance, if not a refusal, on the part of progressives to understand law and policy as attempts to reflect in human relations the higher spiritual principles of an aspirational community. Second, conservatives initiated a bold, albeit divisive, strategy designed conceptually, rhetorically and politically to speak to the fears and hopes of a segment of those disaffected by the political, economic and cultural changes taking place in post–World War II America.

Unlike the progressive liberal community in the post–civil rights era, elite conservatives constructed a community and nurtured a sense of belonging among those whose world was threatened by the civil rights, antiwar, poverty, feminist and youth movements that shook America to its core. Threatened even more by the economic transformations of the seventies and eighties that daily fashioned a world neither made nor controlled by them, the rank and file of the emerging religious right listened intently for a comforting voice that spoke to their spiritual needs, as well as to their material interests, and that offered them a psychological refuge from the egalitarian storms sweeping the land.

It is important to understand the confluence of forces that led to this premature death of the progressive vision, the developments that made the reactionary response to the post–World War II progressive agenda so effective. Just as economic, demographic and social transformations created the possibilities for a progressive liberal vision of American democracy, these same transformations created the conditions for the conservative challenge to that vision.

This should come as no surprise. In many ways American history is a series of tumultuous socioeconomic transitions that play themselves out in culturopolitical contexts. These transitions have fostered different understandings of what it means and might mean to be American. For instance, the period from 1850 to the present encompasses transitions from slavery to freedom, from rural to urban to now largely suburban existence, and from agrarian to industrial to now information- and technology-driven economies. These transitions prompted profound demographic, social and psychological changes among the American citizenry that have resulted in perennial reconceptualizations of American identity and politics.

The transition from a slave, rural and agrarian society to a free, urban and industrial one required a strong federal government to preserve the union, end slavery, protect federal rights, prohibit and mitigate industrial abuse and ameliorate the precarious conditions of an increasing class of urban dwellers cut off from agricultural subsistence. From Abraham Lincoln's Emancipation Proclamation of 1863 to Lyndon B. Johnson's Great Society a century later, progressives tried to give birth to a new conception of community, one that would actively promote and realize an egalitarian vision of American Democracy.

This vision sought to extend the promise of equality and opportunity to slaves and their descendants, immigrant workers and their children, the poor and their families and other groups vying for their place in the American dream. The post–Civil War Reconstruction, the turn-of-the-century Progressive Era, the 1930s' New Deal, the post–*Brown* Second Reconstruction and the antipoverty Great Society programs of the late sixties all represented attempts by progressives to use government to better the condition of the most marginal and vulnerable segments of the American population, those most harmed by the transitions from a slave, rural and agrarian society.

To be sure, the progressive liberal vision has seldom benefitted from consistent pursuit. For as Robert L. Allen pointed out in his seminal text, *Reluctant Reformers*,[1] racism has clouded the vision of many progressives and cheated them of the promise of democracy. Furthermore, the progressive vision has never been without its ably financed and strategically stationed detractors. Indeed, a reactionary movement to contain and ultimately repeal progressive gains has quickly followed every reform era in this country. In this sense, the conservative temperament of our present time is no anomaly. Notwithstanding the historic and current opposition to the progressive vision, however, its mission to extend the promise of democracy to the least powerful, wealthy and accepted of the American population has been a noble and courageous struggle.

The transitions from an urban to a suburban and an industrial to a postindustrial/service oriented society have fomented changes no less momentous than those of earlier times. Yet it seems that here the progressive vision has faltered, if not fallen altogether. Unable to redefine its mission for a post–civil rights generation, progressive liberalism in the late sixties tried to mediate the conflict between reactionary forces attempting to contain and to reverse the limited redistributive gains of the post–Brown era and the more radical voices calling for a wholesale redistribution of economic and/or cultural capital. Recently, however, demographic and economic changes have forced many progressives off the fence, and the side chosen may not bode well for the progressive vision of democracy. In the face of declining political fortunes, some progressive liberals have apparently chosen to bolster their conservative credentials and compete for the same constituency conservative forces have targeted for a generation and successfully pursued for more than two decades.

These conservative forces have crafted an ingenious appeal to the suburbs and to a segment of the population that feels the pressure of a world made smaller and simultaneously more threatening by the corporate downsizing, restructuring and economic uncertainty fostered by technological advancements. The appeal is a simple one that plays on the fears and frustrations of a significant cross section of the voting public. The sometimes not-so-subtle message is this: government will protect you from the threats of urban life by getting tough on crime, building more jails, hiring more policemen and allowing you to purchase and carry firearms. Government will protect you from those who would take your wealth and opportunity and give it to those who are less qualified and deserving through affirmative action, entitlement programs, lax immigration enforcement and general government largesse.

Government will protect you from the promoters of cultural decay who threaten to corrupt your children by taking prayer out of the schools, promoting nonheterosexual understandings of marriage and relationships in law, art and literature, trampling the rights of the unborn and tolerating an entertainment industry that glorifies unbridled passion, sex and violence. Government will protect you from the threat of military and economic violence perpetrated by international hoodlums who would jeopardize vital American interests and ultimately rob you of your freedom.

As with all appeals tuned to exploit fears and frustrations, scapegoats are offered to appease sometimes-legitimate concerns. Blacks, immigrants, the poor, Hollywood, gays and lesbians, liberal intellectuals—and the list goes on—are all to blame for the woes of America and, thus, for the problems of the favored group. The focus on the blameworthiness of the scapegoat obfuscates the undesirability of some conservative solutions. Indeed, possible progressive solutions to legitimate concerns are seldom raised or considered, because scapegoating breeds cynicism and suspicion of these alternatives. By inculcating an us-against-them mentality, scapegoating creates a hostile and alienating world where vendetta and incivility are commonplace in both public and private life. The divisive message of us against them constructs barricades of dogmatic belief that end up imprisoning those who seek protection as well as those from whom protection is sought.

At its best, however, the progressive liberal vision has attempted to break down these rhetorically, socially and politically constructed barriers that separate us from them. Focusing on our inherent sameness and fundamental unity, liberalism has sought and sometimes been successful at transcending the limitations of race and clan to reflect in earthly relations a spiritual understanding of our humanity. In the context of governmental policy, a concern for the least of these is an institutional opportunity, meant to reflect rather than to supplant our ever present personal opportunity, to transcend the limits of status and station and, from that higher vantage point, to see the reality that we and the other are one.

Yet, even at its best, the desire to transcend identity to embrace a universal spiritual unity is problematic, for we are creatures who must struggle with the limitations of our finiteness. And if we are to grasp the possibilities of infinity at all, it must come through a right appreciation of the finite identities to which our spirits have given expression. At historical junctures such as the social gospel and civil rights movements discussed in this book, where progressive liberalism and religion have shared a common vision, this truth of grasping the infinite through an embrace of rather than an escape from the finite seems compelling. To acknowledge God expressed through the most wretched and despised of the earth is no longer to see them as appropriate objects of disdain and persecution. To gaze finally upon those cast out from our hearts and say of them, "there God is and there I am too," is to foment an internal revolution capable of toppling the mightiest of internal tyrannies and inaugurating a truly democratic spirit. And is not this, as John Dewey came to see, the only insurance against tyranny?

Unfortunately, liberalism has too often traveled a path of metaphysical abstraction that denies the most important dimensions of human identity in a postwar America—race, class, gender and religious belief. Rather than attempt to grasp the infinite through a sincere appreciation of how the divine expresses through finite identities, liberalism has too often ignored these finite identities and, in so doing, ignored the paths that lead to God, oneness and progressive democracy.

Critical scholarship is replete with race, class and gender critiques of liberalism. I want to focus attention on something seldom examined by the literature—the damage wrought by the absence of any religiospiritual discourse in contemporary liberal theory. I am convinced that such a discourse is vital to the resurrection of a progressive liberal vision in American politics and that such a discourse can provide new and healing approaches to some of the race, class and gender dilemmas we face today. First, what accounts for the absence, and second, what effect has the absence had on contemporary progressive politics?

Perhaps we can account for the absence by examining the very nature of liberalism. Perhaps liberalism is theoretically incompatible with a desire to undergird progressive liberal politics with religiospiritual meaning. That is, some might suggest that this desire is itself illiberal, a violation of the fundamental tenets of liberalism. This book argues, of course, that this is not necessarily the case, that much depends on the kind of religious and spiritual understanding one has in mind. But we must take the argument seriously, if for no other reason than this: at a very visceral level, many of us feel threatened by religious talk and practice. Religious conceptions of self and community are often very oppressive by liberal standards, shot through with guilt, repression and a blind adherence to dogma masquerading as faith. Most of us have had some negative experiences with close-minded religionists who are intensely intolerant of views different from their own. Something in the liberal human spirit recoils from any suggestion of limitation on human potential and freedom of thought.

This intuitive explanation for why contemporary liberal politics seems to shun religiospiritual understanding and discourse supplements more historical, philosophical and political explanations of the same phenomenon. Historically, the modern political theory that developed in England and Europe in the sixteenth through the eighteenth centuries was inspired by an ongoing conflict between religious faith and a scientific or instrumental reason that dared to question many of the former's most cherished beliefs. Science relied on empirical knowledge, knowledge attained through the five senses, which frequently conflicted with the teachings of the Church. Church officials found many of the suggestions and findings of science blasphemous and heretical, no matter how conditionally they were posed.

Copernican science was condemned for suggesting that the earth was not the center of the universe, and the Catholic Inquisition convicted Galileo in 1616 for scholarship suggesting support for the Copernican view. The historical conflict between the Church and the proponents of the new science whose works would later influence liberal thinkers such as Hobbes, Locke, Hume, Kant and Mill assured that the relationship between liberal thought and religion would always be in tension and permeated with mutual suspicion and even paranoia.

Philosophically, liberal political theory sought to break free from medieval conceptions of community that entangled the individual in a web of duties to Church and King. Even medieval government bowed in deference to the Church, since theology established the supremacy of popes over kings through its declaration that the former ruled by divine right and the latter by right of the people alone. The individual was seen, then, as an obedient servant to the will of God and God's earthly representatives. The question of what I as an individual am to do was not to be resolved by an appeal to conscience, personal belief, desire or self-interest. Rather, knowing to whom the duty was owed and the nature of the duty was decisive.

It took the Renaissance to rediscover and liberate the individual from the strictures of this subservience. Excavating the humanist strands of classical Greek and Roman culture, Renaissance figures suggested a humanist philosophy that used the individual and not the community as the relevant point of departure. Followed by a Reformation that was both influenced by Renaissance individualism and yet tried to constrain that individualism's most antireligious implications, the Renaissance fomented an intellectual tidal wave that would ultimately sweep Europe into the Modern Age.

Under premodern, medieval conceptions of community, the individual was made for community and not community for the individual. Indeed, the community preexisted the individual in that the highest good and fulfillment of the individual, the end to which the individual naturally inclined, was to be part of and to fulfill one's duties to the community. Modern liberal theory introduced the idea of the autonomous individual who preexists the community and whose natural rights communities are obligated to protect. Thus, under early liberal political theory like that of Hobbes and Locke, the community is made for the individual and not the individual for the community. Positive rights run from the community to the individual, protecting the individual's natural rights that preexist the community itself.

This autonomous individual is imbued with varying attributes, depending on the liberal theorist in question. But the one attribute common to all, from Descartes and Hobbes to Rawls, is that of rationality. In liberal theory, the individual is capable of and expected to follow reason. Being present in most men, reason leads to consensus and thus provides a bridge back from a potentially anarchist individualism to a rationally ordered community to which the individual owes limited duties.

The individual is perceived by liberal political theory as not only rational but rationally self-interested, that is, the individual is constituted to act in what it perceives to be its own self-interest. Under the empiricist school of liberal theory represented by Hume and Locke, self-interest provides the only true measure of good, for it can be empirically known by the individual subject through the senses. Under the rationalist school of liberal theory exemplified by Descartes and Kant, categories of thought are necessarily prior to what the senses experience. But the mind generates its own laws that are consistent with an enlightened self-interest that conditions our duties to others on what is also good for ourselves.

Religious belief systems are always in tension particularly with the empiricist school, at least in the public domain, because belief in the existence of God is a question of speculation and faith rather than empirical knowledge or fact. Religious belief systems are normally in tension with rationalist approaches because the rationalist's dependency on ideals constructed by the human mind is thought to be self-sufficient and not in need of a supernatural God that is independent of the human mind's capacity to think God into existence.

It is ironic that most of the early liberal thinkers did not see themselves as making religious belief irrelevant to the new paradigm of knowledge. Most provided elaborate defenses of religious belief as did Locke in *The Reasonableness of Christianity* and Descartes in his crucial dependence on God in the *Meditations* to account for why we can trust reason to give us certain knowledge. But their frameworks implied, leaving to subsequent theorists to make the case more forthrightly, that religious faith and spiritual understanding were "medieval" and thus outside the purview of rational deliberation. Thus liberal philosophy embodies in its presuppositions a quiet skepticism and even hostility toward religious belief and spiritual understanding. This philosophical skepticism and hostility have a political corollary.

Politically, liberal theory sought to direct religious belief and spiritual understanding out of the realm of public deliberation into the private realm of personal belief and civic activity. If kept in the private spheres of conscience, home and church, they might not offend modern sensibilities. The problem was that the fixed truths and immutable laws of religion were viewed as much too static for a dynamic liberal sensibility that sought to liberate the individual from the fixed preconceptions of self and community that characterized medieval thinking. This liberation from custom and tradition was essential, because transformed economies were bringing more and more strangers together into the new communities of cities and factories. Government and laws had to be rationally ordered by bureaucracies and the rule of law to mediate the clashing and changing self-interests of those who often did not share common backgrounds or values.

Liberal political theory was destined to see religion as too dogmatic about the substantive ends of government and law, believing it to mandate a particular conception of the good and virtuous life. According to liberal ideology, there was no common good around which society could be ordered in this way, as medieval society assumed. Rather, there was only a multiplicity of individual goods that society had to protect from mutual destruction and permit to be safely pursued and developed. Thus, for liberal political theory, rational government and law had to focus on freeing individuals to determine and pursue their own conceptions of the good, free from the constraints of a predetermined religious end.

To put it bluntly, liberalism has long been conceptually predisposed to see religion and spirituality as simultaneously silly, dangerous and ignorant. In reality, progressive liberals have not always acted on this predisposition, because politics often make for strange bedfellows. But events in post–World War II America have brought, I believe, the conceptual hostility of liberalism to religious and spiritual discourse more clearly into view.

Stephen Carter claims in his book, *The Culture of Disbelief*, that the big rift between liberals and religionists in the post–World War II era came on the heels of the 1973 Supreme Court decision in *Roe v. Wade*, which held that a woman's decision to have an abortion in the first and second trimesters of pregnancy was protected by her constitutional right to privacy under the Fourteenth Amendment. Carter writes of the era:

> Christian fundamentalists who had preached for decades that their followers should ignore the secular world, perhaps not even vote, looked around and decided that the secular world was on the verge of destroying the tight religious cocoons in which they had bound their communities.... And so the public rhetoric of religion, which from the time of the abolitionist movement through the era of the "social gospel" and well into the 1960s and early 1970s had largely been the property of liberalism, was all at once—and quite thunderously, too—the special province of people fighting for a cause that the left considered an affront. Since the 1970s, liberals have been shedding religious rhetoric like a useless second skin, while conservatives have been turning it to one issue after another, so that by the time of the 1992 Republican Convention, one had the eerie sense that the right was asserting ownership in God—but that the left had yielded its rights.[2]

Carter is correct to focus our attention on the impact of *Roe v. Wade.* It truly was an important factor in the mobilization of the Christian right. Perhaps it was even the proverbial straw that broke the camel's back. But the shift of which Carter writes actually has its roots in a more fundamental schism created by the conservative white backlash against the gains of the civil rights era and the concomitant splintering of the civil rights coalition in the mid-1960s. I will argue that white Southern fundamentalists and political conservatives around the country needed an acceptable political conduit through which to vent their anger and frustration in the wake of hostilities engendered by the civil rights movement.

That political conduit was not sufficiently in place to elect Barry Goldwater in 1964. It was building momentum by the time Richard Nixon won the White House in 1968 with what his advisors called the Southern Strategy. The conservative backlash reached its height of political organization when Ronald Reagan was elected in 1980 and when the political mouthpiece of the Christian right, the Moral Majority, challenged and defeated a long list of senators, congressmen and state officials in 1984. *Roe v. Wade* was a mere rallying point in this wave of counterrevolutionary resistance, a refueling station on the new conservative coalition's march to power.

The political conduit through which an alienated and disenchanted electorate expressed its frustrations with the racial politics of the post–Brown era was the handiwork of a skillful Republican Party that brought together political and religious conservatives in the South and, ultimately, throughout the country. This is a crucial point because if the rise of the religious right to power is rooted in the splintering of the old civil rights coalition and the conservative white backlash to the movement's achievements, any rapprochement between progressive liberalism and religion will have to take this history of racial politics into account. The implications are threefold for the future direction of progressive liberal politics in America.

First, progressives must seek to understand and reshape the conceptual limits of a liberalism too often hostile to religious and spiritual understandings of community. The historical, philosophical and political dimensions of this hostility discussed above must be understood and reinterpreted to allow for the development of a progressive liberal spirituality that avoids the problems associated with the dogmatic and divisive uses of religion that have been so popular through the ages.

Second, progressives must develop a new mode of discourse. They must find a way of communicating their conception of community in a way that connects with the human struggle to give meaning and purpose to life. They must find a way of connecting with that spiritual understanding that comes when we sometimes see through the alienation of our separate selves and glimpse the oneness of all creation. That is, progressives are in need of a new religious discourse, a democratic spirituality that freely talks about God or a power greater than ourselves, but in a way that allows the Christian, Jew, Muslim and humanist, the fundamentalist, liberal and progressive to see their potential in the projected vision. Only through such a discourse can the progressive liberal vision of a community of equals take root in a soil exhausted by the political, economic and cultural transformations of the past forty years.

Finally, progressive liberals must develop a new political strategy that directly challenges the political right's subtle and sometimes overt use of race to forge a community maintained by fear and hostility. The Willie Horton ads used by the Bush campaign, the anti-affirmative-action ads used by the Jesse Helms campaign and the Reagan administration's portrayal of welfare fraud, drugs and crime as primarily African-American problems are all clear examples of how conservatives have played the race card to garner support from segments of a fearful and frustrated white community. Progressive liberals must challenge the racial politics so common to our nation's history and resist the temptation to engage in the same.

This book explores how progressive liberal politics might be resurrected from its premature death by correcting these three problems of conceptual limits, mode of discourse and political strategies. Part I examines the work of an American progressive philosopher, John Dewey, as an illustration of the American progressive liberal's uneasiness with religious discourse. Dewey is a particularly interesting figure to examine because his work struggles mightily with the problem this book addresses—the relationship between a progressive politics on the one hand and religion on the other. Dewey ends up rejecting, for understandable reasons, a role for traditional religion in progressive liberal philosophy and politics. He offers instead a thoroughly secular spirituality he calls "a Common Faith".

There is much that contemporary progressives can learn from Dewey, a progressive philosopher struggling with the good and bad of a belief system like Christianity that both debilitated and inspired, limited and freed, its followers. His project was to expunge the most undesirable elements of religious commitment and export the most desirable qualities into his new, secular, Common Faith, a faith intended to tap the infinite potential of humans to create a truly democratic society. In his emphasis on the infinite potential of the human being to self-create, Dewey expanded the conceptual limits of traditional liberalism. The expansion of those limits should have suggested to him a different understanding of the traditional religion he critiqued. He apparently failed to see the connection. But had he seen it, his secular Common Faith could have found common ground with some of the progressive variants of Christianity being developed during his time. These progressive variants could have provided the substantive and not just process orientation so badly needed in his theory to assure that a commitment to unfettered human freedom and democracy did not end up exploiting the weak and oppressed.

Dewey's efforts at constructing a secular spirituality were unsuccessful, then, precisely because he rejected too much of the substance or content of the traditional religious faith he found at once so attractive and yet so dangerous. Progressive theologians and preachers were refashioning the vision of community reflected in traditional religion in much the same way as he was refashioning liberalism. The Social Gospel of Walter Rauschenbusch, which was later expanded by Martin Luther King, Jr., is an example of how progressive theologians were modernizing the Christian message at the turn of the century. An appreciation of the substance of this revised Christian faith could have provided a valuable link between progressive liberal politics and progressive liberal religion if Dewey had understood the powerful implications entailed by his expansion of the conceptual limits of liberalism.

His failure to make this connection profoundly impacted the development of law in the early twentieth century. American legal realism was deeply influenced by American pragmatism and the expansion of liberalism seen in Dewey's work. Consequently, there was too little reflection, in realism's glorification of majoritarian democracy, on the need to elaborate a normative vision of community that would assure the protection of the least advantaged in society. Lacking any substantive vision of community toward which to orient the law, American legal realism opened the door for a conservative jurisprudence of neutral principles as that substantive vision. This quest for neutral principles of adjudication eventually produced a jurisprudence of color blindness that became the centerpiece of a judicial counterrevolution against the progressive gains of the fifties and sixties.

Part II explores how Dewey and, by implication, American legal realism might have avoided the conceptual tension between liberalism and religion. This part examines both the works of Walter Rauschenbusch and Martin Luther King, Jr. to assess the possibilities of a substantive, progressive, liberal spirituality and faith. These progressive figures were proponents of a Social Gospel whose task it was to communicate religious and spiritual understandings to a secular world. Traditional theological categories such as sin, the Kingdom of God, love and salvation were reinterpreted to bridge the gap between personal faith and social ill. The substantive religious and spiritual principle of love for the least of these was communicated to both religionist and humanist in a way that put each in harmony with the other. If progressive liberals today could develop a similar way of communicating a progressive vision of community, alternatives to a conservative reactionary agenda might be found.

Finally, Part III speculates about how this progressive liberal discourse based on love for the least of these might answer some of the most troubling questions associated with the political, economic and cultural transitions of the post–civil rights era. But as I have suggested from the outset, these are problems for which progressive liberals have, on the whole, found no solutions. This is attributable, in substantial part, to the failure of progressive liberals to admit and confront the use of racial politics in America. This politics of race has fueled a conservative backlash against the strides of the fifties and sixties, strides that have benefitted a vast cross section of the American public for whom the egalitarian promises of democracy have been increasingly fulfilled.

The progressive vision faltered and fell shamefully silent because progressive liberals did not have a progressive religiospiritual vision to offset the crude and divisive use of race, law and religion to forge repressive communities based on fear and frustration rather than love and liberation. It is now time for progressives to reclaim the high road by developing, articulating and implementing a profoundly spiritual vision of a Beloved Community where commitment to the least of these reflects a deeper understanding of our spiritual oneness and spiritual movement towards democracy and justice for all.

Part I

The Quest for a
Common Faith in
American Progressive
Liberalism

Introduction

I suggested in the introduction to this book that traditional liberalism might have an inherent bias against the religiospiritual discourse that, I argue, is necessary to the revival of a progressive liberal vision of American politics. I want to examine this claim more fully by looking at two political and legal philosophies that are progressive variants of American liberalism—American Pragmatism and American Legal Realism. These progressive variants of American liberalism represent, in many ways, the American civil religion. Thus it is important to understand what position they adopt toward religion and why they adopt it. We will then be in a better position to assess the problems engendered by such an understanding of religion and to determine whether this is the only or most desirable position for progressive liberals to hold.

I realize that neither of these traditions is monolithic. The pragmatisms of Charles Sanders Pierce, William James and John Dewey are quite different in many respects. Similarly, the legal realisms of Oliver Wendell Holmes, Jerome Frank and Karl Llewellyn vary significantly on certain points. My discussion of legal realism is admittedly general, but I believe it accurately reflects a problem common to all of the major writers of this tradition. As to pragmatism, there is one central reason why John Dewey's brand of pragmatism is particularly relevant to my project.

I am primarily interested in the compatibility of religion and progressive liberal politics in America. For Dewey, more than Pierce or James, pragmatism was a way of fostering more vibrant and democratic political communities. In Dewey's hands, pragmatism was more a cultural and political intervention, a method of inquiry and mode of communication facilitating the realization of a democratic community's political potential.

Thus, by examining how Dewey's brand of progressive liberalism perceives and interacts with religious beliefs and institutions, we might gain some insight into why the tension between progressive forms of liberalism and religion exists. Put another way, Dewey was, for reasons I'll elaborate shortly, a harsher critic of traditional religion than either

Pierce or James, but yet was more politically progressive than both. Understanding the nature of his criticisms, then, could be the first step toward reconciling the differences between American progressive liberalism and religion.

Chapter 1 explores how and why Dewey saw traditonal religion as a threat to the progressive variant of liberalism he embraced and the particular culture of democracy he envisioned. The chapter then examines how Dewey's dependency on experimental logic, consequentialism and process oriented democracy remains dangerously indeterminate and lacks the normative guidance needed to protect the most vulnerable segments of the community.

Chapter 2 probes the relationship between Dewey's pragmatism and American legal realism. It suggests that a similar dependency on experimentalism, consequentialism and democracy in American legal realism failed to provide normative guidance toward substantive ends of law capable of protecting the most vulnerable and marginal segments of the American population. The failure to develop this normative vision opened the door for a conservative variant of liberalism commited to a jurisprudence of color blindness that fueled the reactionary backlash to the civil rights movement.

Part II will demonstrate how the problems associated with pragmatism's and realism's failure to elaborate a substantive egalitarian vision of American Democracy might have been avoided. It examines the works of one of Dewey's contemporaries, Walter Rauschenbusch, and of a subsequent espouser of the Social Gospel, Dr. Martin Luther King, Jr., in order to illustrate the paths not taken but still available to progressive liberals today. I want to explore whether Rauschenbusch's conception of the Social Gospel and King's understanding of the Beloved Community might have provided a plausible common ground for progressive liberalism and religion, thereby ameliorating the rifts and tensions between the two that we experience today.

Chapter 1

John Dewey and the Quest for a Common Faith

There is a conceit fostered by perversion of religion which assimilates the universe to our personal desires; but there is also a conceit of carrying the load of the universe from which religion liberates us. Within the flickering inconsequential acts of separate selves dwells a sense of the whole which claims and dignifies them. In its presence we put off mortality and live in the universal. The life of the community in which we live and have our being is the fit symbol of this relationship. The acts in which we express our perception of the ties which bind us to others are its only rites and ceremonies.[1]

The above quotation best summarizes John Dewey's approach to religion. America needed a national religion, something capable of bringing people together with a common sense of purpose; but it was not to be a traditional and supernatural form of religion like Christianity or Judaism, rather, it was to be thoroughly secular and humanist in its orientation and ends. This religion would inspire individuals to see and act on the divine capacity of humans to self-create, to make and reshape their worlds. But Dewey was not always so skeptical of the traditional and transcendental religions he later rejected.

John Dewey was born in 1859 in Burlington, Vermont. The son of a pious mother, he was raised a liberal, evangelical Congregationalist. As late as his thirties, the Church played a significant role in his life, garnering much of his time and affection. Dewey grew impatient, however, with the seemingly irrelevant preoccupation of religion with the supernatural and the curse of a religious faith so heaven-minded that it retained no earthly good. In the face of unprecedented human suffering wrought by the massive dislocations of an ever expanding and urbanizing industrial America, Dewey directed his critical energies toward this world's pervasive ills, bringing with him a zeal common to religious devotion.

In 1886, Dewey, then a young professor at the University of Michigan, married Alice Chapman. She ultimately convinced him that "a religious attitude was indigenous in natural experience, and that theology and ecclesiastic institutions had benumbed rather than promoted it".[2] Over the next few years, Dewey would move from seeing the Church as "the highest product of the interest of man in man"[3] to a belief that the role of the Church was to universalize itself and, like the withering away of the state in Marxist theory, pass out of existence.

Thus, although Dewey was a critic of religion in its transcendental and otherworldly sense, he was greatly commited to what he called the "human abode of the religious function." Indeed, one could characterize both the substance and style of his work as a move toward "a Common Faith."[4] For Dewey, this was a secular religion grounded in lived experience, guided by the light of creative intelligence, and inspired by a Renaissance-like faith in the protean powers of man. This secular faith urged the converted to see the world through the eyes of the believer as no longer a hopelessly evil wasteland impervious to the transformative efforts of mere mortals but, rather, as a vast experimental laboratory where limitations are transformed and transcended by the powers of human imagination, creativity, intelligence and will.

Dewey believed that this experimentalism was the only suitable orientation for life in an America being reshaped by the Industrial Revolution and transformed daily by the discoveries of science, the advances of technology, urbanization, dislocation and increasing inequality. Any understanding of the world predicated on either natural or supernatural conceptions of immutable laws, timeless principles and changeless values was in stark contradiction to the apparent flux of temporal life. Thus Dewey fervently rejected the institutional trappings of ritual, liturgy and dogma that provided traditional religion with its static supernatural grounding.

Instead he sought to find in the everyday interactions of human beings the sacred and divine and to understand the God-like powers of man to create through thoughts, words and actions, a new beginning.

He sought to extrapolate from religion its evangelical zeal and its capacity to bind individuals spiritually and to use these in the purely human pursuit of ends illuminated by the light of creative intelligence.

These dimensions of traditional religion were sufficiently universal, he believed, to serve his Common Faith, while the supernatural aspects expunged by his unabashedly humanist and secular religion could lead only to internecine conflict and division. The function of traditional religion was to nurture a faith in ideals and to promote a discourse and experience of community sustaining those ideals.

Because those who have committed to traditional religion in thought, word and deed so fervently believe in the tenets of their faith, they bear witness to God's divine intervention in the affairs of men. Because they stand willing to take the leap of faith, they experience the ideal more profoundly than those who move by sight and not by faith alone. It is this kind of faith that Dewey calls for in his new gospel of the Common Faith, his revision of the Emersonian theodicy of unfettered self-creation.

Dewey felt compelled to elaborate an alternative to the faith of traditional religions because he believed they diminished human agency by nurturing the believer's abject dependency on supernatural intervention. He lamented the impoverishment of a secular faith that was distorted by the anachronistic commitment to religious faith: "Were men and women actuated throughout the length and breadth of human relations with the faith and ardor that have at times marked historic religions, the consequences would be incalculable."[5] Thus, Dewey wrote, "[t]he objection to supernaturalism is that it stands in the way of an effective realization of the sweep and depth of the implications of natural human relations. It stands in the way of using the means that are in our power to make radical changes in these relations."[6]

Just as Dewey saw supernatural religion as an impediment to the refashioning of social relations, he saw aspects of traditional liberalism in the same way. Thus one way of understanding Dewey's opposition to traditional religion is to understand his criticisms of those theories of liberal thought that attempted to project certain conceptions of the individual and community as universal truths to be placed beyond question and modification. As with traditional religion, these conceptions were simply too static for Dewey's dynamic pragmatism.

Dewey understood that the central political philosophers of Western liberalism attempted to justify certain forms of government and social order by reference to static conceptions of human nature. For him, this was a terrible mistake, for the approach of these thinkers was predicated on the belief that conclusions about how to order society flowed from theories about the essence of human nature.

For Dewey—and this is important to understand—human nature was not substantively or teleologically oriented toward any specific set of ends. This brand of liberalism was merely religion by another name. Human nature was ever-changing and dynamic, always in the process of becoming. This foreclosed the desirability of creating institutions impervious to change by founding them on static, unchanging conceptions of humanity. If humans are always in the process of becoming, engaged in the divine act of self-creation, the institutions they develop to facilitate interaction and community must also be thought of as malleable and capable of transformation.

Dewey believed that American culture had also traveled this disastrous course of embracing static conceptions of human nature, notwithstanding the rapid and dynamic changes that had characterized most of its young life, changes that belied the static conceptions on which it based many of its institutions and their practices. By fastening its attention to values that had long outlived their usefulness, American democracy disguised the experiential context of theory and limited the capacity of creative intelligence to respond to novel circumstances. American theorists and traditionalists had not learned from the mistakes of early liberal thinkers on this point.

Hobbes maintained, for instance, that human nature was acquisitive, attracted to wealth, fame and power. Life in a state of nature was intolerably precarious, nasty, brutish and short. In Hobbes's political philosophy, then, insecurity of life and possessions were in tension with a love of life and its acquisitive pursuits. This tension necessitated a social structure promoting the individual's fundamental inclination for self-preservation, security and the attainment of power, fame, and wealth.

Locke's view of human nature, although less brutal than Hobbes's view, nevertheless held that human nature was acquisitive. The individual fulfilled natural desires and inclinations through the appropriation of private property once held in common. In sharp contrast to Hobbes's view, life was basically pastoral and idyllic in this garden of Golden-Age acquisitors. Yet with the introduction of money into Locke's state of nature, events altered dramatically. Individuals could now accumulate property for investment purposes in excess of their own needs or abilities to cultivate without spoilage. They might also appropriate the property of another for their own purposes.

These new developments left many without the ability to appropriate property, a reality that created much frustration, given the individual's supposed human nature as an appropriator of private property. Ultimately, this frustration lead to those with property being threatened by those without property. In Locke's political philosophy, this necessitated a social structure to promote and protect the accumulation of private property. In this manner, Locke's scheme lifted private property to an inviolable individual right fully protected by the resources of collective power.

Immanuel Kant and John Stuart Mill identified autonomy and liberty as the defining features of human nature and similarly envisioned a society designed to protect against their infringement. In a synthesis of all the eighteenth- and nineteenth-century strands of essentialist liberal thought, American democracy proclaimed that all men are created equal and endowed by their Creator with certain inalienable rights, among them, life (Hobbes), liberty (Mill/Kant), and the pursuit of happiness (Locke) (an early draft of the Declaration of Independence read "pursuit of property").

Like supernatural religion, these static conceptions of human nature are no more than the product of idealizing human minds, the projection into the future of what individuals considered important at various moments in history. Such abstractions conceal the historical and cultural context that gave birth to such concepts as the power-seeking, property-appropriating, liberty-loving or freedom-fighting individual.

An examination of this context reveals the social forces that led many to believe that nature provided in abundance what, in reality, cultural forces had developed and exaggerated. By ignoring the historical and cultural context, philosophers mistook effects for causes and turned their attention to a different kind of heaven, one of universal abstractions of human nature based on the partially real and, consequently, Dewey implies, as unreal as the supernatural God of religion.

Such abstractions fetter individual freedom, if one understands freedom experientially rather than abstractly. Dewey pointed out:

[If] our American culture is largely a pecuniary culture, it is not because the original or innate structure of human nature tends of itself to obtaining pecuniary profit. It is rather that a certain complex culture stimulates, promotes and consolidates native tendencies so as to produce a certain pattern of desires and purposes.[7]

Dewey was concerned that static conceptions of human nature—such as the belief that humans desire to obtain pecuniary profit—diminish the willingness to think experientially, even about our conceptions of freedom.

Experiential understandings of the values that we accept so uncritically—such as freedom—reconnect the meaning of the value to a specific time and location. This linking opens up the possibility that we will understand how events, conditions and contingencies constructed the meaning of the value in the first place, and thus how, if those conditions have changed, why meaning should change as well.

Understanding freedom experientially, that is, as acquiring meaning within a specific cultural context, requires a dismissal of the philosophical isolation of the individual as the starting point of theories of community. Dewey wrote:

The idea that human nature is inherently and exclusively individual is itself a product of a cultural individualistic movement. The idea that mind and consciousness are intrinsically individual did not even occur to anyone for much the greater part of human history.[8]

Redressing the relationship between culture and human nature permits Dewey to argue for the primacy of the former and thereby to remove human nature as a limit to the possibilities of creative intelligence and democracy. Culture and human nature are interactive. Economic, political, artistic, legal and linguistic traditions and practices colonize and mold our native tendencies and capacities.

Yet our common faith in the power of intelligence, if we would but stand fast, could also shape these cultural structures and thereby promote the creation of a different conception of human nature, one that would perceive itself free to fulfill changing potentialities as warranted by the enhancement of knowledge. Dewey placed his trust, then, neither in a supernatural God nor in the many conceptions of social order deduced from liberal abstractions of human nature, but in a democratic culture in which life is guided by the experimental method and inspired by a commitment to a mutually reinforcing conception of individuality and community. He paints a picture of this New Jerusalem in some of the most eloquent words American philosophy has known:

> When we have used our thought to its utmost and have thrown into the moving unbalanced balance of things our puny strength, we know that though the universe slay us still we may trust, for our lot is one with whatever is good in existence. We know that such thought and effort is one condition of the coming into existence of the better. As far as we are concerned it is the only condition, for it alone is in our power.[9]

Dewey's language is moving, his aspirations laudable, but his faith ultimately misplaced. It is a "faith in the power of intelligence to imagine a future which is the projection of the desirable in the present, and to invent the instrumentalities of its realization."[10] For Dewey, this virtually untapped reservoir of human capacity is our salvation. Dewey represents, then, the culmination of the modern project, the Enlightenment's deification of the powers of man.

In Dewey, God and the secular analogues of Reason and Nature are dethroned, and the reign of a pragmatic and flexible critical intelligence is inaugurated. In Dewey, American pragmatism reaches its zenith, with everything following in its wake being mere imitation or explication. My primary contention is that Dewey failed to provide sufficient normative guidance for his conception of creative democracy. The absence of such normative guidance reduces deliberative and creative democracy to a dangerous majoritarianism, which can be quite oppressive of the least powerful groups involved in the democratic process.

Dewey's new gospel is intent on removing both religious and secular liberal limits to human potential, so that human capacity can develop to its fullest. What Dewey's gospel fails to appreciate is that such flourishing is not possible without a philosophy of purpose, a teleology that normatively orients us toward a Good that is greater than the process through which it is pursued. Without limits, without this substantive vision of what it is we should be pursuing, even an enlightened majoritarianism will go astray.

Dewey's Common Faith, his quest for an American civil religion, rested on three pillars. The first was a faith in the ability of the experimental method of inquiry to produce knowledge and truth. The second was a faith that a focus on the consequences of proposed action was sufficient to answer the normative questions arising from inquiry. The third was a faith that the context of American democracy, nurtured by the orientation of the Common Faith, would impose sufficient limits on and provide sufficient guidance for the inquiries of creative intelligence.

A. A Common Faith: The Limits of Experimental Inquiry

Dewey was enthralled by the experimentalism of the scientific method. We can attribute his attraction to the scientific method to his fascination with both the temperament and mode of inquiry it required. While Pierce was satisfied to contain scientific method within the traditions and purposes of science, thereby acknowledging the legitimacy of different modes of inquiry in other fields, Dewey sought to extend the scientific mode of inquiry into even cultural concerns. What was so compelling to Dewey about this way of understanding and intervening in the natural world?

First, it was widely held that science required a particular kind of person with particular sensibilities, one largely free from dogma and tradition, one open to new possibilities and capable of revising or rejecting prior beliefs if the evidence of controlled investigations so warranted. Unlike the dogmatic traditions of the Church, the experimental method revels in, rather than recoils from, doubt. Dewey saw doubt as the appropriate mood of a truly scientific mind. It was the seed of greater knowledge and understanding waiting to be cultivated by the tools of critical inquiry.

Dewey thought many disciplines, such as law and religion, maintained an uncritical allegiance to the past and a paralyzing belief in the inherent value of certain moral and legal rules. To him, such allegiances represented a deification of fixed essences dogmatically foreclosing critical inquiry and limiting our human power to revise, modify and transcend anachronistic rules, procedures and goals. The removal of such limits was intended to free individuals to explore the full possibilities of their powers of critical intelligence.

In essence, Dewey believed experimentalism would end the debilitating practice of assessing what is of value in the present by virtue of what was of value in the past. By prompting a critical engagement with the past, the experimental method would question our "[r]eliance upon precedent, upon institutions created in the past, especially in law, upon rules of morals that have come to us through unexamined customs, upon uncriticized tradition."[11] In all fairness, Dewey does not purport to "get away from enjoyments experienced in the past and from recall of them, but from the notion that they are the arbiters of things to be further enjoyed."[12]

Second, the experimental method of science is an empirically based critical inquiry into the relations and connections of physical phenomena. It asks one to assess the conditions and consequences of a thing's coming into existence, its maintenance and demise. Thus it is a method in which the process of inquiry is more important than the outcome of that inquiry.

Dewey contended that experimentalism would challenge our faith in rigidly fixed standards, principles and norms. All such abstractions would be recognized as "hypotheses" and "treated as intellectual instruments to be tested and confirmed—and altered—through consequences effected by acting upon them."[13] This would have the favorable effect of causing them to "lose all pretense of finality—the ulterior source of dogmatism."[14]

Dewey's contention challenges the notion that traditional values hold a special claim on truth. The truth that values possess is instrumental rather than transcendent, functional rather than ultimate. We can ascertain truth only within a concrete context that establishes the conditions for its actualization and the consequences of our allegiance. Dewey wrote:

> If one stops to consider the matter, is there not something strange in the fact that men should consider loyalty to "laws," principles, standards, ideals to be an inherent virtue, accounted unto them for righteousness? It

is as if they were making up for some secret sense of weakness by rigidity and intensity of insistent attachment. A moral law, like a law in physics, is not something to swear by and stick to at all hazards; it is a formula of the way to respond when specified conditions present themselves. Its soundness and pertinence are tested by what happens when it is acted upon. Its claim or authority rests finally upon the imperativeness of the situation that has to be dealt with, not upon its own intrinsic nature—as any tool achieves dignity in the measure of needs served by it.[15]

This process of critical inquiry, to which even the most traditional of values are to be subjected, requires the articulation and continuous refining of a problem to be solved, the positing of hypotheses as to what intervention will best solve the problem, the development of a controlled and experimental intervention to test the chosen hypothesis, the subsequent gathering and evaluation of evidence, and the tentative offering of conclusions based on the preceding inquiries.

For Dewey, anything surviving this process had warranted assertability and thus could be said to be true in this limited sense. Thus Dewey answered the epistemological question of how one can know truth by sidestepping the great philosophical debates of his and earlier times. The question for epistemology was whether we, as knowing subjects, could ever really know the objects of our inquiry and thereby know the truth about anything.

Philosophy proposed various answers to this question. Dewey was satisfied with none. Some, inspired by Plato, said we could know, through the mind's contemplation of ideal forms, the truth about our objects of inquiry. Others, drawing from Aristotle, said the path to truth and knowledge was the empirical study (knowledge acquired through five-sensory perception) of particular forms.

In the first case, the ideas of the mind were antecedent to the objects of the world we thought were real but which were really a distortion of a more transcendent reality. In the second case, the objects of the "real world" were "truly real" and not illusions. Knowledge was attained by turning not inward but outward toward their study and evaluation. In the first, our minds constructed the world of inquiry. In the second, the ideas of the mind were constructed by our engagement with the world of particulars.

In essence, Western philosophy has been but variations on these two traditions inaugurated by Plato and Aristotle and predating them in other cultures around the world. Skeptics of various stripes argued that both idealistic and empirical modes of knowing were flawed, that genuine doubt persisted, even if philosophers refused to acknowledge it.

As to the conflict between rational and empirical approaches, Dewey is clearly in the Aristotelian camp in most respects. He rejects, however, at least initially, any Aristotelian-like teleology. That is, the particulars that are the objects of critical inquiry do not yield a natural order that compels our allegiance. Dewey is not a realist in this sense. Rather, we remain free to value the orders and findings of our studies according to whatever other set of values we deem important.

Is doubt eliminated by this neo-Aristotelian approach? Dewey would be the first to deny it. We never know if we truly have it right. That is because there is no "having it right to have." We determine what it means to "have it right." Knowledge of "having it right" is neither something that exists totally outside of us, embedded in the object to be known through our study and evaluation, nor totally within us, embedded in the ideas we carry in our minds or souls. Rather, it is produced by the interaction of the two.

This interaction is dynamic rather than static. Since our ideas and their objects are changing, knowledge and thus truth are also changing. They resist permanent fixation, static categorization and universal application. As Dewey observed: "There is no knowledge self-guaranteed to be infallible, since all knowledge is the product of special acts of inquiry."[16]

If knowledge is something that is produced rather than something that is discovered, our emphasis must turn to the processes of production, the modes of inquiry that create knowledge and truth. It is these processes that create *truth* but not *Truth*. It is truth because it was produced by the process of critical inquiry. But it is our truth, for such a time as the contextualities, contingencies and conditions that constitute its existence persist.

The epistemic doubt of philosophy is a fiction generated by another fiction, the detached spectator theory of philosophy, the separation of the knower from the known, the subject from its object. Only when we entertain the possibility of such a separation does the epistemological question of whether the knowing subject can know the known object make sense. Only then does the question of epistemic doubt become such a crucial issue.

Dewey was able to answer the question about epistemic doubt, because he rejected traditional philosophy's formal separation of the subject and object. We are neither totally separated nor totally one with that which we seek to know. We are in a state of dynamic interdependency with it. While this interdependency creates doubt, it is not the epistemic doubt over which philosophy obsesses. It is the doubt that attends any commitment to the dynamic process of becoming.

Doubt, then, is welcomed by Dewey. It does not occasion the passivity accepted by those who see no possibility of philosophical certainty. Nor does it justify the dogmatic arrogance embraced by those who, through rationalist or empiricist approaches, find abundant certainty. Rather, it is an opportunity to exercise the Common Faith of Dewey's new civil religion. Let me be clear about where uncertainty and doubt enter Dewey's system in order to be clearer about the nature of the leap of faith he would have us make.

The problem begins with the transplanting of a mode of inquiry more appropriate for investigating relations governed by fixed laws of nature into a domain of inquiry governed by metaphysical questions about values, purpose and being. Even from an empiricist's perspective, these are questions that are subject to the difficult-to-predict variation in human dynamics and social processes. As I stated earlier, the scientific method of inquiry through which knowledge is produced consists of the identification of a problem, the development of a hypothesis to solve the problem, the testing of that hypothesis through controlled experimentation, and the drawing of conclusions warranted by the protocols and tests of experimentation.

It is easy to see the relevance of this mode of inquiry for certain problems of human existence. For instance, the benefits of the method are readily apparent when testing the hypothesis that if subjected to a certain temperature, liquid substances should alter their state and become gas. That is, that a certain intervention in the natural world (increasing temperature) will produce a certain result in the natural world (vaporization). When a hypothesis has been validated through countless tests under varying conditions, it becomes the basis for a law of nature such as the law of thermodynamics.

But extrapolating laws from human interaction with the purpose of anticipating the probable consequences of certain interventions into the social world is complicated precisely because human personality and relations are dynamic, ever-changing, incapable of exact measurement. That a certain intervention in time period 1 produced certain consequences is no indication that a similar intervention will result in the same consequences in time period 2. Indeed, the process of measurement varies the thing measured, even while measuring. That is, our observational perspective (background, experiences, class, identity) and the nature and quality of our evaluative tools will alter our evaluation of the consequences of interventions we seek to compare. Through its own theories of indeterminacy, modern physics has conceded no less for its field of inquiry.

Yet it is precisely this evaluation of the probable consequences of hypothesized interventions that Dewey's experimental theory requires. I want to suggest that Dewey's consequentialism does not provide enough normative guidance on what kind of community we should desire, and it is precisely this lapse that is exploited in subsequent elaborations of the pragmatist approach to law. However, progressive theologians developed a conception of democracy that provided normative guidance through the process of critical inquiry. That normative guidance consisted of a substantive understanding of democracy intended to protect the least advantaged of the society.

B. A Common Faith: The Limits of Consequentialist Analysis

Pragmatism, thus, presents itself as an extension of historical empiricism, but with this fundamental difference, that it does not insist upon antecedent phenomena but upon consequent phenomena; not upon the precedents but upon the possibilities of action. And this change in point of view is almost revolutionary in its consequences. An empiricism which is content with repeating facts already past has no place for possibility and for liberty. . . .

> Pragmatism thus has a metaphysical implication. The doctrine of the value of consequences leads us to take the future into consideration. And this taking into consideration of the future takes us to the conception of a universe whose evolution is not finished, of a universe which is still, in James' term "in the making," "in the process of becoming," of a universe up to a certain point still plastic.[17]

I want to explore more closely the metaphysical implication of pragmatism, its consequentialism, acknowledged by Dewey in the above quotation. I contend that consequentialism does not solve the problem of insufficient normative guidance created by his commitment to a scientific mode of experimental inquiry.

Consider the normative questions posed by the remedies phase of the famous 1954 desegregation decision of *Brown v. Board of Education of Topeka*[18] and the indeterminacy that would permeate a Deweyan approach to the questions raised by that case. The first step under Dewey's experimentalism is to identify the problem to be solved. This is a crucial first step, because how one defines the problem will often determine what interventions are considered and ultimately chosen to solve the problem.

For instance, was the problem of legally sanctioned racial segregation in public schools merely that government sanctioned and enforced segregation on the basis of race? If so, a remedy that prohibited government from segregating students on the basis of race but permitted racial segregation of students to continue when achieved on some other, race-neutral basis, such as residential zoning would be a plausible intervention.

Yet, if the problem was that government-sanctioned segregation resulted in black students being deprived of certain intangible benefits, such as self-esteem, that only direct contact with white students could provide, a purely *de jure* desegregation that permitted *de facto* segregation to continue would not be sufficient. Blacks and whites would need to be brought together—integrated—in educational settings even to begin to solve the problem.

If the problem was that a pervasive ideology of white supremacy, supported by governmental and private forces and by legal and extralegal devices, had created gross racial inequalities across the centuries, one might see the need to adopt a more multifaceted approach than either of the two approaches summarized above. The interventions might range from a restructuring of school curricula designed to inculcate a greater respect for difference and to directly challenge white-supremacy indoctrination. The intervention might focus on a greater equalization of educational resources between races, the development of special programs to compensate for historic disadvantages, the integration of a minority of white students into black majority settings, the integration of students on a short-term and project-oriented basis rather than on a permanent and full-time basis. The possibilities are many.

My point is that Dewey does not seriously reckon with the multiplicity of ways in which problems can be defined. The choice among competing definitions cannot be decided by reason alone, for what will strike a person as reasonable will significantly depend on that person's experiences, orientation and sensibilities. The question of which definition of the problem should be chosen often comes down to whose voice or story, whose experiences, will provide the interpretive vehicle for understanding the facts under inquiry. Dewey does not provide much guidance here for what is, principally, a set of normative questions about what people value and how they prioritize those values.

But let us assume for a moment that the second phrasing of the problem is chosen. Actually, the Court seemed at times to define the problem in the first way and at times in the second. This ambiguity created considerable confusion in subsequent developments. But let me assume agreement on the second characterization of the problem.

The Court concluded that the separate-but-equal doctrine accepted by the Supreme Court in 1896 in *Plessy v. Ferguson* now had no place under our Constitution. In substantial part it relied on evidence that the segregation of students on the basis of race in public education affected the hearts and minds of Negro children in ways they were not likely to overcome. Even accepting this characterization of the problem, there are still multiple interventions one might hypothesize to solve the problem.

One might hypothesize, as did the Court, that the appropriate remedy is "desegregation with all deliberate speed," that is, only a permanent reassignment of students within a unitary school system on a nonracial basis would be faithful to the holding of *Brown*. One might hypothesize that local authorities must act immediately to integrate black and white students in order to solve the problem. One might hypothesize that separation on some basis other than race could have a different effect on black children. Thus, once the stigma of government-sanctioned discrimination was removed, the problem would be solved. One might hypothesize that some form of interaction short of full-scale integration—mandated and integrated enrichment programs or summer programs, for instance—might sufficiently solve the problem.

Again, the point is that at the second stage of critical inquiry— hypothesizing interventions to solve the problem—multiple possibilities present themselves. What will be the criterion of value in choosing among them? Will not the choice, once again, reflect the experiences, values and sensibilities of the chooser in ways Dewey does not fully acknowledge?

It is at the next stage, the stage of testing the various hypotheses presented, that Dewey's theory attempts to provide some guidance. Hypothetical interventions and questions about how we ought to value certain choices presented to us are to be decided by reference to the consequences of implementing one intervention over another. If one finds one set of consequences more favorable than another, the issue of how to choose among alternative possibilities is decided. My concern, however, is that Dewey merely reproduces at another level of inquiry the confusion and indeterminacy with which his experimentalism struggles from the beginning.

For instance, before we can decide whether the consequences likely to attend a particular intervention are desirable to us, we must agree on what the consequences of the proposed intervention are likely to be. The complications should by now be apparent. With respect to the empirical question of what consequences are likely to follow integration, consider the varied possibilities that might present themselves: one study suggests that integration of black and white students, faculty and administration into a unified school system will enhance the self-esteem of black children; and another suggests that integration will damage it. One study suggests that blacks will likely suffer losses in administration and teaching in unified systems, and another suggests that blacks will gain from an overall enhancement of the facilities and job opportunities available to black children. Some studies anticipate widespread social unrest and resistance to integration, the duration and total effect of which is uncertain. Other studies anticipate massive white flight out of cities that will eventually erode tax bases and reduce the overall quality of life and education within cities.

This brief survey of empirical studies does not begin to exhaust an examination of the possible consequences of integration, not to mention a critical inquiry into the assumptions, methodologies and samples of the tests used to justify even these few consequences. Clearly, such an inquiry could continue almost *ad infinitum*. Which of these consequences are more likely than others, looking out onto the world as it was in 1954 and 1955? Even this determination needs a normative framework, lest we lose ourselves in the endless production and critique of empirical studies.

Dewey's theory leaves us even more in the dark when we ask not which consequences are more likely, but which we should find more desirable. For instance, the latter question of what should be preferred is not answered by empirical studies that suggest the consequences of integration will be violent resistance by whites, substantial flight to the suburbs, and a gradual erosion of the quality of inner-city life and education. We may still prefer to integrate because we believe that the consequences will be short-lived or that these consequences are to be preferred over those of maintaining the status quo because the latter is morally reprehensible. In other words, ascertaining the answer to what we should prefer, even more so than ascertaining the answer to what are the likely consequences, is a complex inquiry in search of a normative framework. The inquiry requires a criterion of value that can provide greater guidance than the mere dependence on a process of inquiry can provide.

Now, I do want to be careful not to portray Dewey as a moral relativist or explanatory nihilist. To be sure, given the choice between the experimental logic and consequentialism of Dewey's Common Faith and the vast majority of what has followed in both philosophy and law, I would gladly cast my lot with Dewey. Yet I believe it is important in trying to unpack the tension between American progressive liberalism and religion to see the missed opportunities of the leading school of progressive liberal politics and philosophy America has produced.

Why does Dewey place such faith in the consequentialist analysis he offers to determine the value and priority of possibilities with which we are forced to grapple in his process theory of inquiry? Consequentialism, as we've seen, can be greatly indeterminate in choosing among alternatives that require some normative criterion of value to discriminate among them.

There is one possibility for why Dewey places so much faith in the consequentialist analysis of his experimentalism. Maybe he sees in the world of lived experience—the world that constitutes his experimental laboratory—some unity, some normative orientation, which he believes all reasonable inquirers converting to his Common Faith will see. That is, perhaps Dewey is more of an Aristotelian than he cares to admit. Philospher Bertrand Russell has noted that the only way the mere process of inquiry can be determinate enough to do the work Dewey prescribed for it is if Dewey has an undisclosed metaphysic of unity that assumes a natural order lurking beneath the temporal flux of experience:

> I do not see why inquiry should be expected to result in "unified wholes." If I am given a pack of cards in disorder, and asked to inquire into their sequence, I shall, if I follow Dewey's prescription, first arrange them in order, and then say that this was the order resulting from inquiry. There will be, it is true, an "objective transformation of objective subject-matter" while I am arranging the cards, but the definition allows for this. If, at the end, I am told: We wanted to know the sequence of the cards when they were given to you, not after you had re-arranged them, I shall, if I am a disciple of Dewey, reply: Your ideas are altogether too static. I am a dynamic person, and when I inquire into any subject-matter I first alter it in such a way as to make the inquiry easy. The notion that such a procedure is legitimate can only be justified by a Hegelian distinction of appearance and reality: the appearance may be confused and fragmentary, but the reality is always orderly and organic. Therefore when I arrange the cards I am only revealing their true eternal nature. But this part of the doctrine is never made explicit. The metaphysic of organism underlies Dewey's theories, but I do not know how far he is aware of this fact.[19]

Russell's criticism goes too far, I believe, but it is pointed in the right direction. Dewey is not a realist in the philosphical understanding of that term. That is, he does not believe that behind the flux and appearance of life stands a static reality, transcendental or material, that critical inquiry can disclose and creative intelligence can elaborate. On the contrary, what we might be led to believe is an underlying and ontologically privileged reality is, for Dewey, also socially constructed. Its worth is also to be measured by our assessment of the consequences entailed in valuing it.

Perhaps an illustration drawn from theories of legal interpretation will help illuminate the difference between Dewey's theory and philosophical realism. Dewey possesses a historical consciousness about institutions and processes, yet he is aware of the ways in which the past is too frequently deployed as a conservative tool to control and limit the possibilities of the present and future. Therefore, he would consider it ridiculous to reduce constitutional meaning, as originalists do, to the question of whether the intention of the Framers of the constitutional provision or the public meaning of the provision at the time of ratification should control our assessment of the issue today.

Under Dewey's approach, such inquiry into the past is strictly instrumental and not determinative, not even probative of how one should act in the present. If inquiry into the past provides a better understanding of the possible consequences of an action, it is encouraged; if not, it is rejected. So the precedent established by prior cases and the ability to consult the past and uncover the intent of those acting in the past do not constitute a static underlying "reality" that, if grasped, is any more privileged than other values we might find important. Every value must clear the hurdle of whether commitment to the value in the present context will have consequences that we deem desirable.

But yet Russell is on to something in his criticism of Dewey. Even if Dewey does not believe that there is only one way to arrange the cards in the above illustration, he seems to have faith that the inquiry into the sequence of the cards will take place within certain limits, that inquiry presupposes some order, some way things ought to be. Perhaps Dewey is hoping that democracy will provide this sense of unity and normative guidance his theory so badly needs. Dewey is more Aristotelian, perhaps, than he cares to admit. That is, perhaps he believes that the American context, its history, people and values provide creative intelligence with a purpose and end.

Perhaps Dewey's faith is that when open minds seriously reckon with the American tradition, they will see what his eyes behold—the opportunity to fulfill human potential within limits that acknowledge and safeguard certain fundamental values indispensable to the pursuit of "putting off mortality and living in the universal."[20] But does this faith in the infinite potential of human creativity provide the kind of normative guidance needed for a just society committed to the protection of the least of these? Perhaps Dewey has an understanding of democracy that balances human possibility/freedom with the limit/duty needed for a progressive vision of community.

C. A Common Faith: The Limits of Democratic Process

Dewey envisioned a radical democratic culture as the institutional conduit through which his Common Faith would be practiced and society saved. He wrote:

> Faith in the power of intelligence to imagine a future which is the projection of the desirable in the present, and to invent the instrumentalities of its realization, is our salvation. And it is a faith which must be nurtured and made articulate, surely a sufficiently large task for our philosophy.[21]

Democracy, for Dewey, was the institutional framework within which the power of intelligence would speak new worlds into existence. It was the vehicle through which we are to imagine a future that is the projection of what we find desirable in the present. If it is democracy that Dewey looks to for the foundational support of his Common Faith, then democracy cannot be simply a grand process embracive of all possibilities. It must embody both possibility and limit, duty as well as right. To be sure, it must say something about the good to which we are capable of aspiring, but it must speak as well of the evil to which we have proven capable of falling. It must speak of what should be the just and proper limits to freedom in a society that dares to call itself free.

I will argue that the reduction of faith to a trust in "the power of intelligence to project the desirable" into the future provides no normative guidance as to what we should find desirable in the first place. And without the normative orientation that religion at its best provides, Dewey has removed important limits on the abusive use of power. To understand the work left undone by Dewey's dependence on a process-oriented understanding of democracy as the normative foundation of his Common Faith, we should first try to appreciate what work the idea of democracy does accomplish.

Dewey envisions a culture of communicating and interacting citizens engaged in the challenging process of shaping their worlds in accord with visions that know no limit to the potential of creative intelligence. In this culture one imagines citizens in every walk of life debating the issues of the day, interrogating the assumptions of others as well as themselves, and attempting to craft solutions to the problems that confront them and their fellow citizens. One can almost imagine the frequent town meetings and gatherings organized for the purpose of collectively working out the institutions, processes and normative ends that will govern community life.

Dewey's understanding of democracy is more a process-oriented understanding of democracy. Dewey does not seem to see the possibility of his democracy slipping into something less noble than he intends. His faith is in the power of intelligence to project what is desirable in the present into the future, but he does not seem to understand how power often bends knowledge toward purposes that undermine democracy. He needs a substantive understanding of democracy drawn from its egalitarian impulse that safeguards the interests of the most vulnerable members of society, but no such safeguard is forthcoming. These safeguards are particularly needed in representative democracies such as ours.

In representative democracies, complications arise due to the agency costs associated with having others represent one's interests in a context where effective monitoring is difficult, if not impossible. Because of these costs, it is necessary to provide those represented with rights that protect them from the workings of governmental and market processes over which they may have little effective control. American liberalism has not been slow to articulate individual rights against the state and other individuals, but it has been slow to provide such rights against the market and on behalf of groups, not just individuals, who may need special protection from state and market forces.

Let me better explain why such safeguards are needed and why I believe Dewey's process-oriented democracy falls short of the mark. In theories of representative democracy, individuals represent their constituency's "best interest." According to some theories, the "best interest" is merely the result of an assessment of the preferences of the constituency. Opinion polls and a measure of lobbying intensity often suffice to determine preferences. The representative is but a conduit through which the preferences of the constituency are channelled. While elected representatives in modern democracies often portray the nature of the relationship with their constituencies in such a manner, it is seldom this one-directional and simplistic.

A more power-centered and cynical theory, Machiavellian in many ways, contends that elected representatives make decisions on the basis of whether they are likely to get reelected or accrue some other personal benefit. Representatives tell their constituencies, through the manipulation of images and issues, what is in their "best interest." Such calculations may coincide with what is actually in the "best interest" of the general constituency, or they may only coincide with the best interest of a small portion of the constituency—those who are more likely to vote for the representative, to contribute to campaign fund-raisers, or to repay favors when the representative has returned to private life.

Still other theories, like the Burkean theory of virtual representation, contend that "best interest" is determined by the honest and enlightened reflections of the representative. Representatives are expected to exercise judgment that reflects their superior vantage point, education and enlightenment. Thus, even those decisions which may be disagreeable to the majority of those whose interests are represented are to be accepted by the constituency. Of course, the danger in this theory of representation is that elite representatives will transform democracy into an aristocracy.

To the extent Dewey's radical democratic culture would accommodate a system of representative democracy, it would certainly reject the first theory mentioned above, an uncritical reflection of popular preferences. It would also reject the second theory, an abuse of delegated power for personal ends. Dewey would likely embrace some variant of the third alternative, which encourages the enlightened judgment of the legislator, but, of course, without the conservative and paternalistic slant the theory is given by Burke. That is, Dewey's enlightened representative would undoubtedly reflect a more experimental, critical and open-ended disposition.

The policies enacted by Dewey's legislator would be subject to the rigorous demands of critical inquiry discussed above. That is, alternative ways of solving problems would be subjected, when possible, to controlled testing. If such testing is not possible, one would attempt to map out meticulously the likely consequences of alternative policies. When particular interventions were implemented, they would be subjected to the careful gathering of data and the setting forth of conclusions open to revision and modification in light of new evidence. All of this would be done in an environment of open exchange and lively debate that maintained the integrity of the process of inquiry and thus the production of truth and knowledge.

This system might constitute an improvement over crass political decisions made on the basis of opinion polls and spin doctors. In some cases, however, it might be disadvantageous, serving as a pretext for inaction, with there being always one more hearing to be held, one more test to be conducted, and one more study to be completed. Whatever practical problems attend the application of Dewey's model of critical inquiry, none of the normative questions posed in the preceding section is answered by this process-oriented understanding of democracy. Ultimately, one is still saddled with a plurality of reasonably probable and desirable consequences, each of which might rationally be preferred based on empirical analysis and comparison. How does one decide among them?

At some point, even with Dewey's enlightened theory of democracy, a vote is called and the majority's preferences win the day. Let us call this outcome, then, enlightened majoritarianism, and stipulate that it is superior in some significant sense to the majoritarianism that is common today. My concern is that, this enlightenment notwithstanding, the process has not safeguarded the interests of the least powerful elements of the community.

Perhaps the "power of intelligence" will assure that this enlightened majoritarianism will impose stricter limits on unjust and oppressive outcomes, although I hardly see why we should have faith that this is true. The outcomes that this process could nevertheless produce, notwithstanding the norms of that process, might often be an abuse of power resulting in the systematic oppression of the least powerful. What objections could be marshalled against an informed decision, arrived at after an enlightened process of critical inquiry, to enslave, exterminate, separate or detain a race of people? If substantive limits on the process are to be imposed, as I believe they must, they can be justified only by some commitment to normative values lying outside the consequentialist framework established by Dewey's experimentalism.

Let me make the point more emphatically. I do not believe Dewey would have approved of the vote of Southern legislatures to segregate black citizens in the American South, even if blacks had voted against the measure and lost, and even if all of those voting had commissioned and reviewed detailed studies indicating that the consequences of segregation were more favorable than not. The problem is that Dewey does not talk enough about how to evaluate those decisions that we should not want to subject to a utilitarian formula of maximizing favorable consequences.

On what grounds do we say that certain decisions coming out of even an enlightened democratic process are not to be accepted? Of course, the ready answer to this question is that the sometimes-unpredictable legislative process is guided and constrained by constitutional norms ultimately enforced by the courts. Thus in our republican democracy we place regulation of certain aspects of speech, religion, property, privacy, equal protection, voting and more beyond the reach of majoritarian democracy.

This raises questions as to whether the courts, as opposed to legislatures, are the better keepers of democracy. While I will return to this question later, I do not believe that the problem of institutional competency is the most difficult or interesting problem posed by Dewey's theory. The more interesting question is whether Dewey provides any substantive vision of community beyond his process concerns that nurture a desire to protect and promote the interests of the least advantaged in society.

As I stated earlier, if it is democracy that Dewey looks to for the foundational support of his Common Faith, then democracy cannot be simply a grand process embracive of all possibilities. It must embody both possibility and limit. It must say something about what we are and are capable of becoming and about what should be the just and proper limits of a society that calls itself democratic.

To be sure, process is important, and Dewey is right to alert us to its importance. But process must be oriented toward something other than itself in order to avoid being consumed by itself. Dewey's enthusiasm over the unleashed material and intellectual energies accompanying the American industrial revolution and the potential of critical intelligence to favorably direct those energies toward the common good often blinded him to the need to develop a substantive vision of what the good actually consists.

One result of this blindness was that Dewey failed to grasp the relationship between the production and dissemination of knowledge, on the one hand, and the distribution of power, on the other. He seemed to lack a critical appreciation of the structural and cultural forces that might lead democratic processes away from rather than toward the common good, away from liberation and toward novel forms of oppression, away from warranted assertability based on critical inquiry and toward self-serving manipulation of democratic processes for the benefit of parochial interests. In traditional theological terms, one might say Dewey lacked an appreciation for the weight and gravity of individual and collective sin.

Only by taking evil seriously, as I will later argue Rauschenbusch's Social Gospel does, can one even begin to safeguard the hope for democracy. Kierkegaard once wrote, paradoxically, "Without God I am too strong."[22] This insight is important. For without an understanding of ultimate purpose and the proper limits in which that purpose is to be lived out, an understanding that can still provide great flexibility as to means or process, those with money and political power will exert their influence over the processes of critical inquiry in a creative democracy and will provide the normative framework that determines which ends are to be preferred over others.

If normative philosophy or theology has any role, it is to put in place a framework that challenges, as much as possible, this potential corruption of democratic processes. Here I must concur fully with the conclusions of the philosopher Bertrand Russell about Dewey's pragmatism. Russell explains:

> In all this I feel a grave danger, the danger of what might be called cosmic impiety. The concept of "truth" as something dependent upon facts largely outside human control has been one of the ways in which philosophy hitherto has inculcated the necessary element of humility. When this check upon pride is removed, a further step is taken on the road towards a certain kind of madness—the intoxication of power which invaded philosophy with Fichte, and to which modern men, whether philosophers or not, are prone. I am persuaded that this intoxication is the greatest danger of our time, and that any philosophy which, however unintentionally, contributes to it is increasing the danger of vast social disaster.[23]

The danger, then, is that when programs and policies are supported by hypotheses duly tested by empirical studies and evaluated by reference to human values based in human experience, dissension will persist. Why? Because creative intelligence will forever prove manipulable, directed here, then there, for this cause and that, cloaked by subtle interpretations of fact that warrant different and conflicting truth assertions.

This danger has long been one of the central problems of modern political theory—the rights or powers of majorities over individuals. Again, Dewey's inability to define and explicate a theory of human limit to supplement his theory of human possibility proved problematic. In the end, I believe, he understood this danger, but the checks that he proposed were insufficient.

Ultimately, Dewey understood the dangers of a purely process oriented understanding of democracy. He had placed his "faith in the power of intelligence to imagine a future which is the projection of the desirable in the present, and to invent the instrumentalities of its realization."[24] But the Nazi horror, the Stalinist nightmare, and the spread of fascism and totalitarianism around the world reminded him of the popular saying first heard in the days of his religious youth: "The road to Hell is paved with good intentions." Confronted with the incontrovertible evidence of a person's negative potential, the abuse of human intelligence, the lapse into retrograde and selfish behavior, all cloaked in the lamb's wool of the "common good," Dewey recoiled, seeing perhaps the beast his project might unleash with little hope of containment.

Faced with such a monumental challenge to his Common Faith, Dewey doubted the God of critical intelligence and searched for a workable limit to the dangers of placing too much "faith in the power of intelligence":

> It has been shown in the last few years that democratic institutions are no guarantee for the existence of democratic individuals. The alternative is that individuals who prize their own liberties and who prize the liberties of other individuals, individuals who are democratic in thought and action, are the sole final warrant for the existence and endurance of democratic institutions.[25]

Dewey's shift is significant. He acknowledges that democratic institutions and processes of critical inquiry are "no guarantee for the existence of democratic individuals."[26] He implies a need to transform society at the most personal and psychospiritual level, that of individual consciousness. What does it mean to desire a community in which individuals are democratic in both "thought and action"? To the extent Dewey understands this concept merely as the protection of personal liberties, he is backsliding into a more conservative liberal perspective in which individuals are protected from various forms of collective coercion and duty by the shields of personal rights and liberties.

But if Dewey is not slipping into this traditionalist conception of liberty, he may be on the verge of something quite significant. When we begin to inquire into the conditions for producing individuals who are democratic in thought and deed, we are talking about the need for a normative vision that Dewey now seems ready to remove from the open-ended consequentialism of his experimentalist logic. Certain policies, institutions and purposes must be preferred over others, and they go beyond mere preferences for process. Dewey is forced to make the foundational presuppositions of his theory clear, to bring to the surface his assumptions about what is essential to and desirable for human existence that seeks to make democracy a way of life.

He is compelled to specify what values should be the preferred values of those engaged in the human project of building community.

Most importantly, he is forced to concede that any legitimate theory of justice must confront the stark possibilities of human evil and depravity, and seek to protect the most vulnerable from a process that simultaneously makes possible their liberation and persecution. Paradoxically, I believe that dimensions of the traditional religion lambasted by Dewey provide some insight into what these substantive values should be.

Religion was also undergoing important changes around the time Dewey was writing. Interestingly, I believe, some theologians were developing answers to the questions left open by Dewey. These answers did not reject, but did substantially revise, traditional conceptions of God, evil and the Kingdom of God. The expansion of liberalism in Dewey's Common Faith and the development of progressive liberal religion provided, I believe, a common ground on which progressive religionists and liberals could have found comradery. That ground may still provide the basis for a reintroduction of religion into progressive liberal politics in America.

In summary, what is needed is a way of simultaneously building on the best of the individual creative power Dewey embraced as society's savior, yet with a real awareness of proper limits on that power—limits that nurture democratic individuals through an accentuation of human interdependence and its possibilities. This sensibility can never be achieved by a blind faith in the human capacity for self-creation. If critical intelligence without a normative orientation of what is good and just is enshrined as a god, that god can be made to speak in many voices, seldom with a true sense of responsibility for one's fellow travelers.

Dewey ate the sour grapes of idolatry, and the children's teeth were put on edge. The implications of adopting Dewey's pragmatism were significant for legal realism, creating problems with which contemporary jurisprudence grapples even today.

Chapter 2

Legal Realism and the Quest for a Common Faith

Introduction

The pragmatic turn in American philosophy was accompanied by a similar reorientation in law. This innovation came to be called the American legal realism movement. The influence of Dewey's secular faith was apparent in the development of American legal realism. In realism one could see Dewey's commitment to a science-based method of experimental inquiry, his use of a consequentialist analysis for assessing and prioritizing competing values and ends, and his devotion to the possibilities of creative democracy.

The cataclysmic changes in American life initiated by the industrial revolution had, by the turn of the century, created serious maldistributions of wealth and power. During what came to be called the progressive period of American history, many sought to enlist government in the struggle against the ever-increasing concentrations of private wealth and power. Antitrust and child labor laws were legislative initiatives spawned by this progressive period of American democracy.

As was the case before the Civil War and after the civil rights movement, however, the conservative backlash was greatly facilitated by a federal judiciary that raised constitutional hurdles to progressive legislative initiatives. In a seminal case of 1905, *Lochner v. New York*,[1] the Supreme Court ruled unconstitutional the New York State legislature's attempt to regulate the number of hours employers could require bakers to work each week. The Court ruled that the legislature's intervention in such areas interfered with the contract and property rights of employers and employees. The legislature was, of course, attempting to redress the disparity in bargaining power between employers and employees in this industry through the exercise of its police powers. In siding with the rights of contract and property, the Court sent a clear message that the progressive movement would not go unopposed in its effort to redistribute power from the wealthy to the poor and powerless.

Lochner spurred the pragmatists of the law—legal realists—to action. They leveled harsh critiques against the opinion and the countermajoritarian posture it adopted. Indeed, a figure commonly recognized as one of the fathers of legal realism, Justice Holmes, wrote a dissenting opinion in the case. Realists developed a sophisticated and sustained critique of what came to be called the Lochner era.

Their principal target was the courts, and their critical methodology demystified the claim that judges were neutral arbiters or umpires of constitutional disputes, engaging in neutral, objective and determinate decision-making. The Court of the Lochner era, the realist argument contended, was engaged in the political protection of class-based interests. The Court was, in effect, usurping the power of the people to engage in self-governance, to use, as Dewey might say, the power of intelligence to project what is most desirable in the present into the future. But the influence of pragmatism on legal realism was also problematic, precisely for the reasons explored in the previous chapter.

First, as we have seen, the question of what ends should be valued was reduced, in Dewey's brand of pragmatism, to a question of which set of probable consequences were found most desirable. Empirical experimentalism made value a function of empirical research into the probable consequences of proposed courses of action. Thus, the scientific temperament of experimentalism brought to American legal realism a tendency to separate empirical questions about what "is" from normative questions about what "ought" to be. This distinction between "is" and "ought" failed to understand that normative questions permeated even an examination of the "is." The very enterprise of defining the nature of the problem examined was normative. In this sense the subject and the object could never be separated in the way the scientific method assumed. The Realist judge was bringing a set of perspectives, values and orientations to the very conceptualization and understanding of the problem.

Of course, normative questions about what we ought to do permeated other dimensions of the inquiry as well. If we agree on the nature of the problem or issue to be solved, which remedies among competing remedies do we impose? How do we even decide what the probable consequences are of proposed remedies? Even if we agree on the range of probable consequences for each proposed remedy, how do we prioritize consequences for each remedy and across proposed remedies? It should be clear that in the absence of some normative guidance, relativism was all that remained.

The difficulty of these questions led many realists to defer to legislative branches to make such normative judgments, and some have argued that this was precisely the intention of the movement. The legislative branch, it was argued, possessed superior access to empirical research and occupied a better vantage point from which to assess and value the broad scale consequences of proposed laws. Thus, the impoverished normative discourse of pragmatism profoundly affected legal realism with, as we shall see, quite serious consequences.

Second, Dewey's instrumentalism made value and truth contingent on shifting bases of knowledge, with little appreciation for the relationship between knowledge and power as manifested in the social forces defining the production and dissemination of knowledge in the American culture. Similarly, legal realism was too uncritical of the majoritarianism of the democratic processes it vindicated. The empirical knowledge these processes produced was, not surprisingly, a function of certain power relations that general judicial deference only legitimated.

Finally, although legal realism promoted the possibilities of creative intelligence to reconstruct the world, like Dewey's pragmatism, it underestimated the limits and normative guidance necessary for such flourishing. The absence of such a discourse created an intellectual vacuum soon filled by a reactionary jurisprudence that undermined the transformative potential of *Brown*.

Legal realism, like pragmatism, assaulted the use of concepts and categories abstracted from a context of lived experience and insulated from critique by the mystique of transcendental logic. Dewey understood that through this process of abstraction, law, like so much philosophy, conditioned people to mistake the socially constructed for the divinely sanctioned and, in so doing, limited the possibilities of human agency and intelligence. A more detailed description of how Dewey's philosophy influenced critical developments in the law through American legal realism follows. I will then turn to an analysis of the problems created by realism's failure to develop a normative discourse about the appropriate ends of law.

A. Pragmatism's Influence on American Legal Realism

In an article entitled "Logical Method and Law,"[2] Dewey distinguished experimental logic from syllogistic logic. The latter represents the logic he understood Justice Holmes to have condemned in his often-cited statement, "The life of the law has not been logic: it has been experience."[3] For Dewey, the problem was not so much one of preferring logic over experience as it was preferring a logic abstracted from experience over one born of experience.

Syllogistic logic, quite prevalent in classical jurisprudence, assumes the fixed meaning of certain abstract categories by which human existence is ordered, for example, all men are mortal, or the state cannot deprive any person of "liberty" without due process of law. The task of reasoning is to ascertain particular facts and their relation to the universal categories: Socrates is a man, or a state law regulating the number of hours employees may work for employers deprives the parties of their liberty to contract. The final step is a simple one of deducing conclusions: Socrates is mortal, or the state's legislation is unconstitutional.

Roscoe Pound called this kind of syllogistic legal reasoning "mechanical jurisprudence."[4] Dewey concurred in this characterization, but understood the place of syllogistic reasoning. "[T]he syllogism sets forth the *results* of thinking, it has nothing to do with the *operation* of thinking."[5] The meaning and consequences of being "mortal" and a "man" or having a right to "liberty" and "due process," the major premises used in the *Lochner* case described above, are assumed by the syllogism. The meaning of these terms is not open to inquiry, dispute, verification, or revision. The syllogism obscures the fact that the meaning of its critical categories is social, determined by reference to some cultural context. It is this cultural meaning alone that makes the abstractions of the syllogism intelligible.

Unlike syllogistic logic, experimental logic operates and explicitly depends on the workings of a culture-bound creative intelligence. Once again, Dewey brings us back to one of the fundamental tenets of his Common Faith:

> If we trust to an experimental logic, we find that general principles emerge as statements of generic ways in which it has been found helpful to treat concrete cases. . . . The "universal" stated in the major premise is not outside of and antecedent to particular cases; neither is it a selection of something found in a variety of cases. It is an indication of a single way of treating cases for certain purposes or consequences in spite of their diversity. Hence its meaning and worth are subject to inquiry and revision in view of what happens, what the consequences are, when it is used as a method of treatment.[6]

In other words, the liberty of which the Fourteenth Amendment speaks might syllogistically be used to prohibit the kind of infringement made by the New York state legislature in *Lochner v. New York*,[7] but the abstract concept of liberty in no way requires this result. A particular conception of liberty, like the one used in *Lochner*, should be the result, not the beginning, of the thinking process. A choice among the competing interpretations of liberty remains a matter of choice in light of our assessment of which definition's use will have the most desirable consequences.

Even if the court did not recognize it or would not admit it, the meaning attributed to liberty in *Lochner* was a shorthand way of promoting certain purposes and securing certain consequences in the lives of individuals. During the *Lochner* era, this conception of liberty arguably facilitated the accumulation of capital by employers, who were given great latitude by the court to exploit the labor potential of workers. Embracing this conception of liberty was, then, a specific policy decision made to secure certain ends. Thus, the meaning of liberty was not a changeless essence hovering above and beyond human experience, fixed according to some mystical natural order reflected in the prohibitions of the Constitution and used to resolve conflicts mechanically through an uncritical syllogistic logic. Under the experimental logic of Dewey and the American legal realists, we are free to explore the purposes and consequences of certain conceptions of liberty and to judge for ourselves whether certain meanings remain viable or have been made obsolete by time.

This means that, for the American legal realists, as was the case for Dewey, knowledge and truth were produced by the process of critical inquiry—not from the static interpretation of constitutional precedent, but from the dynamic assessment of consequences associated with alternative meanings and interventions.

But the priests of the late nineteenth-century orthodox legal theology were adept at making that which found its meaning in a specific historical context appear universal and unalterable. Thus the theory of laissez-faire enshrined by the meaning given to liberty in the *Lochner* era made a historically specific and culture-bound conception of human interaction seem timeless and universal. Through this process, a particular vision of human interaction was abstracted into the sanctuary of transcendent bliss, and thus made sacred and protected from human manipulation by an act of human rather than divine intervention.

Legal realists like Felix Cohen believed that pragmatism's experimental empiricism could redeem law from its sanctuary of abstractions and return it to its rightful place, service to humanity.[8] The most pressing question for the new jurisprudence was "[how] to substitute a realistic, rational, scientific account of legal happenings for the classical theological jurisprudence of concepts?"[9] Cohen saw the classical tradition of law, as Dewey saw the classical tradition of philosophy, as an uncritical faith siphoning off valuable energies needed to critically engage the world's problems. "*Legal concepts* . . . are supernatural entities," Cohen asserted, "which do not have a verifiable existence except to the eyes of faith."[10]

Cohen believed, as did most realists, that there were only two significant questions in the field of law. The first, "How do courts actually decide cases of a given kind?" called for an objective and scientific descriptive analysis. The second, "How should courts decide cases of a given kind?" was explicitly normative and required an elaboration and prioritizing of human values. This separation of the empirical "is" from the normative "Ought" was critical to the scientific approach to legal phenomena. It permitted a thorough understanding of the patterns, histories, and trajectories of observed phenomena, and an informed value assessment about how that phenomena should be treated. Thus the separation of is and ought focused the legal scientist's attention on the experience behind abstract legal concepts. Cohen noted:

> Our legal system is filled with supernatural concepts, that is to say, concepts which cannot be defined in terms of experience, and from which all sorts of empirical decisions are supposed to flow. Against these unverifiable concepts modern jurisprudence presents an ultimatum. (Any word that cannot pay up in the currency of fact, upon demand, is to be declared bankrupt, and we are to have no further dealings with it).[11]

Just as Dewey saw supernatural faith as a fetter on creative intelligence and the possibilities of democracy, Cohen and the legal realists believed supernatural legal concepts maintained the same limitations in the arena of the law. Echoing Holmes, the realists lauded experience as the life of the law. The cultural meanings embraced by abstract legal concepts had to be articulated in terms of human experience, lest they take flight to the heavens of transcendental nonsense.

Legal realists, then, would have us understand law in terms of natural relations rather than supernatural concepts. We are to accept or reject rules of law on the basis of an understanding of their contextual purposes and consequences. Such an understanding entails a quasi-scientific descriptive analysis of actual objects, events and processes in life. However, Cohen, unlike many realists, admitted that this inquiry was extremely open-ended and had to be supplemented with a critical theory of values if it were to be workable. In perhaps one of the most telling and prophetic utterances in all of legal literature, Cohen observed:

The prospect of determining the consequences of a given rule of law appears to be an infinite task, and is indeed an infinite task unless we approach it with some discriminating criterion of what consequences are *important*. Now a *criterion of importance* presupposes a *criterion of values*, which is precisely what modern thinkers of the "sociological" and "realistic" schools of jurisprudence have never had. . . . Contemporary "realists" have, in general, either denied absolutely that absolute standards of importance can exist, or else insisted that we must thoroughly understand the facts as they are before we begin to evaluate them. Such a postponement of the problem of values is equivalent to its repudiation. We never shall thoroughly understand the facts as they are, and we are not likely to make much progress towards such understanding unless we at the same time bring into play a critical theory of values.[12]

The inability or unwillingness to articulate a criterion of importance, a critical theory of values, led many legal realists to depend on democratic bodies to do so. Mindful of the countermajoritarian power of the Court and its historically conservative role, many realists struggled to define a role for the judiciary that would not threaten the more progressive inclinations of legislative bodies held accountable through democratic processes.

In his *Lochner* dissent, Justice Holmes articulated what would become a common legal realist position. "General propositions do not decide concrete cases. The decision will depend on a judgment or intuition more subtle than any articulate major premise." It is interesting, however, that his criterion of values ultimately rested on majoritarian processes. "I strongly believe," he contended, "that my agreement or disagreement has nothing to do with the right of a majority to embody their opinions in law. . . . [T]he word liberty in the Fourteenth Amendment is perverted when it is held to prevent the natural outcome of a dominant opinion."[13]

An almost blind faith in democratic and majoritarian processes caused many politically minded realists to pursue the program of bureaucratic reform inaugurated by the New Deal administration of President Franklin D. Roosevelt. For these realists, both the experimental empiricism and consequentialism of the new pragmatism, as well as its normative questions about values, were best played out in the political arena, with the judicial sphere playing only a *de minimis* role in safeguarding the process by which democratic decisions were reached.[14]

This faith in majoritarian processes also caused some realist scholars to believe that the scientific analysis of actual social processes, such as market relations, permitted them to capture the real rules at work behind the written rules perfunctorily applied by courts.[15] Judges could utilize their pragmatic insights in those areas, like the common law, left to judicial policy-making, and use their discretion to articulate rules and principles that promoted more desirable consequences than the rules on the books.

Under this approach, the questions of what actually happens in the real world and what ought to happen in the real world were conflated, since the backdrop for determining which consequences were most desirable would often be a set of market-oriented or private-property-oriented priorities ultimately legitimating and protecting the status quo. The criterion of value never developed because it was too often assumed that the real rules were also the right rules, that the empirical question somehow answered the normative one. Thus, while the realists purported to separate temporarily the is and the ought, in actuality they collapsed the latter into the former, thereby impoverishing normative discourse about the aims and purposes of law. The reluctance to articulate a criterion of values, along with a willingness to blindly accept majoritarian processes, proved both unworkable and, in many respects, catastrophic for the very democratic aims pragmatism and realism desired to promote.

B. The Quest for Neutral Principles: The Frankenstein of American Legal Pragmatism

By the 1950s, realists and their antagonists, those formalists upholding the objectivity, neutrality and determinacy of judicial decision-making, had declared a truce. Each conceded some ground and forged a new alliance, a neoclassical jurisprudence, that purported to synthesize the insights of each position. Traditionalists conceded a moderate version of realism's indeterminacy critique, the contention that abstract constitutional concepts such as liberty, invoked in the *Lochner* case, were indeterminate and thus susceptible to manipulation by democratically unaccountable judges. Thus the traditionalists conceded that courts should defer more than they did during the *Lochner* era to democratically elected bodies which were better suited to engage in empirical study, consequentialist analysis and problem-solving. But this deference did not mean that courts would become no more than rubber stamps for legislative determinations. The question, then, was on what grounds the courts should intervene to overturn the decisions of legislative majorities. This question set the terms of the jurisprudential debate for the next two decades.

For their part, realists conceded that, in the absence of Cohen's criterion of value, there was a problem with the open-endedness of the empirical and descriptive aspects of their legal pragmatism. Therefore, they accepted the traditionalists' search for a criterion of value that would clarify when majoritarian institutions had overstepped their boundaries and when courts could overrule the will of the majority expressed in legislation.

The compromise between legal realists and traditionalists took many forms, but the origins of the compromise are best illustrated by a remarkable speech delivered by Herbert Wechsler at the Harvard Law School in 1959, entitled "Toward Neutral Principles in Constitutional Law," a speech prompted by his reflections on the *Brown* decision of 1954 and subsequent developments.

It was a remarkable speech for many reasons, not the least of which was the background of the speaker. Wechsler, by all accounts, was a liberal. He morally opposed segregation and worked with Thurgood Marshall and other members of the NAACP to fight the system in the courts. He agreed with the outcome of the decision, but had deep reservations about the way the decision was reached. His reservations about the empirical/consequentialist basis for the court's decision, along with his preference for a "neutral" basis, constituted a full-frontal assault on legal realist thinking. It was the first major critique, by a professed liberal no less, to question a cornerstone of realist judicial reasoning, one relying substantially on empirical research and consequentialist analysis in reaching its conclusion that the separate-but-equal doctrine of *Plessy v.*

Ferguson was unconstitutional. How did Wechsler's speech embody this compromise between legal realist and traditionalist perspectives?

Conceding the legal realist critique, in part, Wechsler conceded the realist contention that judicial action "invariably involves value choices." But in making such choices, now echoing traditionalist sentiments, courts are duty-bound to "function otherwise than as a naked power organ." They are obliged to be "entirely principled." As he understood it,

> [a] principled decision . . . is one that rests on reasons . . . that in their generality and their neutrality transcend any immediate result that is involved. When no sufficient reasons of this kind can be assigned for overturning value choices of the other branches of the Government or of a state, those choices must, of course, survive.[16]

Wechsler's renewed quest for "transcendent" neutral principles on which to base judicial decisions constituted the ground that traditional jurisprudence was unwilling to concede to realism. That is, judicial decision-making need not and could not be thought as completely political. It could be guided by neutral principles. By the same token, Wechsler's approach also made clear that legal realism had a point. Courts needed to defer more than they did to majoritarian institutions. Wechsler was prepared to honor such deference whenever the courts could not base their decisions on neutral principles. The troubling implication of this conclusion was that Wechsler was uncertain as to whether neutral principles could be found to overturn the state segregation laws at issue in *Brown*.

To illustrate the degree to which Wechsler's jurisprudence of neutral principles promoted judicial deference to majoritarian processes, one need but cite the judicial decisions he condemns as lacking a justifying, transcendent, neutral principle. First, Wechsler argues that the inability of courts to find a neutral principle to constrain federal commerce powers meant that the courts should defer to federal legislation in this area. All of the federalism-based concerns against federal regulation of commerce had already been presented and debated by the states through their elected representatives in Congress. Thus Wechsler sides with the realists in their support of Congressional commerce powers to

regulate corporate power. Second, because courts seem unable to articulate a neutral principle to explain why states cannot regulate the number of hours worked by employees but can regulate other aspects of
employer/employee relations under their police powers, the courts
should defer to majoritarian processes by upholding such legislation if
it meets the less demanding test of reasonableness. Thus Wechsler sides
with the realists in their critique of *Lochner* and their support of legislatures' regulation of corporate power. In both cases Wechsler's inability
to articulate a transcendent neutral principle meant that the federal
courts should defer to the democratic processes of federal and state legislative bodies.

But most troubling to those engaged in the struggle for racial justice
was the realization that Wechsler was unable to think of a transcendent
neutral principle that could justify the Court's overturning of the challenged practices in *Smith v. Allwright*,[17] *Shelly v. Kraemer*,[18] and *Brown
v. Board of Education*.[19] Wechsler, then, indicated a reluctant willingness
to defer to majoritarian processes that validated or promulgated race-
based classifications excluding blacks from privately operated white
political primaries, residential areas maintained by private restrictive
covenants and white public schools. Thus Wechsler continued to defer
to the majority as a good realist would, but he did so for a reason that
would be offered by a *Lochner*-type traditionalist—the failure to find a
transcendental and neutral principle.

Wechsler's equivocation on the rights of states to legislate Jim Crow
called into question the holding of *Brown*, which even he conceded was
a *morally* correct decision. It certainly problematized the attempt by
many to use *Brown* as the stellar example of the right kind of activist
court, to be distinguished from *Lochner*, the wrong kind of activist court.
For Wechsler, however, the Court should have deferred to majoritarian
legislatures in both *Lochner* and *Brown*, since it lacked any neutral principles to distinguish one from the other.

Wechsler's speech illustrated the inherent dangers of the pragmatists' and realists' failure to develop a criterion of importance for such
an inevitable conflict over ends and values. Because that criterion
was not developed by progressives, nonprogressive forces ultimately
defined it, and the former were, henceforth, always on the defensive
about the role of the courts in a constitutional democracy. Had such a

criterion been developed, realists would not have found themselves in the precarious position of struggling for a normative justification of the *Brown* decision, being unable to distinguish Brown from Lochner.

The criterion of values urged by Cohen might have been both a testament to human imagination and possibility as well as a limit on majoritarian politics and gateway to a just society. Instead, Cohen's prophecy came true, and the calamity of too great a dependency on majoritarian politics and empirical analysis loomed on the horizon. In the wake of Wechsler's critique, scholars feverishly struggled to capture and rationalize *Brown* as an example of judicial review at its best, while satisfying Wechsler's demand that the Court engage only in principled decision-making. Nothing less than the legitimacy of the judiciary in a constitutional democracy was at stake.

The solutions proposed by legal scholars to Wechsler's musings are discussed below. These solutions were problematic precisely because they continued to shy away from the development of a criterion of importance by which conflicting values could be compared and prioritized. Instead, institutional competency and neutral decision-making became the blindfold behind which judges tilted the scales of justice to their traditional imbalance of white power and privilege, thereby rationalizing a pervasive system of racial injustice.

The obsession either closed the eyes of many to the reality of particular histories of oppression and traditions of struggle, or it marginalized those experiences to the point of trivializing them. Process theory, rights theory, original understanding, and the synthesis of law and economics were all offered as solutions to Wechsler's dilemma. All these solutions were ultimately unsatisfactory, particularly in light of what might have happened had pragmatism and realism not created the value vacuum exploited by conservative forces.

C. The Battle over *Brown* and the Retreat from Racial Justice

In the wake of the *Brown* decision, conservative and progressive variants of liberalism battled over the right to define *Brown* and thus to determine its legacy. I will describe two conservative variants—original understanding, and law and economics—and two progressive variants—rights, and process theory—involved in the battle over *Brown*. The final variant discussed is a synthesis of a conservative conception of individual rights and process theory. It became known as the strict scrutiny and colorblindness approach and became the dominant framework for resolving the legacy of racism in American society. This conservative synthesis succeeded in both confirming and containing *Brown*.

Let me explain the problem created by the *Brown* decision and why this battle over the meaning of the decision was necessary. *Brown* reversed the almost-sixty-year reign of Supreme-Court-sanctioned segregation of African-Americans inaugurated by the 1896 ruling of *Plessy v. Ferguson*. By holding that the separate-but-equal doctrine of that case had no place under our Constitution, the *Brown* decision threatened to topple the edifice of segregation constructed to subjugate African-Americans throughout the South in the wake of slavery's abrogation. But not only state-sponsored segregation was threatened by this decision. The Court seemed to suggest, based on realist-type empirical research, that racial separation itself was the violation. If this was the violation, judicial remedies might decree the integration of every public institution—schools, businesses and governments—in order to repair the history of societal discrimination against African-Americans.

Because of *Brown*'s potential to reconstruct the American landscape by deinstitutionalizing the white power and privilege accumulated under slavery and segregation, conservative forces quickly reacted to fill the value-vacuum made undeniably apparent by Wechsler's critique. The central objective of the conservative reaction was to put forth a theory of the judiciary's role that could simultaneously accept *Brown* and hold the line against further reconstruction of American society.

The Framers' intent or original understanding school of jurisprudence admitted that judges were making value choices, but the implications of the realist critique could be avoided so long as judges were applying the values of a higher, democratic source, rather than their own. For instance, when interpreting constitutional values such as equality, the constitutional value at issue in *Brown*, the question was not whether the petitioner's or respondent's conception of equality should be applied; nor was it whether the state legislature's or Congress's conception of equality should be applied. The proper question was: What did the Framers of the Fourteenth Amendment mean by equal protection or, alternatively, what was the public conception of equal protection at the time the provision was ratified? I suppose that this approach satisfies Wechsler's concern that the principle chosen to resolve the case needs to transcend both the subject matter of and the parties to the case.

Yet this methodology would be all too static for pragmatists and legal realists. As we've seen, for them the inquiry into the past is purely instrumental, never controlling. That equality meant a particular thing to a segment of the American population in the 1800s would not be a good enough reason to apply that same understanding of equality in the mid-twentieth century. A dynamic society requires dynamic values. But because neither the pragmatists nor the realists elaborated a more substantive vision of community designed to protect and promote the interests of the least powerful, conservative forces intolerant of the change suggested by *Brown* provided their own normative conception of community. For some proponents of the original understanding hermeneutic, such as Robert Bork, *Brown* was correctly decided. Yet, Bork contended that his methodology would not permit affirmative action in the absence of a clear showing of a history of intentional discrimination by the state implementing the policy. This effectively held the line at *Brown*, robbing it of its transformative potential. That is, the problem with *Plessy* and the separate-but-equal doctrine was that states were allocating students to schools on the basis of race. It was permissible, then, to use race to correct this violation, as *Brown* purported to do. But institutions that had not committed such violations did not need to nor should they voluntarily use race to determine where students attended school. Such noncorrective race-based classifications would not be consistent with the intent of the Framers or the intent of their times and, therefore, should be held unconstitutional.

The law-and-economics school of jurisprudence also admitted that judges were making value choices, but the implications of the realist critique could be avoided so long as judges were applying values that did not simply reflect their own personal biases. Like Dewey and the realists, they were ready to engage in a consequentialist analysis of values. The normative question of which values should be preferred was answered by deferring to the logic and ends of market capitalism, unless

some higher law like a statute or constitution required a different interpretation. Thus, for common-law questions or questions clearly left
open by statutes, judges were encouraged to support and overturn
precedent based on their consequentialist analysis of what rule best promotes the goal of efficiency, or, the highest return at the lowest cost.

Under the law-and-economics approach, efficiency became the criterion of value needed to orient critical inquiry normatively. Because of
the normative vacuum established by pragmatism's and realism's failure
to develop a substantive vision of democracy, law-and-economics proponents were able to promote efficiency over equity concerns.

For constitutional questions, many law and economics advocates
became strict or plain-meaning constructionists. This position turned
out to be practically indistinguishable from the position taken by the
proponents of original understanding on both state-imposed segregation and affirmative action. Some, however, brought economic analysis
to bear even on these constitutional questions. They argued that _Brown_
was correctly decided because governmental segregation on the basis
of race created wasteful and inefficient duplication of resources.
Maintaining two separate schools for blacks and whites, when one unified school system was sufficient, simply did not promote the goal of
efficiency.

The law-and-economics analysis held the line, however, as did the
original-intent analysis discussed above, at _Brown_. Again, in the absence
of a clear showing of state discrimination, no affirmative remedy would
be forthcoming. State-imposed affirmative action programs that created "special preferences" for minorities and women, denying positions
and opportunities to "more qualified" persons, were inefficient and thus
a violation of the equal protection clause of the Fourteenth Amendment.

In contrast to these two conservative postrealist reactions to _Brown_,
legal liberalism produced two progressive responses to the Wechsler
critique. One response was a renewed jurisprudence of rights set forth
by Ronald Dworkin. The other was a jurisprudence of democratic
process put forth most notably by John Hart Ely. In his renaissance of
natural-rights theory, Dworkin also agreed with the realist critique that
judges were making value choices. But he argued along with the traditionalists that judicial review need not be an instance of naked power.

For Dworkin, judges exercised bounded discretion. The values they applied should flow from a particular reading of the traditions within which interpretation took place. Thus, Dworkin's reading of those traditions led him to reject the kind of open-ended consequentialism embraced by pragmatists and some of the realists. He also rejected the particular set of values embraced by original-intent, law-and-economics and other schools of thought. Dworkin specifically privileged the value of equality over liberty, thereby directly challenging the legacy of *Lochner*-era jurisprudence.

For Dworkin, the moral theory most consistent with our constitutional traditions, the moral theory that casts those traditions in their best possible light, was that individuals have a right to be treated with equal respect and concern. For Dworkin, this concept of equality was the bedrock of Western civilization and American democracy. The history of social struggles has been the movement of this concept from theory to practice, from rhetoric to reality. While there have been many different conceptions of equality, one had to distinguish, Dworkin would argue, conceptions of equality from the concept of equality. The concept of equality was unchanging and constituted the aspirational pull of our community.

Dworkin saw liberty as a species of this concept of equality, and thus an understanding of the former had to be worked out within the limits established by the latter. This meant that *Brown* was correctly decided, because segregation did not treat African-Americans with equal respect and concern. It stigmatized them as inferior on the basis of something over which they had no control—race and the color of their skin. The liberty right of whites to freely associate only with whites in public schools and thereby to exclude African-Americans had to give way to the equality rights of African-Americans to be treated with equal respect and concern.

On the other hand, affirmative action, as it is normally practiced, does not violate the equality rights of whites who are excluded by a preference for African-Americans. Whites have no inherent right to society's scarce resources, such as positions in state medical schools. The allocation of these scarce resources can be achieved in accordance with the varied goals of society—diversity, restitution, community needs and so on. The only limit on these utilitarian goals is that the process of selection must not violate the rights of individuals to equal respect and concern.

Equal respect and concern do not require that one sole determinant of merit be employed to determine qualification for a scarce resource. When institutions use race as a factor in distributing scarce resources, resulting in the inclusion of some African-Americans and the exclusion of some whites who might have been included had race not been used as a factor, the exclusion of the latter does not violate their right to equal respect and concern. The reason is that there is no presumption of inherent inferiority that attaches to their exclusion. The exclusion does not indicate that those excluded are intrinsically less worthy than those included. So long as the exclusion is random and does not by design single out some particular segment of the applicant population, it should be upheld.

A different progressive response can be seen in the works of the new process theorists. Their focus on assuring that democratic processes operated within the bounds of egalitarian concerns provided a much-needed limit for Dewey's open-ended consequentialism. Legal-process theory divided into two camps, one progressive and the other conservative. The first promised to pursue the implications of *Brown* and intensify the challenge to American racism. The second became the dominant paradigm for Fourteenth Amendment equal-protection analysis and eventually served, like the original-intent and law-and-economics approaches discussed above, to contain the radical implications of *Brown*.

The progressive approach to process relied on the concept of "insular and discrete minorities" first mentioned in footnote 4 of the *United States v. Carolene Products* case of 1938. The primary role of the courts was to make sure the majoritarian democratic processes did not trample the least powerful and most vulnerable segments of the American population. Thus, when certain insular and discrete groups were impacted by majoritarian processes, the Court had to subject the results of those processes to a stricter judicial scrutiny in order to protect the equal-protection rights of these discrete and insular groups. Under this analysis, *Brown* was an easy case. African-Americans were totally excluded from the majoritarian processes that resulted in their state-imposed segregation. The Court could invalidate segregation laws on that basis alone.

But what if African-Americans had participated in the process but had simply failed to convince a majority of voting citizens in Topeka, Kansas that segregation on the basis of race was a bad thing? Something else was clearly needed if process theory was to guard against this undesirable possibility. The answer given by some process theorists was that certain groups in American society required special protection by the courts. History had proven that, because of the insular and discrete status of some groups, they were particularly vulnerable to majoritarian processes. Thus, even if such groups, like African-Americans, participated in the process of deliberation and voting, the court was justified in looking particularly closely at majoritarian results affecting them.

Obviously this approach would have gone far in responding to the historically specific oppression of African-Americans and the need to treat that history uniquely. For instance, the insular-and-discrete analysis would reach those cases in which majorities cloaked their racism in race-neutral language that used the effects of slavery and segregation as criteria for allocating scarce resources. For instance, the education, income, wealth and residence of African-Americans were all clearly affected by centuries of oppression. The new racism perpetuated the domination of African-Americans by structuring competition for scarce resources on the basis of these nonracial criteria, knowing that African-Americans would have fewer of these resources because of past and present racism.

The discrete-and-insular group analysis would have reached much of this because it would not try to distinguish between those color-blind majoritarian outcomes motivated by an invidious intent to discriminate against African-Americans and those lacking such intent but which, in their pursuit of other legitimate objectives, adversely impacted African-Americans, thereby incidentally reproducing the exclusion and marginality created by historic forms of racism.

That is, the insular-and-discrete analysis would not require an inquiry into the motives of lawmakers, as the present approach requires. Rather, since African-Americans would qualify as an insular and discrete group, the burden of proof would be on the government to prove that a race-neutral method of allocating scarce resources which also disproportionately impacted that group did not violate the equal-protection rights of African-Americans. Under the insular-and-discrete groups' analysis, for instance, courts would pay close attention to a state's use of testing to allocate scarce resources. The burden of proof would be on the government to demonstrate the relevance of the test to job performance and the unavailability of less exclusive devices to achieve its objectives. Today, of course, the burden of proof is on African-Americans to show the invidious intent of those legislating the policies under review.

Finally, the insular-and-discrete group analysis would probably uphold the vast majority of voluntary affirmative action programs under siege today. One proponent of this progressive version of process theory, John Hart Ely, has argued that when the majority race decides to limit its own opportunities in order to redress historical imbalances and injustices or to achieve other objectives such as diversity and meeting community needs, courts should not intervene. The process is working properly. Those whites who might lose out are not a discrete and insular minority. Their losing out is not entitled to the same judicial concern as that of groups like African-Americans. Yet, when African-Americans allocate scarce resources to other African-Americans through political entities they have come to control, this is subject to closer scrutiny, though perhaps not the highest scrutiny, unless the excluded individuals are members of an insular and discrete class also in need of protection.

The final post-*Brown* approach was a conservative synthesis of rights and process theory. This synthesis eventually became the dominant paradigm for equal-protection analysis of racial justice issues. It wedded a traditional conception of individual rights to a realist deference to democratic processes. Like other conservative approaches, it managed, eventually, to both capture and contain *Brown*. It can be traced to the strict scrutiny analysis of suspect classifications used in the 1944 case of *Korematsu v. U.S.*[20]

The methodology required that the Court largely to defer to democratic majorities in the area of social and economic legislation, subjecting them to the lowest of judicial scrutiny. Courts would, however, overrule democratic majorities when those bodies used illicit criteria to distribute benefits and burdens to its citizens. Race was an example of an illicit criterion, and, thus, its use by democratic bodies would be subjected to the Court's strictest scrutiny. Race was to be subjected to such strict scrutiny because decisions on the basis of race were most repugnant to the modern democratic sensibility. Race was an immutable characteristic, a trait about which one could do nothing. It would violate the most fundamental tenets of modernity, emphasizing agency, mobility, change and self-creation, to condition the pursuit of good on something outside one's own control to affect. So the Court saw itself as a postrealist protector of democratic processes. It also utilized a conservative understanding of individual rights to check the redistributive potential of democratic bodies.

While liberty was the fashionable personal right in the *Lochner* era, the right of equality was given special status in the post–*Brown* era. But unlike Dworkin's progressive interpretation of equality, this school defined the right as the right to color-blind or race-neutral laws. Thus, color-blindness, a general prohibition against the use of race as a basis for legislating, was embraced as the neutral and transcendent value called for by Wechsler. It assured that legislatures would not use the concept of "group rights" to trample "individual rights." The Court had used individual rights to trump legislative efforts to rectify class or "group" injustices in the *Lochner* era. Now, in the post-*Brown* era, it would use individual rights once again to trump legislative efforts to rectify racial or "group" injustices.

The benefit of the insular-and-discrete group analysis discussed above was that it permitted a conversation about the historical significance of slavery and segregation for the social location of African-Americans. It did not suppose a symmetry of experiences among individuals and groups in the American culture. Some more than others had group-oriented experiences of protracted subordination. The strict scrutiny of racial classifications, color blindness, abstracted the analysis from one historically and contextually sensitive to group dynamics to one concerned about the use of race in general. Under this second approach, then, it was the use of race that was problematic and not the fact that the race burdened happened to be an insular and discrete minority. The implications were clear.

As for *Brown*, the problem was that government used race as a criterion by which to allocate scarce resources. There was no rational relationship between race and a decision about where and with whom one should pursue educational goals. Thus, *Brown* was correctly decided, even if for the wrong reason.

As for those disparate-impact cases discussed above, since race was not used as a criterion to distribute resources, no remedy was forthcoming, unless one could prove that the legislators actually had an invidious purpose to discriminate against African-Americans in their use of a race-neutral classification.

As for affirmative action, since the problem was defined as the mere use of race, even a so-called benign racial classification intended to help African-Americans would be subject to strict scrutiny. If the problem is in the use of race to classify people to receive benefits and burdens, then whites have as much of a right to protection from such generalizations as African-Americans. The middle-of-the-road position contended that, if race was used as one factor among others in deciding the distribution of a scarce resource, a lower-level scrutiny would be appropriate. But in the reality of constitutional adjudication, this commitment appears to have vanished. The trend is toward viewing any use of race in the distribution of scarce resources as pernicious to the constitutional norm of equality. Thus the symmetrical and color-blind approach adopted by the more conservative variant of process theory, intent on devising neutral principles to both capture and contain *Brown*, drained equal-protection analysis of its potential to reckon with the specific and unique history of American racism and the subordination of African-Americans it produced.

In summary, the problem with the approach of strict scrutiny of suspect classes under process theory is that it abstracts the historical causes of black oppression, a reality the "insular and discrete" language tried to tap, to a "suspect racial classification" that makes discrimination on the basis of race suspect regardless of its context. Thus it is unable to respond effectively to the realities of American racism because it characterizes the problem as the conscious use of race in general, rather than the specific use of race to dominate African-Americans and other discrete and insular groups. Like original-intent, law-and-economics and other conservative postrealist approaches, this approach also succeeds in capturing and containing the *Brown* decision.

Given this resolution of the legal process dilemma, the primary question is whether contemporary race jurisprudence has sacrificed a more efficacious balance of the possibilities and limits of democracy on the altars of the neoclassical compulsion for abstract neutrality, a compulsion seen most vividly in Wechsler's call for neutral principles. As we have seen, this desire for abstract neutrality was precipitated by the pragmatist and realist failure to elaborate a normative vision of democratic community that safeguarded the interests of the most marginalized and vulnerable segments of the population. This failure ended up imposing debilitating limits on the use of law to remedy the effects of slavery and segregation.

Just as the insular-and-discrete analysis of progressive legal liberalism understood that an appreciation of democracy's history of oppression required a heavy presumption against racial classifications disadvantaging African-Americans, the neoclassical quest for neutrality typified by Wechsler's speech required the same presumption when democracy purported to act in favor of African-Americans through racial classifications designed to reconstruct America's racist patterns. Thus, strict-scrutiny analysis required that so-called benign racial classifications could be used only to remedy a specific and provable constitutional violation committed by the unit employing the classification, when the remedy did not injure innocent third parties and was also narrowly tailored to achieve its objective.

With such "neutral" limitations, it is not surprising that few affirmative action programs have survived the Court's scrutiny. As the events of the post–Great Society era unfolded, it became apparent that the avowed symmetry of the legal-process approach was asymmetrical in operation, if not in theory. As Justice Marshall often said, strict scrutiny may have been strict in theory, but it was fatal in fact. It was much easier to invalidate racial classifications than to validate them.[20] In the history of strict-scrutiny analysis, for instance, only one Supreme Court case has survived its rigorous review. Unfortunately, the conception of neutrality being settled upon, decades after Wechsler's much-heralded intervention, was one that saw any use of race, hostile or benign, as a breach of neutrality. Color-blindness had become a proxy for neutrality and the revolution inaugurated by *Brown* was halted in midstride.

In Part II, I want to suggest how two progressive and activist intellectuals of the Christian clergy who were writing and organizing during this crucial period of American history offered a different approach to the problems we have been examining. Their approach might well have avoided some of the problems discussed above, and might also have provided a vehicle through which progressive liberalism and religion might find and maintain common ground. I refer to the works of Dr. Walter Rauschenbusch and Dr. Martin Luther King, Jr. Based on a discussion of these two figures, I will suggest a framework within which this synthesis might be achieved and a new spirituality infused into both national public discourse and ordinary daily life.

Part II

God and Democracy

Defining the Role of Religious Discourse in a Secular Culture

Introduction

Part II offers an alternative to the Common Faith urged by Dewey. Walter Rauschenbusch's development of a Social Gospel and Martin Luther King, Jr.'s expansion of that concept in his theology of the Beloved Community help us to resolve many of the difficulties faced by progressive liberalism in general and John Dewey and the American legal realists in particular.

First, these theologies provide us with ways of thinking and talking about the relationship between a progressive liberal agenda and religious and spiritual life. Second, their theological and programmatic commitment to "the least of these" provides us with a mechanism through which we can address and challenge the uses of race to limit and defeat progressive agendas. Third, the normative commitment entailed by this focus on "the least of these" provides a badly needed understanding of limit to supplement Dewey's philosophical liberation of the individual from strictures limiting unfettered self-creation. By democratizing and institutionalizing the Christian value of love and by developing a love-based conception of social justice, these theologies provide us with a substantive vision of democracy that is inclusive and pluralist. This substantive vision embraces the progressive liberal theme of self-empowerment developed by Dewey, but within a system of overlapping duties to God and others that limits the dangerous quest for personal empowerment.

Chapter 3

Institutionalizing the Christian Value of Love through the Social Gospel

In *1861*, only two years after Dewey's birth, Walter Rauschenbusch was born. His father was the sixth in an unbroken line of German Lutheran pastors. When asked as a youth what he desired to become, the precocious Rauschenbusch exclaimed, "John the Baptist." Little did his family realize the prophetic nature of his utterance, for Rauschenbusch would long be remembered as the most significant figure in an influential cultural movement known as the Social Gospel,[1] a prophetic voice crying in an industrial wilderness of disruption, dislocation and despair.[2]

Writing and preaching during the period of Dewey's disaffection with religion, how much of an effect would Rauschenbusch have had on Dewey's conception of religion were the latter acquainted with the former's thought and activism? Very much a product of the progressive liberal era that greatly influenced Dewey at the turn of the century,[3] Rauschenbusch's writing also exemplifies a faith in the human capacity for good and a belief in the indefatigable march of human progress urged onward by the discoveries of science and the possibilities of its technologies.[4] Yet Rauschenbusch's ability to see the importance not just of the religious function but of religion itself in the struggles for liberation marks a crucial difference between the two intellectuals.[5]

First, Rauschenbusch articulates an understanding of God consistent with the most profound insights of the pragmatist critique. Yet that understanding provides normative guidance and thereby avoids both a disempowering relativism and an oppressive absolutism. Second, Rauschenbusch's Christian faith requires a greater appreciation for sin and evil than does Dewey's secular faith. This orientation makes Rauschenbusch much more attuned to the structural and institutional realities of oppression than Dewey. Third, Rauschenbusch takes sin and evil seriously because he has a vision of the Good by which he can define deviations as sin. This conception of the Good is more than a commitment to the process of critical inquiry. Rauschenbusch's vision of a reconstructed America is wedded to the prophetic Christian scripture that commands a concern and commitment to "the least of these"—the disenfranchised, despised and downtrodden of the world.[6] Such a concern requires an affirmative program designed to institutionalize the Christian value of love through democratically accountable structures in which the common good is sought and promoted in an atmosphere that is largely, though never completely, free of subordination. Rauschenbusch referred to this as the Kingdom of God. Each element of the Social Gospel is important in understanding the relevance of religion for a secular culture and the kind of criterion of value needed to give pragmatism and realism[7] a vision of substantive justice.

A. The Social Gospel's Conception of God

The conception of God on which Rauschenbusch constructed the Social Gospel's theology accentuated three dimensions of the Christian message not often stressed by the orthodox Christianity of his day.[8] First, the God of Christianity was democratic by nature in that His grace had reckoned all as equals before Him. Second, the Christian conception of God laid the foundation upon which a true unity of the human race might be achieved, one that simultaneously respected individuality but extolled commonality. Finally, God was deeply moved by the suffering of the world and was not the cause of, or indifferent to, the evil that perpetuated that suffering.

For Rauschenbusch, the traditional conception of God that secularists such as Dewey rejected was outmoded. The real God was buried beneath centuries of ritual, doctrine and bureaucracy devised by those wishing to make religion the handmaiden of political power. Rauschenbusch frankly admitted, then, that: "The conception of God held by a social group is a social product, even if it originated in the mind of a solitary thinker or prophet."[9] The sin of traditional Christian theology was that it failed to distinguish the eternal truth of Christianity from its temporal trappings. In so doing, Christianity mistook the temporal for the eternal, elevating the former to a status that robbed the latter of its redemptive power.

Although the liberating gospel of Christianity was nurtured in the womb of Hebrew oppression, it was born into a world of Roman imperialism and nourished in the fields of a feudal medieval Europe. By the turn of the twentieth century, Christianity still walked boldly in search of earthly command, all too often aligning itself with autocratic forces of wealth, prestige and power. Along the way it appropriated the discourse, imagery and trappings of its secular contexts, and projected a conception of God that was detached, legalistic, authoritarian, and a mere imitation of earthly rule. For Rauschenbusch, such a conception was bankrupt. He observed:

> The old conception that God dwells on high and is distinct from our human life was the natural basis for autocratic and arbitrary ideas about him. On the other hand the religious belief that he is immanent in humanity is the natural basis for democratic ideas about him. When he was far above, he needed vice-regents to rule for him, popes by divine institution and kings by divine right. If he lives and moves in the life of mankind, he can act directly on the masses of men. . . . [T]hat would be a God with whom democratic and religious men could converse as their chief fellow-worker, the source of their energies, the ground of their hopes.[10]

Rauschenbusch's theology conceived of God as "living and moving in the life of mankind," a "God with whom democratic and religious men could converse." Unfortunately, Dewey did not see that here was a conception of God that could bridge the gap between religiosity and progressive liberals. God had paved the way for democracy by so loving the world "that he gave his one and only Son, that whoever believes in him shall not perish but have eternal life."[11] Just as all had sinned and fallen short of the glory of God, all were redeemed in the faith that came through Christ Jesus.[12] With one momentous act of redemptive love, history was forever altered, the veil torn asunder, and men of every station, nationality and creed elevated as equals upon the pedestal of faith in Christ Jesus. As Rauschenbusch so aptly put it:

> When [Jesus] took God by the hand and called him "our Father," he democratized the conception of God. He disconnected the idea from the coercive and predatory State, and transferred it to the realm of family life, the chief social embodiment of solidarity and love. He not only saved humanity; he saved God.[13]

For the proponents of the Social Gospel, it was a short step from the democratizing impact of God's act of redemptive love to the unity of the human race in the Beloved Community. If all were equals in the sight of God, with an equal opportunity to enter the Kingdom of God through faith in Christ Jesus, then Christianity could bridge the historic chasms that separated men from women, blacks from whites, Asians from Europeans, Catholics from Protestants, and rich from poor. "You are all sons of God through faith in Christ Jesus," the apostle Paul reminded the Galatians, "There is neither Jew nor Greek, slave nor free, male nor female, for you are all one in Christ Jesus."[14] Rauschenbusch understood that "[t]he Christian God has been a breaker of barriers from the first. All who have a distinctively Christian experience of God are committed to the expansion of human fellowship and to the overthrow of barriers."[15] Bringing this fact home to the Christian consciousness was "part of the mission of the Social Gospel, and it looks to theology for the intellectual formulation of what it needs."[16]

The danger in such a religious mission was that it would serve as the sheep's wool beneath which imperialistic ambitions masquerade: "As long as there are great colonizing imperialisms in the world, the propaganda of Christianity has a political significance."[17] Rauschenbusch sought to avoid this dreadful possibility by emphasizing the value of and

respect for plural cultures and the need to humbly search for commonalities that form the core of spiritual solidarity. "The reign of love," he
pointed out, "tends toward the progressive unity of mankind, but with
the maintenance of individual liberty and the opportunity of nations to
work out their own national peculiarities and ideals."[18]

The source of the commonality was God, which Rauschenbusch saw
as the common denominator of our plural existences. "Our human personalities," he observed, "may seem distinct, but their roots run down
into the eternal life of God. . . . The all-pervading life of God is the
ground of the spiritual oneness of the race and of our hope for its closer
fellowship in the future."[19]

Here Rauschenbusch struggled with one of the perennial problems
of philosophy and law, the dilemma posed by the conflict between
monist and pluralist conceptions of reality, the tension between the universal oneness of God and the particular manyness of God. By what
right could the Christian conception of God be forced upon those with
a different or no conception of God? Rauschenbusch rightly implied
that such an enterprise must be undertaken with a degree of humility
and an abundance of love. The One and the many may at times coexist,
when the many are but varied expressions of the One that is universal.
Pointing out the linkages between the many and the One may then be
a way of bringing groups from the particularities of their own identities
to a shared oneness of God.

The shared identity may be called by various names and distinguished by this or that ritual and creed, but the essence of the identity,
the criterion of value, was what was of most importance. Rauschenbusch believed that the "consciousness of solidarity is the essence of all
religion." Because of this human longing for solidarity, all religions and
groups attempted to define who they were by reference to a circle
denoting the boundaries of fellowship. "But the circumference and spa-
ciousness of the fellowship within it," he observed, "differ widely. Every
discovery of a larger fellowship by the individual brings a glow of religious satisfaction."[20]

The human longing for solidarity, to be a part of something greater
than oneself, is the universal of all religious experience. In this sense,
then, religion is not incidental but essential to who we are and shall
become. Rauschenbusch contended that, with its conception of the

human family and the Beloved Community, Christianity offered an international religious consciousness that might facilitate the unity of the human race. These values were present in all religions, though perhaps not as explicitly developed. The mission was to tease out these implications until the ideal of human unity came to be consciously embraced by all.

One had to be ever-cautious that the quest for unity not lead to an oppressive assimilation of others to standards that perpetuated the very oppression the Christian conception of God intended to eradicate.[21] Rauschenbusch put it best when he said, "If we invite men to come under the same spiritual roof of monotheism with us and to abandon their ancient shelters, let us make sure that this will not be exploited as a trick of subjugation by the Empires."[22] The Social Gospel's conception of God as one concerned with and moved by the suffering of humanity was significant in checking this tendency to corrupt good for evil purposes. I will say more about this important limit below but suffice it to say that Rauschenbusch grapples with cultural pluralism and power relations in a way that Dewey and the realists failed to do.

Rauschenbusch also answered an important question that nontheologians like Dewey seldom pose: Why do the good suffer? It is a timeless question to which men and women in every generation and from every walk of life have provided sundry answers. The answers have said much about the conception of God prevalent from time to time and place to place. In Christian literature, the answers have run the gamut from "because they have committed some secret sin or possess some critical flaw of character" to "because evil is so pervasive in this world that suffering randomly affects all" to "because God chastises those he loves, putting no more on us than we are able to bear." The first sees suffering as a form of desert for the sins committed in this life, a warning issued in advance of burning hellfire. The second sees suffering as endemic to the human condition, something to be patiently tolerated until the next life when there will be no more suffering and the weary shall be at rest. The third reckons suffering as a loving God's encouragement to become more righteous.

Rauschenbusch disagreed with all such interpretations of God's role in human suffering. The Christian God was above all one of love and mercy. The preceding interpretations all characterized suffering as an individual phenomenon, as something afflicting the individual in isolation, apart from the rest of the human community. Although some forms of suffering certainly satisfied this criterion, most did not. The modern-day suffering of poverty, hunger, homelessness and exploitation was a collective suffering put in place by collective social processes with collective consequences. "[W]e can not stand for poor and laborious people being deprived of physical stature, youth, education, human equality, and justice, in order to enable others to live luxurious lives."[23] Such a condition was caused not by God, but by humans who have failed to follow God's will. Rauschenbusch contended that true Christians should be repulsed to see the conditions of social suffering "perpetuated by law and organized force, and palliated or justified by the makers of public opinion. None of the keys offered by individualistic Christianity fit this padlock."[24]

Social suffering, then, like the individual suffering of bodily pain, is but a warning "of the existence of abnormal conditions."[25] It prods us to search out the causes and restore the social body to health. Anesthetizing the human body disguises the pain but never heals the cause of the pain. Indeed, we become indifferent to the pain because we no longer feel it. Similarly, modern rationalizations for the existence of grave inequity and suffering, rationalizations that taint the victim as unworthy or as falling short of the mark and that see exploitation as the necessary by-product of advanced civilization, are akin to drugs that conceal the true causes of social misery and pain by numbing us to the reality of human suffering. Rauschenbusch wrote:

> The innocent suffering of great groups through social solidarity simply brings home to us that the tolerance of social injustice is an intolerable evil. The great sin of men is to resist the reformation of predatory society. We do not want God to be charged with that attitude. A conception of God which describes him as sanctioning the present social order and utilizing it in order to sanctify its victims through their suffering, without striving for its overthrow, is repugnant to our moral sense.[26]

If my account of Rauschenbusch's conception of God is correct, he both answered the criticisms of secularists such as Dewey and defined a prophetic role for religion in a secular culture. By historicizing the conception of God, he demonstrated the ways in which it had been appropriated for authoritarian purposes quite contrary to the teachings and life of the historical Jesus. When God is once again projected as a universal truth by which people should order their lives, the abstraction is quite different from the transcendental nonsense critiqued by realists such as Felix Cohen.

This abstraction contains a criterion of value by which the common good can be known and pursued. Because its normative assumptions are clearly stated and elaborated, it is less likely that the concept will be exploited and manipulated to serve purposes for which it was not intended. God is democratized, conceived of as a promoter of equality, respectful of difference but yet longing for a unity in diversity in which certain differences can be respected because our commonalities are understood. Rauschenbusch's abstraction is always envisioned as a God of the people, intimately concerned and involved in the lives of His creations, encouraging them to see evil and suffering as the opportunity for good rather than as one's fate or punishment for sin.

Before discussing the Social Gospel's criterion of value more substantively, we must first develop its conception of sin and evil. The Social Gospel has been accused of having too optimistic a view of human goodness and the capacity of human effort—in other words, of being merely the religious analog of Dewey's Common Faith. Scholars have attributed this to a deficient appreciation of the pervasiveness of sin and evil. I believe this criticism is misplaced. Indeed, I believe, the balance struck by the Social Gospel between an appreciation of the limitations imposed by sin and a faithful struggle against those limitations[27] is precisely the kind of balance needed by the pragmatist and realist theories.

B. The Social Gospel's Conception of Sin and Evil

Living in sin is living outside the will of God. The will of God is that we love Him fully and love our neighbors as ourselves. Thus the will of God is that we consume ourselves at every level of existence with a love for God that transforms our self-love into a liberating love for others. Sin, then, is selfishness, a love for self that draws us out of communion with God and humanity.

This understanding of sin is somewhat different from the conception of sin in classical theology.[28] The latter account views sin as human rebellion against God. Little concern is paid to the sinner's relationship to other individuals. Yet if Jesus' commandment of love speaks both to the individual's relationship with God and to other individuals, an account of sin that fails to incorporate this dimension is surely incomplete. "Sin is not a private transaction between the sinner and God. Humanity always crowds the audience-room when God holds court. . . . We rarely sin against God alone."[29]

Classical theology's preoccupation with sin as a rebellion against God is rooted in the doctrine of original sin. This doctrine attempts to explain the pervasiveness of sin and evil in the world by reference to the sin of Adam and Eve in the Garden of Eden. Their rebellion against God inaugurated Satan's reign in human affairs and began the genetic, biological transmission of sinfulness from one generation to the next. The dimension of man's sin against man is not an issue in this context because, according to the story, Adam and Eve are the only two people on Earth.

Surprisingly, Rauschenbusch does not totally reject the notion of original sin, a central pillar in the classical Christian story of the Fall, Redemption and Salvation of the world. Part of his attraction to this fanciful myth of religious literature is classical theology's willingness to account for individual sin by reference to the unity of the human race. Rauschenbusch sees this unity as a rare opportunity for an individualistic theology like classical Christianity to emphasize Christianity's social and collective underpinnings.

The solidaristic account of sin and evil that pervades all of human existence should alert us to our common origin in God, our common fall from grace and our common struggle for redemption. Unfortunately, traditional scholars have distorted a story capable of illuminating the commonality of human struggle into an individualistic account of our isolated and fractured relationship to God. Although Rauschenbusch would not deny that some evil traits might be transmitted biologically,[30] his emphasis is clearly on the process of social transmission through tradition and culture. "That sin is lodged in social customs and institutions and is absorbed by the individual from his social group is so plain that any person with common sense can observe it. . . ."[31] These customs, traditions, cultures and the institutions that express them create a superpersonal force connecting us with the past, present and future. In one of many illustrations of this connection, Rauschenbusch writes:

> When negroes are hunted from a Northern city like beasts, or when a Southern city degrades the whole nation by turning the savage inhumanity of a mob into a public festivity, we are continuing to sin because our fathers created the conditions of sin by the African slave trade and by the unearned wealth they gathered from slave labor for generations.[32]

Rauschenbusch takes evil seriously. But unlike classical theologians, he does not see it as a brooding omnipresence, a Satan with evil spirits, abstracted from historical context, forever denying the possibilities of social transformation. Instead, Rauschenbusch's Social Gospel argues that although the Western theological understanding of original sin is needed to appreciate the present limitations of the human capacity for good, these limitations are neither natural nor fixed. They are social rather than metaphysical in nature, their causes and consequences substantially discerned from the study of behavior, custom, socialization and acculturation. Sin and evil are primarily communicated through natural institutions like the family, school, job and church. If these institutions could be refashioned in the spirit of Christ, they could better constrain evil and better promote the social good.

Rauschenbusch saw the concept of original sin as an abbreviated reminder of the pervasive and intractable character of evil, that it is with us until the end of time. "We shall never have a perfect social life," he wrote, "yet we must seek it with faith. . . . At best there is always but an approximation to a perfect social order. The kingdom of God is always but coming. But every approximation to it is worthwhile."[33] This awareness required a critical orientation prepared to rethink and reform the institutions and practices of the revolution that had ossified into hierarchies of domination—institutions and practices that were themselves intended to challenge domination. Like all contextual insights reified over time, the doctrine of original sin once expressed a powerful insight into the dilemma of human existence, an insight that counselled faith, hope and love in the face of our own sins and inadequacies. Abstracted from the context of human struggle and suffering, however, that which was intended to redeem humanity encouraged instead a faithless, hopeless and loveless people, those who saw only the possibilities of an afterlife compensating them for all that the evil and sin of this life forbade.

Rauschenbusch's historicizing of sin and evil connected it to earthly institutions and practices in a way the supernatural classical account of evil could not. Humans mired in and weighed down by such evil were in need of redemption, even if such redemption could be only partial and piecemeal at best. Overcoming evil was, then, a perennial enterprise, for the very structures erected to transcend evil were themselves capable of evil. Thus, Christians had to be ever-vigilant, lest they in consummate pride think themselves capable of the perfection only God could possess. This critical vigilance would then concern itself with the ways in which old or new institutions marginalized, excluded and subordinated people, for it was through such processes of domination that sin and evil manifested themselves most profoundly.

As one can see from this discussion, the process of critical inquiry is important to Rauchenbusch as well. But it is not nearly as open-ended as Dewey's approach, because, for Rauchenbusch, critical inquiry is always normatively linked to the liberation of the marginalized and the oppressed from the social inequities that squelch their potential as creations of God entitled to equal worth and dignity.

C. The Social Gospel's Conception of the Kingdom of God

If a historicized conception of sin and evil sensitized Rauschenbusch to the plight of the subordinated and alienated, the New Testament's "least of these my brethren"—the command of love—required Christians to struggle against and transform the principalities and practices of evil.[34] Economic, cultural, and ideological structures of domination frustrated freedom, denigrated dignity and blinded individuals to the Divine within. Rauschenbusch wrote that the essential purpose of Christianity is to transform human society into the Kingdom of God by regenerating all human relations and reconstituting them in accordance with the will of God. The Kingdom of God "overlaps and interpenetrates all existing organizations, raising them to a higher level when they are good, resisting them when they are evil, quietly revolutionizing the old social order and changing it into the new."[35]

Thus, when Rauschenbusch spoke of Christianizing the Social Order in his 1912 work of the same name, he was not advocating Christianity as a state religion. Rather, he was urging individuals to extend the values of Jesus—love, intolerance for injustice and oppression and the vindication of the weak—to all of society's practices. To Rauschenbusch, Christianity had lost its public voice. Silenced by the spread of secularism and the separation of church and state, it was deemed unscientific, a relic of a bygone era in which people were ruled by superstition, myth and emotion. The Social Gospel was the restoration of moral voice to the public sphere.

The Social Gospel could not depend on science to provide that moral voice, because science was too visibly tied to the narrow class interests of those who controlled the sources of funding, the focus of scientific inquiry and the fruits of research. At its best, science could merely open a window to the world according to its own categories of understanding. Religion opened yet another window, a window through which one might glimpse the purpose as well as the possibility of life.

The Social Gospel could not depend on philosophy to provide that moral voice because philosophy was too preoccupied with the epistemological and metaphysical foundations of knowledge. Classical philosophy, like classical theology and jurisprudence, had committed the sin of idolatry. It had turned inward and exalted the mind to the status of God, worshipping its capacity to create the world it imagined. It sought to understand the world and God in terms of the mind rather than to appreciate the tension between world and mind that ultimately made knowledge and action questions of faith and not reason alone.

For Rauschenbusch, then, the role of Christianity in a secular culture was to give voice to the voiceless, affirm their humanity, value their experiences, and infiltrate the whole of social life by sanctifying the secular. An appreciation for the residual evil in all human endeavor demanded vigilance in putting an end to the ways in which reformed institutions continued to oppress those they intended to liberate. This critical perspective nurtured a sensitivity for the least of these, as

Christians endeavored through faith, hope and love to move the mountains of poverty, alienation and exploitation that shaped their world.

The conception of God elaborated above is closely connected to the approach to Christian ethics that integrates abstract normative concepts with earthly struggles and pursuits. It is Rauschenbusch's understanding of the dialectical relationship between the two and the problems associated with exclusively pursuing one over the other that makes his work so prophetic. This integration is best represented in his conception of the Kingdom of God. "This doctrine," he noted, "is itself the social gospel."[36]

The central problem with traditional Christianity was that it had erred either by abstracting the concept of the Kingdom of God to another plane—a spiritual plane detached from earthly travail—or by reducing the Kingdom to the particular institution of the Church on earth. Both approaches were catastrophic and led to the development of what Rauschenbusch called individualistic Christianity, a theology that "sees everywhere countless sinful individuals who must all go through the same process of repentance, faith, justification, and regeneration, and who in due time die and go to heaven or hell."[37] Rauschenbusch pointed out that "[t]his religious point of view is above time and history,"[38] transcendental nonsense in Cohen's words, and the antithesis of the Social Gospel's approach, which "tries to see the progress of the Kingdom of God in the flow of history; not only in the doings of the Church, but in the clash of economic forces and social classes, in the rise and fall of despotisms and forms of enslavement."[39] I will now examine the implications of these errors of Christian theology in greater detail.

First, abstracting the Kingdom of God to otherworldly preoccupations neutralizes the democratic impulses of the Christian Gospel implied by the conception of God discussed above. If God's Kingdom has no implications for this world, neither does Christianity's message of equality and human solidarity. Although individuals might be spiritual equals, vast inequality might legitimately define their earthly condition. Although they might commune as brothers and sisters on some abstract spiritual level, they might continue to erect barriers of race, gender, class and nationality that legitimate unjust forms of subordination.

Such an interpretation makes Christians formally equal before God, notwithstanding their actual inequality in life. When the modern discourse of sovereignty substituted human will for God's will and human law for divine law as the normative guide for behavior, the formalism of divine law was transplanted into secular law. Thus, notwithstanding ostensibly democratic revolutions, one could claim that all were equal before the law, though admittedly vastly unequal as to wealth, power and opportunity. It is this schism between rhetoric and reality, the legitimation of actual suffering and oppression, that Rauschenbusch's conception of the Kingdom of God is intended to remedy. By remedying this problem, Rauschenbusch makes the conception of God discussed above a reality, a catalyst for substantive and not merely formal equality.

Rauschenbusch understood, then, that because of the problems that traditional Christian theology had set its sight on solving, Christian theology had convinced many that the Kingdom of God was a heaven beyond this life to which their attention should be devoted. This claim fostered an otherworldly disposition that devalued the importance of human struggle for justice on earth. Rauschenbusch did not, however, totally reject the abstract conception of the Kingdom. Instead, he maintained an idealism intended to inspire those who seek it. The Kingdom could never be replicated in its fullness and glory, for as mere mortals we were incapable of such feats, but surely we could project it as best we could, given the limitations under which we struggled.

Individual salvation, therefore, is inextricably connected to social salvation, for the individual is shaped by the society in which she lives. Because the individual is born in sin and shaped in iniquity, redemption from sin and evil requires that we redeem the individual from the evil society through which she was constituted. This redemption calls for nothing less than the transformation of oppressive structures that deny equality and frustrate the solidarity of mankind.

The second error in Christian theology on the doctrine of the Kingdom is a natural consequence of the first error. Rauschenbusch believed Christianity had given up on the transformation of this world, because it believed the Kingdom of God had already come in the form of the Church. The institutionalization of Christian faith, then, resulted in the debilitation of faith through an abject dependence on ritual, liturgy and creed. This led to a religious formalism in which a form of godliness was embraced, but the substance of faith, its transformative potential, was abandoned. Although the Church was indeed the "channel through which ethical impulses pour into humanity from God," the Kingdom was yet much more.[40] The Kingdom must never be reduced to any of the constitutive elements that comprise it: a specific church, denomination or social program. The Kingdom was "the sum of all divine and righteous forces on earth."[41]

Just as the possibilities of justice are stultified by its pedantic reduction to legal process, so is the potential of the Kingdom stymied by its reduction to the institutional Church. Individuals begin to define the limits of their Christian duty by the regulative ideals of the institution. Often those regulative ideals are foreign to the mission of Christ, for they focus on narrow bureaucratic concerns designed to perpetuate the institution's existence rather than to promote the goals of the Kingdom. Lost amidst the countless rituals, creeds and liturgies designed to mark one body of believers off from another, many churches—having mistaken worship for service and having taken Luther's justification by faith as the end rather than the beginning of Christian commitment—are ill-prepared to be the courageous agents of social transformation Christ desired them to be.

Fortunately, then, the Kingdom of God casts its net wider than the institution of the Church:

> It embraces the whole of human life. It is the Christian transfiguration of the social order. The Church is one social institution alongside of the family, the industrial organization of society, and the State. The Kingdom of God is in all these, and realizes itself through them all.[42]

Although the Kingdom of God was much more than just the Church, Rauschenbusch nevertheless understood the importance of the Church in preserving religion and fostering the religious consciousness needed to transform society. Thus, unlike Dewey, he never envisioned the withering away of the Church. Like Dewey, however, he understood that "the greatest future awaits religion in the public life of humanity."[43] This was to be the role of religion in a secular culture.

Rauschenbusch understood that before this noble role for religion could be achieved, however, there was a need to challenge the most debilitating assumption of the two errors of Christian theology elaborated above. Christianity's abstraction of the Kingdom to another world and its reduction of the Kingdom to the institution of the Church were both predicated on Christianity's assimilation of individual salvation to Western-style individualism.

For Rauschenbusch, the mission of Christianity had become the salvation of the individual soul from the damnation of hell fire in the life to come. As discussed earlier, this mission not only had certain implications for Christian theology's conception of God, but also implied a preoccupation with questions of individual sin and salvation at the expense of considerations of collective evil and social redemption. In effect, it achieved a separation, not just of church and state, but of secular and religious discourse. The separation of these discourses and the relegation of religious discourse to the sphere of private interaction resulted in the most troubling separation of all—a separation of the public from the private self. The source of this separation was seen in the earliest of modern European thought.

What Luther achieved in the Protestant Reformation of the sixteenth century and Hobbes and Locke achieved in the secular realm was a new arrangement between religion and politics. What began in Hobbes as a strictly naturalist justification for a secular authority that did not depend on religion to legitimate it—although Hobbes's absolutism justified the imposition of state religion—ended in Locke as a full separation of church and state. Hobbes's political theory offers informative parallels to Christian theology and helps to explain the move toward the separation of the religious and the secular that Rauschenbusch found so troubling.

As in Hobbes's state of nature and war of all against all, traditional Christianity views human nature as fallen, depraved and in need of redemption. While enlightened reason redeems the fallen Hobbesian soul, grace salvages the Christian soul. Just as deference to the external authority of the Hobbesian sovereign is deemed necessary in secular matters, deference to the sovereign power of God in spiritual matters is deemed equally vital. The Christian is to render unto Caesar that due Caesar, and to God that due God. This bifurcation results in Christianity's preoccupation with strictly private and spiritual matters and the silencing of the Christian voice in the public space, where Hobbes's sovereign would, through the sword, provide security in exchange for the subject's obedience.

The structure of each account is fundamentally the same. Following the laws of fallen nature results in personal disorder and insecurity. Disorder and the feeling of insecurity it engenders eventually lead to contrition and repentance (a willingness to accept the Kingdom of God in Christianity, and to join the social contract in Hobbes's philosophy). This repentance clears the way for divine and secular intervention by a sovereign authority. The intervention restores a modicum of security and peace in exchange for strict obedience to the sovereign's will (government in the secular realm, and God or his appointed representative in the religous realm). Finally, obedience is rewarded and transgressions are punished.

The focus, whether expressed religiously or secularly, is relentlessly on the individual's personal redemption. Such a focus distracts from the societal forces that shape the evil state of nature from which the individual is to be redeemed. The individual in both accounts is an abstraction disconnected from social context and from a history in which sin and evil are transmitted from one generation to the next.

For Rauschenbusch, then, the true meaning of God's Kingdom and the Christian's responsibility for others had long been sacrificed upon the altars of Western individualism, notwithstanding the protestations of the Church. Rauschenbusch's objective was to historicize and contextualize these abstractions fully and to thereby give the conception of the Kingdom of God both a divine and a secular purpose.

Rauschenbusch, therefore, did not reduce the concept of the Kingdom to any one institution, such as the Church, or any one political program, such as socialism or capitalism, but perceived the Kingdom as a much broader spiritual movement pervading all of life. "The Kingdom of God," Rauschenbusch wrote, "is humanity organized according to the will of God."[44] Without the benefit of the preceding discussion, such a characterization would be repulsive to a secular mentality, conjuring up images of a medieval period in which all of society was governed by an autocratic Church with its own armies, courts and magistrates. Rauschenbusch, of course, flatly rejected such a vision of religion's role. It was not the separation of church and state that he objected to in modern culture, but the much more radical and debilitating separation of private religion and public life. Religion was vital to human existence, and the prophetic Christianity of the Social Gospel, he believed, was the key to a more just society.

As interpreted through the consciousness of Jesus, the Kingdom of God stands for, first, the divine worth of life and personality. Jesus demonstrated the divine worth of all life by choosing to associate primarily with those whom society had labelled as outcasts and social plagues, as lacking in all worth, much less divine worth. By situating himself on the margins, he radically democratized the conception of worth and freed it from the trappings of power, wealth and prestige. He was born in a stable and buried in a borrowed tomb, and while He preached, He had no established home to call his own. Because He understood deprivation and marginality first hand, He reached out most to those without hope.

When announcing His public ministry in the temple, Jesus made clear that He was anointed to preach good news to the poor, and sent to proclaim freedom for the prisoners and recovery of sight for the blind, to release the oppressed, and to proclaim the year of the Lord's favor for them.[45] He made His home among the most destitute, derelict and downtrodden elements of the society, healing the sick who could not afford doctors, feeding the hungry who could not afford food and clothing, and sheltering the naked who could not afford even the basics of life. Even in these, "the least of these my brethren," Jesus saw divine worth. Thus His life, from cradle to grave, was revolutionary, toppling socially constructed hierarchies that valued the powerful, rich and elite over the powerless, poor and pedestrian. His allegiances, Rauschenbusch believed, demonstrated that

> the Kingdom of God, at every stage of human development, tends toward a social order which will best guarantee to all personalities their freest and highest development. This involves the redemption of social life from the cramping influence of religious bigotry, from the repression

of self-assertion in the relation of upper and lower classes, and from all forms of slavery in which human beings are treated as mere means to serve the ends of others.[46]

Second, the Kingdom of God implies what Rauschenbusch described as "a progressive reign of love in human affairs."[47] Society must learn to love by practicing love, by creating those institutions that promote and inculcate concern for one's fellow creature. We can see the bounty of love, Rauschenbusch contended, "wherever the free will of love supersedes the use of force and legal coercion as a regulative of the social order."[48] Not that we can ever exist without law, but we must condition ourselves to see law as the beginning and not as the limit of our duty to humanity. Christ came not to destroy the law, but to fulfill it, to supersede it by using it as a springboard to a higher, more spiritual reality. A teacher of law once inquired of Jesus what commandment of the law He deemed most important. Jesus replied, "Love the Lord your God with all your heart and with all your soul and with all your mind and with all your strength. The second is like unto it: Love your neighbor as yourself. There is no commandment greater than these."[49]

To make love real in the world is the quest of the Social Gospel.[50] For Rauschenbusch, "[t]he highest expression of love is the free surrender of what is truly our own, life, property, and rights,"[51] for the advancement of the Kingdom.[52] It requires that we give up "the opportunity to exploit men," draining them for our own ease and convenience. Such self-sacrifice was vividly depicted by Christ in his willingness to bear the cross of redemption. For the Kingdom, Christ was willing to be misunderstood, disparaged, chased, unjustly accused, tried and convicted; he was willing to be bound, stabbed and hung from a cross until death. Greater love has no man than this, He told His disciples, that He lay down His life for His friends.[53] Because His central commandment was one of love, Christ made clear that love begets love which abounds all the more.

In conclusion, the Kingdom of God must be understood as humanity organized according to the will of God, a God conceptualized as a promoter of substantive as well as formal democracy. The Kingdom upholds the divine worth of life and personality for all and, as Christ did, sides with the oppressed and marginalized as a way of remaining true to this ideal. Such a commitment is the best guarantee to all personalities of their freest and highest development.

Finally, the Kingdom is committed to the progressive reign of love in human affairs. It is only through such love, as I have described and will elaborate shortly, that the struggle for the Kingdom of God can be sustained against obstacles no less formidable than those confronted by Christ.

Chapter 4

Dr. Martin Luther King, Jr. and the African-American Religious Origins of the Beloved Community

The life and works of Dr. Martin Luther King, Jr. were significantly influenced by the social gospel of Walter Rauschenbusch. While Rauschenbusch wrote during the tumultuous but promising times of the progressive era, King later led a civil rights movement no less transformative than the progressive era of the early twentieth century. As stated above, Rauschenbusch modernized Christianity in the same way Dewey modernized philosophy, adapting it to the conditions and possibilities of American society. Rauschenbusch's social gospel answered the major problems raised by Dewey's critique of traditional religion, problems that ultimately necessitated Dewey's rejection of supernatural faith in favor of a naturalist Common Faith.

Had Dewey incorporated some of the progressive understandings of religion being developed during his lifetime, progressive liberal thought might have developed differently than it did. As it turned out, both the pragmatist and realist variants of progressive liberalism were too utilitarian to appeal to that deep yearning for a spiritually affirming and just community.

King was obviously influenced by Rauschenbusch's theology of the social gospel as well as the work of Reinhold Niebuhr, Martin Buber and Gandhi. Most often forgotten or ignored by King scholars and biographers, however, is the profound influence of the African-American religious tradition on his theology and activism. An understanding of this influence is essential to grasping King's approach to theology, politics and social reform. It is through this tradition that he developed an understanding of the "Beloved Community," his response to the problems facing the "least of these" in American society.

It was the influence of this African-American religious tradition on King's thought and work that significantly laid the foundation for his religiospiritual understanding of liberal tenets, an understanding I believe is crucial to the resurrection of the progressive liberal vision in American politics and culture. King's appropriation of the African-American religious tradition led him to a spirituality of reconstruction that he did not fully elaborate in his lifetime but which is there, like a seed beneath the surface of all he said and did, awaiting our attention and cultivation.

A. The Role of the African-American Church in the American Slave Experience

In order to fully understand the influence of the African-American religious tradition on King's thought, one must understand the vital role African-American religion played in the community-building enterprise necessitated by the social disintegration and chaos of the American slavery experience. Confronted by practices of social control that destroyed or suppressed their West African heritage, language and traditions, Africans were expected to conform to a community created by their slave-masters. Slave-masters attempted to refashion the African's identity through the eradication of collective memory. In the void created by the socially imposed atomization and amnesia of the African community, the African-American Church served both to legitimate and delegitimate the moral authority of a slave-owning society. An understanding of both effects is essential for understanding King's theology and process of interpretation.

1. The Role of Religion in the Legitimation of Authority

Slave-masters believed Christianity had a stabilizing and disciplining influence on the slaves' dispositions, and they thought it would foster consent by Africans to their exploitation and oppression. The conservative evangelicalism intended to convince Africans of their subordinate status, however, possessed qualities that would eventually allow many slaves to turn its use as a rationalization of slavery against slavery itself. The rationalization of slavery generally went along the following lines: Africans were a heathen class of humans, pagans outside the Christian community. Slavery was, therefore, an institution established principally for the benefit of Africans, intended to save them from God's wrath against pagan worshippers. Through the beneficent institution of slavery, these heathens might gradually be converted from their sinful and evil ways and made fit for the Kingdom of God.

The concern for salvation under this conservative evangelicalism was, of course, a spiritual and not an earthly salvation. Bringing salvation to the slaves was premised on five basic assumptions of a conservative Christian orthodoxy later challenged by Rauschenbusch and King. The first was the fallen nature of human beings—the pervasiveness of human depravity and sin. The second was the need for contrition—a period of mourning characterized by feelings of personal guilt and sorrow for sins. The third was the need for conversion—an intensely personal experience with God in which the burdens of sin were lifted and the soul cleansed and made fit for the Kingdom of God. The fourth was the necessity of coming out of the world—the sometimes-physical but usually psychological separation of the community of believers from sinful, worldly concerns and pursuits. The last was a deference to the state and existing social order—rendering unto God that which was God's and unto Caesar that which was Caesar's. Such an understanding of separation of church and state was predicated on a belief that God had duly appointed civil government to constrain the sinful nature of earthly beings.

These features of conservative evangelicalism were considered rooted in an infallible scripture representing the untainted word of God. They legitimated slave-masters' authority in several ways.

Southern evangelicals elaborated the scriptural justifications for slavery and invoked the will of God to reconcile slaves to their subordinate status. Slavery could not be sin, they reasoned, since God sanctioned it in his infallible Word. Evangelicals frequently cited the Old Testament story of Noah's son, Ham, whose progeny God supposedly condemned to a legacy of servitude for Ham's indiscretion. These and other scriptural evidences were, to the proslavery evangelicals, conclusive proof of God's authorization of African slavery.

Having provided the moral justification for slavery through scripture, evangelicals constructed an argument designed to avert any effort by the Church to transform the institution. Because the scripture supported slavery, and secular authority established and protected it under state law, the Church, mindful of its commitment to the separation of church and state, could not condemn slavery. Because slavery did not constitute sin, God's law did not contradict the civil law. Slavery fell under the latter, and the scriptures dictated obedience to secular authority.

Moreover, conservative evangelicalism dictated that because God would deal with the evil of Southern slavery and apartheid in His own way and time, the eradication of those institutions should await His divine deliverance as evidenced by the changed hearts and minds of men. Like the apostle Paul's letter to the master of the slave named Onesimus in the New Testament, persuasion and not coercion was the preferred strategy for dealing with the slavery question. Thus patience and the implicit acceptance of a slave's subordinate status were exalted as the highest of Christian virtues.

Conservative evangelicalism had made its position on the morality of slavery quite clear. Unresolved, however, was whether the separation of church and state permitted the Church to play any role at all in the relationship between masters and slaves. Although scripture exhorted masters to provide their slaves with instruction sufficient for salvation, evangelicals emphasized that salvation was the sole purpose of giving slaves the Gospel. The evangelical message was that if slaves were faithful to the Gospel—humble and obedient, faithfully serving in the station to which providence had assigned them—they too could enter the Kingdom of God. As one evangelical contended: "Our design in giving them [the slaves] the Gospel, is not to civilize them—not to change their social condition—not to exalt them into citizens or freemen—it is to save them."[1]

2. The Role of Religion in the Delegitimation of Authority

Although the use of religion as an instrument of social control often necessitated oversight by white masters, strict enforcement was not maintained, and slaves often met separately for religious services, including weekly and Sunday evening services. It was within the freedom provided for religious worship that Africans began to assert some control over how the void created by the disintegration of their cultural identities and communities would be filled. In this small space of freedom, an alternative conception of community was defined, and the history of a new American people emerged. African-American religion and its central vehicle of expression, the African-American Church, supplied the needed catalyst for the reconstruction of community destroyed by slavery.

Although slave-masters and evangelicals attempted to limit the transmission of counterhegemonic interpretations of scripture, their efforts were often met with quiet defiance and limited success. African gospel preachers and slaves who learned to read against their masters' wishes (and, many times, against state law as well) were determined to read the Bible in light of their own experiences. Many slaves realized that the message of submission, docility and absolute obedience to the master was a distorted picture of the Bible's eternal truths.

The Africans' appropriation of conservative evangelicalism as a bulwark against the degradation and countless microaggressions of slavery proved that there were alternate interpretations of the texts that supposedly justified their subjugation. Slaves demonstrated that scripture was subject to an alternative interpretation that called for the eradication of the very social structure evangelicals sought to legitimate. In short, in their monumental struggles against oppression, slaves deconstructed and reconstructed religious ideology to reflect their deepest yearnings for freedom and community. To the surprise and fear of many whites, slaves transformed an ideology intended to reconcile them to a subordinate status into a manifesto of their God-given equality. This theological reconstruction was both prophetic and pragmatic in orientation.

Prophetic Christianity involved a critical application of religious principles to the social context of oppression. It measured and judged that context by the normative standards derived from the religious tradition. Thus prophetic Christianity always presupposed a normative or ideal conception of community as a standard from which deviation might be judged, challenged and transformed. For prophetic Christians, slavery might at times have to be tolerated but it could never be accepted. One was obligated to proclaim God's judgment on such an evil and to offer oneself as an instrument through which God's deliverance from slavery might be wrought.

Like the prophets of the Old Testament, prophetic Christians restored the connection between religious devotion and social justice. Under the judgment of God expressed through the prophet, one could not simultaneously claim to be faithful to God and also be an exploiter of the weak and vulnerable. Protection and just treatment of the most powerless segments of the community were inextricably connected to righteousness, and, thus, a devotee of the faith could not have one without the other. Those who maintained otherwise were hypocrites, vipers and the true sinners against God and humanity.

Conservative evangelicalism taught that slavery was a divinely ordained practice instituted by the master race for the benefit of morally deficient Africans. But slaves read of Moses, the Hebrew children and God's mighty deliverance from the hardships of Egyptian slavery. The story provided proof of God's intolerance of American slavery and his intention someday to divide the Red Sea of Southern oppression and lead His people out of Pharaoh's land.

Many slaves found in the Judeo-Christian tradition, then, and particularly in the historical Jesus of early Christianity, a call to revolutionary action. They read of a Jesus who proclaimed that God had anointed Him to "preach the gospel to the poor; . . . to preach deliverance to the captives, and . . . to set at liberty them that are bruised";[2] who commanded those who would follow him to care for "the least of these": the hungry, naked, sick, and those in prison; who entered Jerusalem to the revolutionary cry of Hosannah; and who defiantly asserted "[t]hink not that I am come to send peace on earth: I came not to send peace, but a sword."[3] Denmark Vessey and Nat Turner, for example, recognized the revolutionary potential of Christianity: "since God is on our side, we strike for freedom, confident in his protection."[4] The Reverend Henry Highland Garnet contended: "'To such degradation [as slavery] it is sinful in the extreme for you to make voluntary submission. . . . Brethren arise, arise! Strike for your lives and liberties. Now is the day and the hour. . . . Rather die freemen than live to be slaves'."[5]

Pragmatic Christianity was a functional religion, very much resembling Dewey's pragmatism. It was improvisational, experimental and open to revision. Beliefs, rituals and practices were valued according to their utility in restoring a sense of community to a people whose community cohesiveness had been weakened and destroyed by a relentless persecution. In short, pragmatic Christianity was concerned with the development of understandings that permitted an oppressed people to survive from day to day and maintain a faith in ultimate deliverance, if not in this life, then in the one to come.

Pragmatic Christianity found scriptural support for a more patient opposition to slavery that fostered and preserved a healthy sense of self-worth. It was not focused, as was prophetic Christianity, on openly proclaiming judgment on the evil system of slavery and utilizing every opportunity to defy it. Instead, pragmatic Christianity focused on the internal development of spiritual resources needed to survive slavery.

Against the formidable oppression of slavery, segregation and contemporary forms of subjugation, this pragmatic Christianity would provide the means by which African-Americans could survive their daily travails. Its emphasis on personal faith nurtured a forward-looking people who could sing with conviction the words "I'm so glad that trouble won't last always."[6] Its emphasis on love bolstered a sense of self-esteem diminished by the debilitating and degrading practices of a culture that relegated them to the status of objects. It nurtured an inward-looking people who could sing with reassurance the words "The trumpet sounds within my soul. I know I ain't got long to stay here."[7]

Conservative religious ideology portrayed slaves as inherently inferior and unequal creatures in need of white paternalism. But slaves heard of a God who gave His only Son to die for all humanity. They heard that God did not discriminate among persons—that in Him there was neither Jew nor Gentile, slave nor free—that all were brothers in Christ Jesus. Slave-masters and evangelical preachers admonished slaves to render absolute obedience to their masters and to serve cheerfully in the position to which they were destined. But slaves read of and believed in a master superior to their earthly masters—a master to whom their own masters were held in submission, and whose commandments their masters were obligated to obey. The belief in Jesus as ultimate master undermined the suggestion that complete submission was owed to one's earthly master.

The disparity between what slaves read and heard from their own preachers and the practices of whites in the slave system had two important consequences. First, it preserved and enhanced the self-esteem of the slaves; the realization that some whites were not faithful to the Word provided them with a sense of moral superiority. Even in slavery, slaves could be the light unto the sinner's path.

Second, it provided a standard against which they could measure whites individually, rather than collectively by their social status as master race. It provided a framework for understanding the differences between cruel white overseers and whites who worked on the underground railroad to freedom. Even when the institutions of oppression seemed most intractable, understanding their oppression as the sin of unfaithful whites maintained for the Africans a sense of sanity and hope occasionally given new meaning by the prophetic focus on power and immediate liberation. In short, the pragmatic appropriation of Christian ideology by the African-Americans provided the basis for their survival of slavery's many brutalities and indignities.

Although this appropriation helped to restore the dignity of the African slave, it also had paradoxical effects. Pragmatic Christianity admirably served the cause of survival, but its eschatological and inward orientation simultaneously served the function of social control. It saved black Christians from a debilitating hatred which, if permitted to fester, would have created a pervasive sense of despair and hopelessness that would have substantially impaired the moral will to survive. However, it also promoted as virtues patience and tolerance of the social institutions of oppression. Viewing morality in terms of individual character thus undermined the possibilities of a sustained Christian radicalism against what was perhaps the most debilitating and sustained system of subordination known to the modern world—American slavery.

3. The Role of Religion in the Shaping of Alternative Conceptions of Community

The unique synthesis of prophetic and pragmatic Christianity drawn from slave religion was the African-American religious tradition that significantly shaped King's theology and praxis. This synthesis drew heavily on the interplay between the individualist and spiritual orientation of pragmatic Christianity and the collectivist and social orientation of prophetic Christianity. It encouraged an intensely personal relationship with God while nurturing the possibilities of collective defiance and transformation. I will argue shortly that this synthesis formed the foundation of King's conception of the Beloved Community. But first, let us explore more closely the alternative conception of community implied by the prophetic and pragmatic conceptions of Christianity developed above.

The African-American Church rejected white Christianity's claim that the law and order of a slave society were necessary to constrain the evil proclivities of human nature and should be obeyed. Furthermore, most slaves probably never accepted the view that slavery was justified on grounds of black inferiority and white superiority. For these slaves, the spiritual freedom and sense of equality that accompanied religious conversion threw into question the morality of the social order in which they lived. Conversion was an experience of unconditional love and acceptance from God and those involved in the process. No earthly slave society or system of oppression could refute such a cosmic affirmation of one's inherent worth. One student of this period writes:

> Contradicting a system that valued him like a beast for his labor, conversion *experientially* confirmed the slave's value as a human person, indeed attested to his ultimate worth as one of the chosen of God. . . . [M]eetings encouraged participants to include references to individual misfortunes and problems in their prayers and songs, so that they might be shared by all. This type of consolation . . . [was] the answer to the crucial need of individuals for community.[8]

The religious experience of conversion was central to the alternative belief system of slaves and the alternative community that belief system implied. The process of conversion in African-American religion involved a period of sustained mourning in which the contrite sinner would assemble with worshipers in prayer for as many successive meetings as required to "bring the sinner through"—a phrase used to express the sinner's completion of a right of passage from the alienated existence of sinner to the bonds of Christian fellowship and community. The process of conversion often resulted in a cataclysmic seizure of the person by the Holy Spirit that catapulted all into a rapture of ecstatic joy and praise. The experience was collectively cathartic. In the slave community, uninhibited shouting and praise temporarily obliterated secular distinctions in status between the slaves. It was a process in which personalities disintegrated by the social chaos of oppression found meaning and commonality by fusing with others in a collective act of self-affirmation and even defiance.

The African-American Christianity that resulted from this synthesis between prophetic and pragmatic variants offered the alternative conception of community that would inspire King to struggle to redeem American society from its racist and oppressive history. King's aspiration to rebuild community from the social death of slavery and segregation paralleled the conversion experience in slavery. Nonviolent direct action would inaugurate a period of societal mourning and repentance for the sins of the past. From this collective contrition redemption would follow. New individuals would be forged in the crucible of redemptive suffering. A new community, a beloved community, would evolve from a righteous struggle for the soul of America.

The struggle for a sense of collective as well as individual self-worth was essential to any social conversion; segregation laws and impoverished conditions that diminished not only self-worth but a community's sense of itself as well had to be challenged and abolished. The objective was to break down the barriers of hatred and misunderstanding that prevented individuals from seeing and respecting the God-given humanity of all.

But King knew that only collective action and peaceful defiance of the status quo could achieve the destruction of such barriers and simultaneously engender the formation of a beloved community founded on love and justice. A redistribution of wealth and power through the collectively cathartic experience of social conversion was a necessary part of this conception of community.

In this social conversion, law would have to assist in the obliteration and amelioration of many of the secular distinctions founded on race, class and the deprivation of fundamental human rights. Like the alternative conception of community implied by the conversion experience in African-American religion, social conversion would strive for a universal sense of oneness that appreciated the particularity of the African-American experience. This social conversion of the American culture would require people to change their hearts and minds as well as behaviors. While law could not alone transform hearts and minds, it could edify. It could encourage the kind of introspection that makes such change possible.

I believe King's synthesis of pragmatic and prophetic Christianity drew from the concrete experiences of the African-American struggle for liberation. The communal or social possibilities of religious conversion greatly impressed him in this regard. In the conversion experience of the African-American religious tradition, previously alienated individuals saw themselves as inextricably connected through prayer and praise that placed them on one accord. In the call and response of conversion a special solidarity was forged which, at least for this moment of resplendent rapture, harmoniously integrated class, gender and regional distinctions. Difference became an asset rather than a liabilty, an opportunity to see the same God variously expressed through the particularities of community. King sought to bring this experience of textured solidarity from the shout circle of the African-American religious tradition to the larger American society. Through a social conversion that emulated religious conversions, the Beloved Community might be born. Alienated individuals might be able to glimpse the interrelatedness of their being and begin to act from an orientation of love rather than fear as they worked out their own textured solidarity.

To foster this spiritual and social solidarity, King masterfully used narrative, the story-telling that had long been a cornerstone of African culture in general and the African-American religious tradition in particular. A major attribute of narrative is that it gives voice to those rendered voiceless by discourses, ideologies and institutional practices that objectify them as things to be possessed rather than beings to be revered. It sets forth the irreducible essence of one's humanity and disperses the dark shadows that shroud its beauty from view. Through narrative mere footnotes in history are lifted into the text and read as agents in the making of history and not mere passive appendages to the histories of others. We gain through the stories of those made voiceless by a stultifying cultural imperialism, a picture more complete than before, a chorus of human experience richer than the monotone of the conqueror's refrain.

Another attribute of narrative is that it explains how ideologies, discourses and social orderings are experienced by the oppressed. To be sure, oppression breeds pathologies that the oppressed must strive to overcome, but it also spawns more positive and creative responses. Narrative often provides insight into these more positive responses, the ways marginalized groups transform hopeless conditions into powerful possibilities that might benefit us all. Such understanding informs a more complex reconstructive vision of community than the myopic insights of one-dimensional histories permit. In other words, contained within the harrowing experiences of oppression are rich alternative conceptions of community developed by the oppressed to make sense of their worlds and to inspire their struggle for better worlds still. By examining the concrete ways people have responded to oppression, we often find the proverbial diamond in the rough—the nuanced ways people have reconstructed community from chaos and hope from despair. The theoretical possibilities presented by a conception like the Beloved Community are given practical guidance by the elaboration of such experiences through narrative.

Finally, narrative makes an epistemological claim. We know first and best through experience, emotion and feeling. Only later is this knowledge given expression by the abstract categories of mind that detach it from its true source of creation. Narrative is the language of spirit speaking to spirit, that ineffable sixth sense connecting us with the other through the often different stories we tell of our struggles to be free from and yet belong to something. Through stories we come to know the other not as other but as self waiting to be claimed. Through stories we bridge, even if temporarily, the chasms that seemingly separate our plights, and we know, even if we cannot long sustain its awareness, that we are not alone.

King realized that many African-Americans probably never believed that the assumptions of conservative evangelicalism logically compelled their submission to authority. Their submission was not based on consent to a social order they believed to be legitimate. Rather, coercion and its constant threat of death, injury, humiliation or impoverishment compelled their submission. Individuals may have fully agreed with the theoretical critique of conservative religious ideology and yet been constrained by existential limitations that made collective struggle to attain alternative conceptions of community difficult if not impossible. King eloquently describes these existential limitations through a moving use of narrative:

> [W]hen you have seen vicious mobs lynch your mothers and fathers at will and drown your sisters and brothers at whim; when you have seen hate-filled policemen curse, kick, brutalize and even kill your black brothers and sisters with impunity; when you see the vast majority of your twenty million Negro brothers smothering in an airtight cage of poverty in the midst of an affluent society; . . . when you take a cross-country drive and find it necessary to sleep night after night in the uncomfortable corners of your automobile because no motel will accept you; when you are humiliated day in and day out by nagging signs reading "white" and "colored"; when your first name becomes "nigger" and your middle name becomes "boy" (however old you are) and your last name becomes "John," and when your wife and mother are never given the respected title "Mrs."; when you are harried by day and haunted by night by the fact that you are a Negro, living constantly at tiptoe stance never quite knowing what to expect next, and plagued with inner fears and outer resentments; when you are forever fighting a degenerating sense of "nobodiness"; then you will understand why we find it difficult to wait.[9]

Through such moving narrative as this, King bridged the gap between those who had and had not experienced the brutalities of slavery and segregation. These experiences necessitated his eclectic appropriation of various theologies and philosophies, which he constantly revised in light of his growing understanding of the problems of American life. As I have pointed out, King drew inspiration from the African-American religious tradition, a tradition allowing him to develop innovative approaches to the problems facing oppressed people.

In summary, the history and experiences of African-Americans under oppression taught King several valuable lessons. First, submission to illegitimate authority did not derive exclusively from a hegemonic ideology such as the conservative evangelicalism of slavery and segregation. Public and private coercion played a significant role in maintaining submission. Second, far from being duped by the political and religious ideologies intended to oppress them, African-Americans had often successfully turned those ideologies on their heads and used them as instruments of survival and liberation. Third, within the space created by the interplay of coercion and consent, African-Americans evolved and implemented conceptions of community important to broader visions of a reconstructed society. The interdependency, love, equality and hope that characterized the best of those communities were particularly attractive to King and greatly informed his conception of a Beloved Community.

Chapter 5

The Spiritual,
Social and Strategic
Dimensions of the
Beloved Community

King's conception of the Beloved Community
represents, then, a synthesis of the prophetic and pragmatic variants of
African-American religious thought. Working through the implications
of this synthesis is crucial to appreciate the profundity of King's vision.
Several dimensions of the Beloved Community require elaboration.
The first is King's conception of the spiritual work or soul work that all
individuals need to engage in for purposes of nurturing the possibilities
of a community founded on justice and love. The second is his social
conception of the Beloved Community to which these transformed
individuals are to aspire. The third is his understanding of the proper
strategies for pursuing this aspirational community. That is to say,
King's conception of the Beloved Community has spiritual, social and
strategic dimensions we must more fully understand.

A. The Spiritual Dimension of the
Beloved Community

King understood that the new laws put in place by
the civil rights movement were, in and of themselves, no guarantee of a

just and loving community. Rather, the individuals promulgating, enforcing, interpreting and following those laws must themselves be just and loving individuals. King understood, as Dewey came ultimately to see, that democratic institutions were no substitute for democratic individuals. Thus his synthesis of pragmatic and prophetic Christianity into a conception of the Beloved Community was a way of cultivating spiritual sensibilities capable of producing more democratic, more loving and just individuals.

In 1967, in one of his last written works, King called for a "true revolution of value that will soon cause us to question the fairness and justice of many of our past and present policies." The civil rights era had ushered in a revolution of law with the 1964 Civil Rights Act and the 1965 Voting Rights Act. But King understood that if the legacy of slavery and segregation were to be remedied, if the pervasive poverty that threatened the precarious freedom of so many were to be eradicated, individuals must work at the deepest spiritual level to reorient themselves and reprioritize their values. For King, love was the most important value in the inventory of values

In one of his most memorable sermons speaking to this reorientation, King spoke of the need to cultivate a three-dimensional love for God, Self and Others. God-love was a love of infinite potentiality and unconditionality, a love that reached for but never fully attained the heights of infinite being. God-love was a cultivation of a spiritual relationship with the creator of the universe, having faith in one's connection to divine purpose, and developing practices of prayer and ritual to more fully realize that purpose.

If God-love focused on the heights of love, self-love focused on the depths of love. This was a love that was to penetrate the innermost recesses of one's being in its ultimate recognition that God resided therein. The development of one's skills, gifts and talents, then, was an essential part of a self-love that stood at the intersection of love for God and love for others. Loving oneself enough to develop one's potential could never be selfish in the modern egotistical sense of the word, since it connected with a unifying love for God and others.

If God-love focused on the heights of love and self-love on the depths of love, other-love was concerned with the breadth of love. King understood this to be the great challenge of the new covenant established by Christianity to love one's neighbor as oneself. It was at the core of his understanding of love for the "least of these," which I will elaborate in the following chapters. Most importantly, however, other-love is connected to a self-love that is itself connected to God-love. When other-love is separated from a self-love which is itself rooted in a reverence for and aspiration to attain the unconditional love that is God, it becomes patronizing, judgmental and manipulative. King sought to avoid this dilemma.

A properly constituted love for others was at the core of King's conception of the Beloved Community and his call for a revolution of value. If such a revolution could take place, the changes in law, policy and institutions needed to respond to the legacy of slavery and segregation would be made priorities and would be better insulated from attack by those pursuing agendas that divided the community through a manipulation of fears and hostilities. If God-love, self-love and other-love could be linked through a unified understanding of our being, we would see, as he often put it, that there was no I without thou, no thou without I, that we all were inextricably woven into a single garment of destiny.

So King understood that the Beloved Community was possible only if individuals were willing to do the difficult soul work necessary for spiritual transformation. This soul work consisted of people's willingness to reorient and reprioritize their values, their sense of who they were, their purpose and their duties to God, self and humanity.

The spiritual transformation of individual consciousness that integrated love for God, self and others into a unifying love illuminated the oneness of all creation and nurtured a temperament that sought to recast binary understandings of existence—I and thou, us and them, white and black, rich and poor—as interdependent rather than oppositional, sharing a commonality that difference enhanced rather than diminished. In his unique synthesis of dualities, King would often point out that conflicts were not either/or dilemmas but, rather, both/and possibilities. I want to spend some time illustrating the implications of this synthesizing and wholistic temperament because it was central to King's interpretive approach to the problems faced during his time and thus central to his conception of the Beloved Community, which he offered as a response to those problems.

This synthesizing temperament emanates from a unified conception of love in which self, other and God, though distinct, meet as one. The idea is best illustrated by a metaphoric description of the most cherished Christian symbol—the cross. The vertical extension of the cross represents love for God. The horizontal arm represents love for humanity. God-love and other-love intersect at the center of the cross, a reservoir of self-love continuosly filled by our love for God and humanity. King's interpretive approach to three dualities illustrates the spiritual dimension of his Beloved Community. The dualities brought into conflict the conception of human nature as fundamentally evil versus human nature as fundamentally good, the need for social order versus the need for human freedom and the cultural particularism of black nationalism versus the abstract universalism of autonomous individualism. I will discuss the first of these dichotomies here and postpone a discussion of the remaining two for subsequent sections.

The point of this exercise is to illustrate King's penchant for synthesizing dualities and his understanding that we could spiritually orient ourselves to find unity and wholeness in the midst of diversity, rupture and even chaos. The moral arch of the universe iss long, he would always say, but it bends toward justice. Our seemingly separate paths are woven into a single garment of destiny. Such an understanding would be the by-product of a spiritual transformation that King understood as essential to achieving a true revolution of value. People who otherwise believed they had nothing in common would have to learn to see into each other's worlds, seeing the otherness of themselves and the context of their interrelated being. Binary opposites would have to be recast as interdependent realities. The willingness to see the other as an extension of oneself was a spiritual maturity without which the Beloved Community could never come into existence. One could only achieve this spiritual awareness through a less static understanding of good and evil.

In 1960, King wrote an article entitled "Pilgrimage to Nonviolence." In it he explained his disenchantment with Christian liberalism and his concomitant move to Christian existentialism. Christian liberalism emerged around the same time as pragmatism and the Social Gospel discussed earlier. It challenged the orthodoxy of the conservative or fundamentalist view that, among other things, was the foundation of the master's preachments to the slave.

Evangelical liberalism stressed the power of human reason to discern the moral good of life and possessed an inexorable optimism concerning human capacity for goodness. But the more King "observed the tragedies of history and man's shameful inclination to choose the low road," the more he came to see the "depths and strength of sin."[1] His experiences convinced him that evangelical "liberalism had been all too sentimental concerning human nature and that it leaned toward a false idealism" that failed to see that "reason is darkened by sin" and "is little more than an instrument to justify man's defensive ways of thinking."[2] One might say that this is the insight revealed to Dewey in the wake of Nazi horrors.

At the other extreme from evangelical liberalism was the neoorthodoxy of Karl Barth, which emphasized the intractable nature of sin and evil and the relative futility of utopian aspirations. Barth maintained that many of the social injustices of the world were necessary evils that could be rectified only by the apocalyptic return of the Kingdom of God. Although he recognized the insights of neoorthodoxy, King could not fully accept this view—it cast too dark a shadow upon the possibilities of social change.

King searched for a philosophical middle ground that saw human nature as a struggle between good and evil, a philosophy that conceded humanity's finiteness yet acted on the faith that God could use finite creatures to establish a Beloved Community based on love and justice. He found this philosophical common ground in a Christian existentialism influenced by his study of Kierkegaard, Nietzsche, Jaspers, Heidegger and Sartre.

Like the existentialists, King believed that liberalism failed to give serious consideration to humanity's finite freedom—our existential estrangement from our essential nature of goodness as creatures of God. King described as "perilous" the assumption by some liberal theologians that sin was but a mere "lag of nature that can be progressively eliminated as man climbs the evolutionary ladder."[3] For King, the estrangement from one's essential or true self of goodness ran deeper. It was psychological, cultural, political and economic. Its pervasiveness meant that all movements to project the Kingdom of God into earthly relations were subject to being influenced by the very alienation from goodness the movement sought to overcome. Human programs and institutions could ossify and petrify, thereby becoming the very incarnation of the evil defeated and transformed through struggle. This meant that those engaged in social struggle should always be watchful for the ways structured interventions, like laws and social programs intended to liberate end up oppressing. This always resulted from the deep-seated alienation of humanity from its essential nature of goodness. With awareness of the alienation fostered by our finiteness, a requisite degree of humility was achieved. Good and evil were interdependent and not polar opposites.

As I have argued, this was the great shortcoming of Dewey's thought. By focusing on the infinite capacity of many, he paid too little attention to what existentialists called the finiteness of human existence. King brings the infinite and finite aspects of humanity into constructive tension in his move to Christian existentialism. The ideal of Christian perfection and goodness was always tempered by the realities of human frailty. The realities of human finiteness and limitation were always pulled toward transformantion by the ideal of infinite possibility.

Thus the individual, being both infinite and finite, was always in the process of becoming, never completing the journey toward that perfect good King called the Beloved Community. Nevertheless, King believed that the struggle to actualize the ideal in history could transform social relations. Only perennial struggle to achieve the Beloved Community allows us to experience our essential nature and to change our limited knowledge and understanding of the world. For King, love negotiated the tension between man's infinite limitations and infinite potential. Love, rather than a process of critical inquiry, stood in the gap between what man was and what he might yet be. Because Dewey failed to cultivate a substantive orientation for his process of critical inquiry, his theory became a process without normative protection of the least of these. King's Beloved Community gives the process of becoming an understanding of what we might aspire to become and how we might pursue that aspiration.

B. The Social Dimension of the
Beloved Community

The Beloved Community had a social as well as a spiritual dimension that flowed out of King's synthesis of the pragmatic and prophetic traditions of African-American religion. This social dimension offered an alternative vision of community to the one put forth by those who derived their community from a belief that human nature was fundamentally evil. Many argued that if human nature were fundamentally evil, a strict social order was needed to maintain security and to diminish the threat posed by such evil. The social order of segregation was often justified on grounds that a strict separation of the races was needed to thwart the potential conflict and evil that would develop from a mixing of the races. Thus authorities had to maintain the law and order of a community in the face of civil unrest, thereby constraining the freedom of many within the community.

In other words, the imposition of civil order necessary for the creation and maintenance of community required a curtailment of personal freedom, as all the social-contract theorists understood. Some personal freedom had to be surrendered to achieve a secure and lasting freedom. King examined this duality of order and freedom, however, and provided a synthesis similar to his synthesis of good and evil. For King, order and freedom were not in conflict when normatively oriented toward a substantive conception of justice.

For instance, some white clergy of Birmingham, Alabama claimed that the civil rights protests of 1963 resulted in a loss of law and order, and that King was primarily responsible for the tension and deteriorated race relations that pervaded the community. King understood that conservative evangelicalism assumed scripture required the Christian's deference to the authority of the state. It assumed that God had given magistrates the sword "not as a terror to good works, but to evil." But King pointed out that order, if it were to be distinguished from tyranny, must serve the end of justice, that it must, in other words, be good and just order:

> A just law is a man-made code that squares with the moral law or the law
> of God. An unjust law is a code that is out of harmony with the moral law

. . . not rooted in eternal and natural law. Any law that uplifts human personality is just. Any law that degrades human personality is unjust. All segregation statutes are unjust because segregation distorts the soul and damages the personality. It gives the segregator a false sense of superiority, and the segregated a false sense of inferiority. . . . So segregation is not only politically, economically and sociologically unsound, but it is morally wrong and sinful.[4]

King held that disobeying human law, even though it be unjust law, must be done out of love and with a willingness to suffer the penalty for its breach. Through this redemptive suffering, the transgressor evidences the highest respect for law, order and the possibilities of democracy, while remaining true to his higher duty.

The understanding of justice through which King synthesized coercion and freedom might more appropriately be called the democratizing critique. It was at the very heart of King's orientation toward life, his desire to see the mutual dependency and interconnectedness of creation. This critique took the world as it had been socially constructed to reflect the privileging of certain interests, voices, stories and people over others, and demonstrated how the subordinated other was of equal value to that privileged and, therefore, could not be objectively subordinated in the hierarchy of privilege.

During the Birmingham demonstrations of 1963 referred to above, moderate white clergy criticized King for the breach of law and order precipitated by his "untimely," nonviolent, direct action protests to desegregate the city. In his famous "Letter from Birmingham City Jail," King responded that he had:

almost reached the regrettable conclusion that the Negro's great stumbling block in the stride toward freedom is not the White Citizen's Counciler or the Ku Klux Klanner, but the white moderate who is more devoted to "order" than to justice; . . . who paternalistically feels that he can set the timetable for another man's freedom. . . . I had hoped that the white moderate would understand that law and order exist for the purpose of establishing justice, and that when they fail to do this they become dangerously structured dams that block the flow of social progress.[5]

King examined and exposed the mutual dependence of order and freedom, that is, that the meaning of each was incoherent in isolation of the other. He understood that the primary difference between the two was that a belief in the primacy of order assumed that human nature was fundamentally evil and in need of restraint, while a belief in the primacy of freedom assumed that it was fundamentally good and capable of autonomy. The privileging of order over freedom assumed that the latter was only possible within the constraints imposed by sovereign authority. Otherwise, civil society would degenerate into a Hobbesian war of all against all. Like Hobbes and, at times, Locke as well, the white clergy of Birmingham privileged the conception of human nature as fundamentally evil over the conception of human nature as fundamentally good. Thus the ordinances and injunctions prohibiting demonstrations in the city were necessary restraints on freedom needed to maintain order in the face of the human capacity for evil.

King's critique exposed the white clergy's preference for order over freedom and evil over good, and demonstrated that these preferences lacked any universal foundation. The hierarchy could easily be inverted. If freedom presupposed order, as the white clergy contended, it was no less true that order presupposed freedom. If humans were not also capable of substantial good, no social order was possible, because they would by definition be ungovernable.

In this way, the social order supposedly necessitated by human evil presupposed the freedom and human goodness it denied. If freedom without order was anarchy, order without freedom was tyranny. Each depended on the other for its existence. They were not either/or opposites but both/and necessities. They were inextricably bound in a relationship of mutual dependency.

It is important to understand that the democratizing critique of segregation's privileging did not lead to moral relativism because a substantive conception of justice provided the framework within which freedom and order were to be understood. At the core of that substantive conception of justice was a conception of the least of these and an understanding that, as King said above, "any law that uplifts human personality is just. Any law that degrades human personality is unjust."

This normative orientation of democratic process is precisely what was missing in the pragmatist and realist approaches discussed earlier, omissions resulting in an increasing vulnerability of the least advantaged.

In the social dimension of King's Beloved Community, the relationship between self and other was reconceptualized to challenge traditional liberal understandings of the individual and the community. The individual was no longer seen as an autonomous self separate from a hostile community and in need of protection from the self-negating forces of the community. Neither was the individual to be seen as a mere product of the community due no greater respect than the community was willing to give.

In King's communitarian vision, there is no I without thou, but the interdependency does require acknowledgment and protection of individual rights. But individual rights were to be understood in a radically different way from the prevailing notion of liberal rights. Rights were not just the right to be free from coercion, they were the right to be part of community. This meant that rights entailed a sense of duty or responsibility without which the notion of rights would be incoherent. Rights gave individuals the space and resources to develop their gifts, talents and skills in preparation to serve others.

Much of King's theory of the state depended on the optimistic view of human nature posited by evangelical liberalism. That is, with the evangelical liberals and proponents of the Social Gospel such as Rauschenbusch, King believed that individuals could harness the powers of the state in pursuit of a Beloved Community here on earth. Yet, King also understood, with the neoorthodoxists, the limitations and dangers of this optimism—that human alienation from the goodness of God was pervasive, and humans were forever capable of manipulating reason, law and policy to serve unjust ends. His Christian existentialist synthesis posited a human nature that was alienated from God and knowledge of his divine plan for humanity. Individual rights represented, under this existentialist view, a hedge against our imperfect attempts to reconcile our finite existential and divine essential selves. Thus King's conception of rights extended far beyond the traditional litany of liberties and rights against the state espoused by classical and contemporary liberalism.

These rights were "inherent rights that were God-given and not simply privileges extended by the state."[6] For King, the rights of life, liberty and the pursuit of happiness meant that "all individuals everywhere should have three meals a day for their bodies, education and culture for their minds, and dignity, equality and freedom for their spirits."[7] This required that the state affirmatively create the institutions necessary to realize these natural rights.

Unlike some progressive thinkers, King understood the importance of a system of individual rights. Some, such as Dewey, have contended that rights are incoherent and indeterminate reifications of concrete experiences that obfuscate, through the manipulation of abstract categories, disempowering social relations. King, however, understood that the oppressed could make rights determinate in practice. "Law tends to declare rights, it does not deliver them," he would say. "A catalyst is needed to breathe life experience into a judicial decision."[8] For King, the catalyst was persistent social struggle to transform the oppressiveness of one's existential condition into ever-closer approximations of the ideal. The hierarchies of race, class and imperial domination defined those conditions, and the struggle for substantive rights closed the gap between the latter and the ideal of the Beloved Community. Under the pressures of social struggle, the oppressed could alter rights to better reflect the exigencies of social reality—a reality itself more fully understood by those engaged in transformative struggle.

King's Beloved Community accepted and expanded the liberal tradition of rights. King realized that, notwithstanding its limits, the liberal vision contained important insights into the human condition. For those deprived of basic freedoms and subjected to arbitrary acts of state authority, the enforcement of formal rights was revolutionary. African-Americans understood the importance of formal liberal rights and demanded the full enforcement of such rights in order to challenge and rectify historical practices that had objectified and subsumed their existence.

Although conservatives contended that the emphasis on rights disrupted the gradual moral evolution that would ultimately change white sentiment, King contended that "[j]udicial decrees may not change the heart, but they can restrain the heartless."[9] While law may not make my enemy love me, he would often say, it can keep him from lynching me. But, although radicals contended that such rights were mere tokens and created a false sense of security masking continued violence, King understood that the strict enforcement of the rule of law was essential to any struggle for social justice, whether that struggle was moderate or radical in its sentiment and goals. Freedom of dissent and protest, freedom from arbitrary searches, seizures and detention, and freedom to organize and associate with those of common purpose were necessary rights that no movement for social reconstruction could take for granted.

Furthermore, King saw the initial emphasis on civil rights, I believe, as a necessary struggle for the collective self-respect and dignity of a people whose subordination was, in part, maintained by laws reproducing and reinforcing feelings of inadequacy and inferiority. The civil rights struggle attempted to lift the veil of shame and degradation from the eyes of a people who could then glimpse the possibilities of their personhood and achieve that potential through varied forms of social struggle. King's richer conception of rights provided limitations on collective action while broadening the scope of personal duty to permit movement toward a more socially conscious community. That is, these God given rights were seen by King as an opportunity to develop one's capacity to serve others. Thus individual rights were always oriented toward the common good, the attainment of a Beloved Community.

While King's understanding of the role of rights and duties in a Beloved Community is important, there are other crucial aspects of King's vision. First, King rejected the liberal effort to reconcile the individual's natural freedom and equality with a social order that subordinated human rights to the rights of property. In classical liberal thought, like that represented in the political philosophy of John Locke, the state existed to promote the pursuit and protect the appropriation of private property. To King, this epitomized the misplaced priorities of American democracy. "A life," he wrote, "is sacred. Property is intended to serve life, and no matter how much we surround it with rights and respect, it has no personal being. It is part of the earth man walks on; it is not man."[10]

Second, King's Beloved Community remained fundamentally aspirational. America, King believed, must never relinquish its right to dream—to reach beyond the limitations of its present to grasp the possibilities of its future. The state need not be thought of as a potential enemy of liberty or as some mystified "other" perennially threatening to rob us of individual liberty. King sought to dereify this conception of state by making people see that we, living human beings, are the state. To the extent we have become alienated from the very power we would wield to create the Beloved Community, we must recapture that power and vest it in those who are disempowered by electoral, political and socioeconomic processes of which they no longer feel a part.

This view of the state was based neither on the pessimistic view of human nature espoused by aspects of Lockean theory nor on Christian neoorthodoxy. Nor was it based on the optimistic view of human nature found in some critical theories and the progressive Christian theories of evangelical liberalism. It was based on a synthesis of both interpretations that evinced an awareness of the limitations and possibilities of each. Thus, for King, the Beloved Community would not be satisfied with classical notions of civil order based upon a public/private dichotomy limiting the role of the state to the protection of individual autonomy within a private sphere shaped by capitalist relations of production. Nor could it be content in its slightly more progressive posture of removing publicly created obstacles (legal segregation) to mutual dependency (integration). Rather, the state must serve the greater purpose of promoting human unity and mutual dependency through the removal of both publicly and privately produced impediments to the Beloved Community.

Finally, the disintegration of the civil rights movement in the mid-sixties and the erosion of the liberal consensus undergirding that movement, combined with King's ardent commitment to social justice, compelled his move to the political left. He eventually developed a form of democratic socialism that he believed represented the best of two ideologically opposed systems. King noted that "the good and just society is neither the thesis of capitalism nor the antithesis of communism, but a socially conscious democracy which reconciles the truths of individualism and collectivism."[11]

King's suspicion of American capitalism and the evils of economic exploitation was nurtured by his early witness of the symbiosis of racism and poverty, segregation and economic exploitation. Racism reproduced a distribution of wealth and power that perpetually relegated African-Americans to the lowest rung of the economic ladder. Through early experiences of racism and segregation, King would later recall, "I grew up deeply conscious of varieties of injustice in our society."[12]

Experience would not allow him to be naïve about the creation of such a just community. He clearly realized that his public ministry was at a crossroads in 1966, and that the path of moderate liberal reform down which he had journeyed had now reached a dead end. Faced with the demands of a militant left and an accommodationist right, King, in typical fashion, struggled toward a new ideal that placed him to the left of his previously moderate stance.

The following year, King delivered perhaps his most radical address:

> I want to say to you as I move to my conclusion, as we talk about "Where do we go from here," that we honestly face the fact that the movement must address itself to the question of restructuring the whole of American society. There are forty million poor people here. And one day we must ask the question, "Why are there forty million poor people in America?" And when you begin to ask that question, you are raising questions about the economic system, about a broader distribution of wealth. When you ask that question, you begin to question the capitalistic economy. . . . We are called upon to help the discouraged beggars in life's marketplace. But one day we must come to see that an edifice which produces beggars needs restructuring. It means that questions must be raised. You see, my friends, when you deal with this, you begin to ask the question, "Who owns the oil?" You begin to ask the question, "Who owns the iron ore?" You begin to ask the question, "Why is it that people have to pay water bills in a world that is two-thirds water?" These are questions that must be asked. . . . Now when I say question the whole society, it means ultimately coming to see that the problem of racism, the problem of economic exploitation, and the problem of war are all tied together. These are the triple evils that are interrelated.[13]

Dr. Martin Luther King, Jr. was assassinated before he had the opportunity to develop many of the themes suggested by his newfound commitment to democratic socialism. Thus his program lacks many specifics. Several things are clear, however. First, for King, the Beloved Community required, at the least, a guaranteed minimum income and guaranteed employment, and the democratization of political and economic institutions in order to promote a truly participatory democracy.

King believed that this democratic socialism must be coupled with a program of wealth redistribution to the poor.

Second, this country's experience of more than 200 years of slavery and more than 60 years of Jim Crow segregation and exploitation could not be ignored. Racist traditions, thought patterns and behavior could not be eliminated either with the passage of a "color-blind" statute or by a court ruling prohibiting discrimination on the basis of race under the equal protection clause of the Fourteenth Amendment. The state and its arbiter of the law—the courts—had to take affirmative steps to educate the population on the value of difference and diversity and to provide the victims of discrimination with the education and resources to actualize their potential in a society that had systematically suppressed that potential. Thus certain kind of racial reparations and Afrocentric education would be compatible with King's vision. Further, King seemed to imply, as I will later argue, that the state had to ensure that institutions previously excluding individuals on the basis of race did not continue to do so on the basis of some other "racially neutral" criterion, the neutrality of which has been corrupted by racism itself.

The question of how the legacy of racism was to be treated was a pressing question in the wake of the Voting Rights Act of 1965. It is clear from the above quote that King saw an interrelationship between racism, classism and imperialism. He desired critiques and programs that responded to them all. Black nationalist groups, however, were turning inward, cynical of and embittered by cross-racial alliances. They were quite skeptical of America's resolve to confront the severity of the matter and thus levelled a stinging critique of white supremacy and the legacy of American slavery. King's response to the black nationalist critique provides an opportunity to examine the third dimension of his Beloved Community—strategies of resistance.

C. The Strategic Dimensions of the Beloved Community

King's vision of a Beloved Community was significantly informed by the spiritual and social dimensions explored above. Yet there was another dimension that complemented these two, the strategic dimension. Many urged King to use less disruptive strategies in his quest for black liberation. Wait, they urged, and allow the legal and political process to resolve these problems. Wait, many urged, and allow God to convert the hearts and minds of those who oppose desegregation.

King maintained that while God might be working to change the sinful hearts and minds of white oppressors, collective organization through nonviolent direct action would be His instrument of conversion and salvation. King saw the strategy of nonviolent direct action as an empowering synthesis of the Old Testament's concern for justice and the New Testament's emphasis on love: "Greater love has no man than this, that he lay down his life for his friends."[14] Justice and love were inseparable. The former formulated the ends of struggle and the latter the means of achieving them. It was a necessary expression of one's love for God, then, to lead souls blinded by the darkness of sin to the light, to raise consciousness and to challenge the injustice anywhere that threatened justice everywhere. In his letter from the Birmingham Jail, King explained why "waiting" was no longer an option:

We know through painful experience that freedom is never voluntarily given by the oppressor; it must be demanded by the oppressed. Frankly, I have never yet engaged in a direct action movement that was "well-timed," according to the timetable of those who have not suffered unduly from the disease of segregation. For years now I have heard the words "Wait!" It rings in the ear of every Negro with a piercing familiarity. This "Wait" has almost always meant "Never." . . . We must come to see with the distinguished jurist of yesterday, that "justice too long delayed is justice denied."[15]

King was willing to wait no longer. He expressed his great disappointment with the otherworldly orientation of the white Church that counseled patience and heavenly reward for earthly suffering:

In the midst of blatant injustices inflicted upon the Negro, I have watched white churches stand on the sideline and merely mouth pious irrelevancies and sanctimonious trivialities. In the midst of a mighty struggle to rid our nation of racial and economic injustice, I have heard so many ministers say, "Those are social issues with which the gospel has no real concern," and I have watched so many churches commit themselves to a completely otherworldly religion which made a strange distinction between body and soul, the sacred and the secular.[16]

Because he believed the strategy of nonviolent direct action was the ideal strategy for realizing some of the spiritual and social aspirations of the Beloved Community, King spent his life leading African-Americans and others into direct confrontation with oppressive institutions and practices. Through direct action the African-American community exposed the contradictions and violence endemic to American society.

King called for the social transformation of American institutions and practices, to be sure, but his strategies for social transformation were always consistent with the spiritual dimensions of his Beloved Community. That is, King envisioned a community of equals brought together by their commitment to love-based justice. As both infinite spiritual and finite mortal beings, we were always in the process of becoming. Thus strategies of resistance shaped our sense of who we were and who we were capable of becoming.

The sensibility that inextricably connected strategy to the spiritual and social dimensions of the Beloved Community is an important one to understand and try to emulate. We can see it most vividly, perhaps, in his approach to the black nationalist critique of the civil rights movement in the period between 1965 and 1968. A study of King's encounter with black nationalist ideology is important for several reasons.

First, this encounter illustrates how King was willing to find good in and dialogue with those with whom he disagreed. If we could consistently practice this virtue of understanding and communicating with those whom we perceive as different from ourselves, we could move closer to the Beloved Community. Second, it illustrates how King's conception of the Beloved Community embraced diversity without sacrificing unity. He appreciated the particular history and needs of the African-American community, yet he understood those needs in a way that did not foreclose the possibility of common alliance. If we could better nurture the skill of embracing that which is universal about our disparate experiences through a deep appreciation of our particularities, we could move closer to the Beloved Community. Finally, it illustrates how King synthesized yet another duality, nationalism and integrationism, in a way that was both loving and just. Again, if we could do the same, given the present-day tension between these approaches to racial justice, we could move closer to the Beloved Community he envisioned.

In his 1967 book, *Where Do We Go From Here: Chaos or Community?* King responded to the claims and aspirations of the Black Power movement by arguing that many of the movement's concerns were consistent with his own conception of the struggle and the Beloved Community it sought to create. This understanding moved him considerably beyond his 1963 *I Have A Dream* position, in which he appeared to call for a community committed to moral and legal color blindness—a society that would judge individuals "not by the color of their skins but by the content of their character."

His new position indicated a more subtle and sophisticated understanding of American racism which, I believe, he possessed all along but realized America was not yet ready to receive. This new position fell somewhere between the commitment to integration for which he is so well remembered and the black nationalism that was becoming increasingly popular among the youth of the movement. King understood these approaches were in tension but neatly synthesized them without lapsing into either a liberal universalism or nationalist particularism and insularity. Examining where he drew the lines of distinction between acceptable and unacceptable forms of black nationalism and how he understood integration might give us insight into an important dimension of his Beloved Community. It may help us answer the equally pressing questions of our own day as to how we might reconcile nationalist and integrationist strategies in the African-American community. King begins this line-drawing enterprise by understanding the historical, political and psychological origins of the Black Power movement.

First, he understood Black Power as a cry "born from the wounds of despair and disappointment . . . a reaction to the failure of white power."[17] That is, he historically situated the Black Power movement within a context of past and present black oppression, one in which the daily lynching, brutality and deprivation of blacks went unanswered, one in which governmental promises were broken with impunity, civil rights laws were substantially unenforced and redemptive suffering was an open invitation for greater abuse. Unlike typical integrationists who attempted to suppress the dangers of white power by embracing a norm of color blindness, however, King's recognition of white power's "brutal, cold-blooded and vicious"[18] manifestations led him to understand many of the race-conscious strategies of liberation adopted by nationalists.

Second, King understood Black Power as "a call to black people to amass the political and economic strength to achieve their legitimate goals."[19] Far from adopting a posture of color blindness, he called for racial-bloc voting "to liberalize the political climate and achieve [blacks'] just aspirations for freedom and human dignity."[20] He appreciated the need, then, for race-conscious moral, political and economic empowerment responding to the historical reality that "from the old plantations of the South to the newer ghettos of the North, the Negro has been confined to a life of voicelessness and powerlessness."[21]

Finally, King recognized that Black Power was first and foremost "a psychological call to manhood."[22] That is, it was an attempt to combat the pervasive sense of nobodiness and self-hate conditioned into many by a dehumanizing system of slavery and segregation that "scarred the soul and wounded the spirit of the black man."[23] Thus he supported Black Power's "determination to glory in blackness and to resurrect joyously the African past."[24] King's insights on this facet of the Black Power movement were profound. He explained:

> Black Power is a psychological reaction to the psychological indoctrination that led to the creation of the perfect slave. While this reaction has often led to negative and unrealistic responses and has frequently brought about intemperate words and actions, one must not overlook the positive value in calling the Negro to a new sense of manhood, to a deep feeling of racial pride and to an audacious appreciation of his heritage. The Negro must be grasped by a new realization of his dignity and worth. He must stand up amid a system that still oppressed him and develop an unassailable and majestic sense of his own value. He must no longer be ashamed of being black.[25]

King described the history of white supremacy as a history of "cultural homicide." That is, white supremacy had systematically denied blacks their place in the world and in American history as the builders of civilizations, the architects of culture and critical contributors to the health, wealth and hope of humanity. Thus, King contended, the black man could stave off this "cultural homicide" only by rising up "with affirmation of his own Olympian manhood." "Any movement for the Negro's freedom that overlooks this necessity," he added, "is only waiting to be buried."[26]

The preceding positions are not the positions of an integrationist committed to a liberal norm of colorblindness as the means to liberation. The positions are acutely race-conscious and practically indistinguishable from many of the positions taken by cultural black nationalists on the issue of race.

Notwithstanding these similarities, however, there were important differences. First, King had difficulty with the slogan "Black Power." He actually preferred the slogan "Black Consciousness" or "Black Equality," and urged its consideration to Stokely Carmichael and Floyd McKissick during the Mississippi Freedom March of 1966. His difficulty with the term appears far less ideological than strategic, however. He was concerned that the slogan would nurture and promote an unhealthy insularity that in the end would be self-defeating. Why have a slogan, King inquired, that would "confuse our allies, isolate the Negro community and give many prejudiced whites, who might otherwise be ashamed of their anti-Negro feeling, a ready excuse for self-justification?"[27]

Members of the press were already linking Black Power to violence, and King felt that the slogan would only detract from the substantive issues of racial oppression and poverty. The two factions could not agree on a slogan that essentialized both the frustration and the socioeconomic and cultural concerns of the movement and that the press would not simultaneously sensationalize and link to an advocacy of violence. Instead, the King faction agreed to drop the "Freedom Now" chant for the duration of the March and the Carmichael/McKissick faction agreed to drop the "Black Power" slogan in a show of unity against Mississippi oppression.

Second, King considered Black Power's "unconscious and often conscious call for retaliatory violence" its most "destructive feature."[28] Violence against individuals burned rather than built bridges to a better tomorrow. The feeling of self-preservation among whites was so pervasive that violence evoked irrational fears and unbridled resistance to just claims, thereby trapping the oppressed within the vicious cycles of racism and poverty from which they sought liberation. Thus he objected to violence on both strategic and moral grounds. Interestingly, both McKissick and Carmichael renounced the use of violence as well, Carmichael once remarking that "the question of violence versus non-violence was irrelevant. The real question was the need for black people to consolidate their political and economic resources to achieve power."[29]

But black nationalism was by no means monolithic. King had spoken with many who were unwilling to make such concessions. He realized that talk of violence, even the nonaggressive mode of self-defense, was too dangerous. He pointed out that "the minute a program of violence is enunciated, even for self-defense, the atmosphere is filled with talk of violence, and the words falling on unsophisticated ears may be interpreted as an invitation to aggression."[30]

King saw the freedom struggle in terms of a people in the process of becoming, shaping today what they would become tomorrow. Thus one could not divorce means from ends, as black nationalist advocates of violence were prone to do. Violence might achieve some measurable concessions, but ultimately it was "a descending spiral, begetting the very thing it seeks to destroy."[31] King put it this way:

> Returning violence for violence multiplies violence, adding deeper darkness to a night already devoid of stars. Darkness cannot drive out darkness: only light can do that. Hate cannot drive out hate: only love can do that. The beauty of nonviolence is that in its own way and in its own time it seeks to break the chain reaction of evil. With a majestic sense of spiritual power, it seeks to elevate truth, beauty and goodness to the throne. Therefore I will continue to follow this method because I think it is the most practically sound and morally excellent way for the Negro to achieve freedom.[32]

Finally, a substantive disagreement centered on the role of whites in the movement. This again spoke to the fears of insularity that King resisted. Carmichael and McKissick were prepared to exclude all whites from the Mississippi march, but King adamantly objected, as he always did, to the separatist proclivities of black nationalism. He understood the backlash of black anger resulting from a white liberal paternalism that often overwhelmed and undermined black self-determination and moral development and "increased a sense of blacks' own inadequacies."[33] But his version of Christian existentialism required that he not avoid the tension through separation but face it head on, living with the tension while redefining it through struggle.

The answer to the dilemma, then:

> was not to give up, not to conclude that blacks must work with blacks in order for Negroes to gain a sense of their own meaning. The answer was only to be found in persistent trying, perpetual experimentation, persevering togetherness. Like life, racial understanding is not something that we find but something that we must create.[34]

In summary, King's opposition to the term "Black Power," his objection to the black nationalist's valorization of retaliatory violence as a justifiable response to oppression, and his rejection of black nationalism's inclination toward separatism were important differences between King and many black nationalists. In some ways, however, they were all responses to black nationalism's propensity for insularity. Thus, it may be helpful to flesh out King's response to separatism with a slightly finer brush.

While racial separatism took different forms under black nationalism, with some calling for an actual territorial homeland for African-Americans, the most prevalent understanding of separatism focused on independent political, socioeconomic and cultural development. But King's orientation was to encourage an awareness of and embrace of black humanity as a way of apprehending common humanity, that is, our common origins and destinies. Through the particularity of black experience and the culture it produced, one could see glimmers of universal truth on which blacks could build bridges to the experiences of others. King, therefore, was outward-looking in his racial introspection. This was the critical turn for those committed to building pluralistic mass movements. This rejection of extreme forms of separation and insularity did not lead, however, to a crass acceptance of color-blindness as an appropriate ideological framework. As usual, King found the middle way.

First, King provided a penetrating critique of the formalism and symmetry often associated with liberalism. Again, this critique avoided the traps of a blind integrationism while resisting the temptations of a myopic nationalism. For instance, he understood that while "Black Power is an implicit and often explicit belief in black separatism," it is "inaccurate to refer to [it] as racism in reverse." Racism is a doctrine of the congenital inferiority and worthlessness of a people, and with a few exceptions, King noted, the major proponents of Black Power have never contended that the white man is innately worthless.[35] Thus, as I will later argue, King would find the entire debate surrounding affirmative action as a form of reverse racism or discrimination troubling.

We cannot understand racism abstractly, as the liberal doctrine of color blindness suggests. Instead, the meaning of racism is only assessable through the historical and social context of domination—a context in which Caucasians have utilized the category of race in the service of domination of blacks and not the reverse. Therefore I believe King would view the use of race-conscious measures to reconfigure the social matrix, to deconstruct the hierarchies of dominance put in place by race and maintained by ostensibly neutral markets, as a constructive use of power—"love implementing the demands of justice."[36]

King avoided the myopia engendered by some forms of black nationalist insularity by realizing that Black Power's focus on intraracial development should not be an end in itself, but a means to the formation of empowering potentially transformative coalitions with others, including progressive whites. In this regard, he embraced but critically evaluated the race consciousness of black nationalism. That is, he realized that integration without the strong sense of identity encouraged by Black Power advocates resulted in assimilation and nontransformative accommodation. But, the development of a healthy racial identity without integration resulted in isolation and possible annihilation by white antagonists who, because of black insularity, could attack the latter at little political or moral cost to themselves.

Therefore, while King supported what might be styled black cultural nationalism or Black Consciousness for purposes of countering the psychological effects of slavery and segregation and responding to the inequitable allocation of resources left in their wake, he resisted the dangers of black insularity. Instead, he advocated a more holistic approach to the problem than either the paradigmatic integrationist or nationalist would allow. This holism was apparent even at the psychological level of identity formation. According to him,

> [t]he problem is that in the search for wholeness all too many Negroes seek to embrace only one side of their natures. Some, seeking to reject their heritage, are ashamed of their color, ashamed of black art and music, and determine what is beautiful and good by the standards of white society. They end up frustrated and without cultural roots. Others seek to reject everything American and to identify totally with Africa, even to the point of wearing African clothes. But this approach leads also to frustration because the American Negro is not an African. . . . The American Negro is neither totally African nor totally Western. He is Afro-American, a true hybrid, a combination of two cultures.[37]

Second, King understood racism as much more than an irrational act of conscious predjudice and discrimination. That is, he understood the unconscious and institutional dimensions of racism that black nationalists were beginning to unpack in their writings. In other words, he understood that the material power relations help constitute and reproduce a society that is unconsciously as well as consciously racist. Thus King seldom severed the call for integration from the demand for substantive reallocations of power. "On the one hand," he contended, "integration is true intergroup, interpersonal living. On the other hand, it is the mutual sharing of power."

Rejecting both assimilation and insularity, King rejected the contention that blacks could "totally liberate [themselves] from the crushing weight of poor education, squalid housing and economic strangulation without being . . . integrated, with power, into every level of American life."[38] Thus, while he applauded the internal economic development rhetoric of black nationalists, he was convinced that "the ultimate answer to the Negroes' economic dilemma is in a massive federal program for all the poor along the lines of A. Philip Randolph's Freedom Budget, a kind of Marshall Plan for the disadvantaged."[38] However, given King's evolving understanding of the pervasiveness of racism on the American psyche and culture, he would probably approve of special programs within this larger redistribution to respond to the particular histories of African-Americans.

Finally, as the previous quote indicates, King's assessment of racism, its causes and cures, required not only an examination of the relationship between consciousness and relations of power but a much closer examination of the dynamics of class relations than liberalism's emphasis on individual worth and merit generally permitted. While integrationists complained that the central problem of the American social structure was black exclusion, and nationalists complained that the central problem with integration was black diffusion, King struggled for an integration coupled to transformation of race and class relations—a program bent on restructuring rather than reenforcing prevailing social and economic hierarchies. This required a critique of American capitalism and its relationship to the problematic aspects of American liberalism.

So King stood willing to engage in both a black nationalist type of critique of the legacy of white supremacy and a democratic socialist critique of American class relations. For King, these critiques, combined with a critique of American imperialism, constituted the future of progressive liberal politics. I will argue in Part III that the failure of American progressive politics has been precisely the unwillingness of white progressives, particularly, to follow King's lead.

In summary, King's vision of a Beloved Community flowed out of his synthesis of pragmatic, individualist-centered and spiritually oriented understandings of the African-American religious tradition with the prophetic, community-centered and socially oriented dimensions of the same tradition. This synthesis was the primary source, I have argued, of his conception of a Beloved Community.

This ideal and aspirational community encompassed spiritual, social and strategic dimensions. On the spiritual level, King understood the need for individuals to engage, on the most personal and spiritual level, the issues of the soul—our relationship to God, our love, or lack thereof, for self and others. He understood that social problems like racism and poverty were manifestations of spiritual imbalance that changes in law could only point the way toward correcting. The real work had to be done by the individual engaging in a psychospiritual conversion of his or her very being, which would then serve as the catalyst for social conversion.

The revolution of value that would accompany an understanding of the relationship between the individual, God and others was one in which dualities between good and evil, black and white, I and Thou would be synthesized into a new understanding of mutual dependency rather than binary opposition. The fundamental unity of all things would be made manifest, while the diversity of all things would be more fully appreciated.

The social dimension of the Beloved Community required in its synthesis of order and freedom that both conform to the dictates of a love-based justice. Justice and love, for King, provided normative guidance for critical intelligence and democratic process. At the core of this conception of a loving justice was a commitment to the protection and promotion of the "least of these." By this analysis, individual rights could no longer be viewed as a right to the protection of privileges based on race, class and imperial domination of others. Rather, rights provided the freedom to take responsibility for oneself and one's fellow traveler, to develop one's gifts, talents and skills in preparation for service to others. The state, then, was to be reconceptualized as a facilitator of a radically different understanding of rights, human rights, that would connect us in an interlocking network of mutual dependency rather than separate us into private spheres of self-interested pursuit.

Finally, the strategic dimension demonstrates that the process of pursuing the Beloved Community is as important as the end itself. This is so because both we and the community are in the process of becoming and thus are shaped by the methods we adopt to secure our ends. Therefore, in his synthesis of nationalism and integrationism, King again points the way. We need not be insular nationalists or abstract integrationists. We can avoid the worst of each and embrace the best of both. Within certain limits, we can grasp what is truly universal about our experiences as human beings through an appreciation of the particularities that make us different.

These spiritual, social and strategic dimensions of the Beloved Community provide us, then, with a deeper understanding of the "least of these" than Rauschenbusch was able to develop. It remains now to distill and formulate a framework based on the insights of Raushenbusch and King that we can apply to some of the problems facing progressive liberal politics in America.

Part III

The Beloved Community
Toward a Religiospiritual Vision of Progressive Liberalism

Introduction

I argued in Part I that the progressive liberalism of both John Dewey and the American legal realists failed to develop a normative conception of community capable of protecting and promoting the interests of the most vulnerable and least advantaged segments of the population. Their reliance on democratic process was not sufficiently attentive to the ways process is shaped by power relations that relegate many to the perennial status of marginalized and disempowered outsider. I suggested in Part II that Walter Rauschenbusch's theology of the Social Gospel and Martin Luther King, Jr.'s theology of the Beloved Community provide the normative guidance needed to avoid the pitfalls of American progressive liberalism. These theologies are particularly attractive in light of the fact that much of progressive liberalism, as my study of John Dewey indicated, has found it necessary to reject religious discourse and understanding in favor of a secular humanism that is often politically disempowering and spiritually unfulfilling.

In Part III I want to extrapolate from my treatment of Rauschenbusch and King a normative framework that inclines democratic process towards a substantive conception of justice founded on a radically new, religiospiritual understanding of love for the least of these. This new orientation constitutes a love-based conception of justice. I frame this love-based conception of justice as a religiospiritual understanding because I am aiming for a new progressive liberal approach to religion that enhances the coalition potential of religionists and humanists.

This will require some compromise and concession on both sides, but I believe such a shared understanding is possible. Both Rauschenbusch and King illustrated the movement that is necessary for religionists, the willingness to find social and strategic as well as spiritual meaning in their guiding religious texts. Similarly, humanists must evince a greater willingness to find spiritual, as well as social and strategic, meaning in their guiding texts. Finally, both must appreciate the validity and importance of their respective interpretive enterprises. If such mutual respect and appreciation is nurtured, the most important question becomes what spiritual, social and strategic meanings should have primacy and not whether such a holistic approach to interpretation is itself proper. It is this underlying normative commitment to a love-based conception of justice for the least of these that holds both religionists and humanists together in this enterprise of holistic interpretation. This normative commitment diminishes the threat of interpretive relativism and indeterminacy.

The first chapter in Part III outlines the normative framework extrapolated from my earlier development of Rauschenbusch and King. The second chapter suggests the relevance of this new framework for a very old but still pervasive problem of American politics; how racism continues to limit, retard and defeat progressive political agendas in America.

The third chapter suggests that progressive liberalism must develop a more sophisticated understanding of racism than it has to date and have the courage to act on that understanding in order to forge new coalitions. The final chapter ponders how this framework might have prompted a different approach to the now-defeated progressive initiative of affirmative action. I suggest how progressive liberals might have avoided the tragedy but, more importantly, how future progressive initiatives might avoid a similar fate.

Chapter 6

Toward a Normative Framework of a Love-Based Community

The central problem of liberalism is one consistently overlooked by its critics. The problem is that the liberal conception of community is based too much on fear and too little on love. It is fear of the "other" that generates in liberal thought the fundamental paradox of liberal theory. The liberal subject both desires and fears, needs and is threatened by community. Because community coercion is simultaneously indispensable and yet a threat to individual autonomy— itself the foundation of liberalism—theories of social justice and law are inclined toward conservative understandings of the state and are inherently suspicious of collective power. I want to suggest that we should reformulate the fundamental paradox by moving away from fear and closer to love as the basic motivation for being in community with others.

A love-based conception of community does not purport to transcend the love/fear dichotomy; it attempts only to renegotiate their relationship. A love-based conception of community incorporates but refuses to be stultified by the legitimate concerns of more prevalent fear-based conceptions of justice. The love-based conception of community is not one that is blind to the capacity for human evil, however. It does not repeat the mistakes of early progressives such as Dewey, discussed earlier. Rather, it offers a different understanding of love that embraces both the infinite potential and finite limits of humanity, both the great capacity for good and the considerable capacity for evil. The fundamental difference between love- and fear-based conceptions of community—and this is by no means insignificant—is that the former requires a set of overlapping duties orienting us toward a constructive communion with others, while fear orients us toward a more restrictive focus on self-interest. I believe a love-based conception of community can more easily accommodate the legitimate concerns of fear than fear-based conceptions of community can accommodate the promise of love. I will discuss the particularities of this balance shortly, but first, we need to understand how liberal theory, in general, has too long depended on fear as the catalyst for community.

In early liberal theory, the social order constructed by both Hobbes and Locke is one necessitated by the fear rational subjects have of others. For Hobbes, life in the state of nature is nasty, brutish and short. The individual is imperiled on every side by the threat of those pursuing the power needed for self-preservation. For Locke, the fear of having one's property stolen by those losing out in the struggle for security necessitates a social order that, above all else, protects the natural rights of private property. Long before Darwin and long after him, Western individualism, including its more progressive variants, has presupposed the legitimacy of a survival of the fittest. A just social order was one protecting the acquisitions of the fit from those who were basically unfit.

The most significant difference between conservative and progressive variants of this acquisitive individualism is the belief by progressives that the community has a duty to ameliorate in some way the most devastating effects of the struggle for survival. This sometimes takes the shape of providing safety nets for those who fall through the cracks, creating equal opportunity to compete, and even creating a level playing field to determine who really is the fittest and thus deserves to survive elimination.

The centerpiece of the conservative variant of this acquisitive individualism is that any interference by the government in this survival of the fittest retards the natural evolution of the species, impedes personal and societal development, or fails to optimize the most efficient use of resources. To be sure, the mode of conservative expression has varied from time to time, as is the case with the progressive variant, but the underlying message is the same. A just social order should do little more than protect individuals from the threats to property and person from those within the political community and those outside that community. The rule of law, a strong police and military force are the cornerstones of such a civil order. The state is not to engage in redistributive programs that in effect rob Peter to pay Paul.

Even contemporary variants of progressive liberalism like the political philosophy of John Rawls have found it difficult to base a conception of justice on something other than the fearful self-interest of individuals. Rawls's individuals decide that a just society must protect the interests of the least advantaged in their political community, a progressive liberal commitment. Thus, legislation designed to provide the greatest benefit to the greatest number may go forward only when that legislation benefits, as well, the least advantaged members of society.

Rawls makes clear, however, that individuals will reach this consensus based not on any feelings of altruism but, rather, on the purest of self-interest. Having located them behind a veil of ignorance where they are stripped of any knowledge of their eventual status in the community, Rawls has his participants choose a social order they would deem just. Rawls reasons that all will rationally fear the possibility that they will be among the most disfavored of the society with little hope of altering their status. This fear will provide sufficient incentive to establish, then, a social order protecting and promoting the interests of the least advantaged.

I am proposing that progressive liberalism move from a fear-based conception of justice toward a love-based conception of justice.[1] Again, one can never totally transcend this binary opposition. It seems to be a permanent part of the cosmic relationship between good and evil and the infinite and the finite. We can, however, like King, reorient our emphasis and, in so doing, open up possibilities that will significantly transform our understanding of the relationship between fear and love and their relationship to justice.

The conception of love-based justice I hope to use is one we have seen already in the theologies of Rauschenbusch and King. I believe, however, that this conception of love is one that we can detect in every major religion, and not just Christianity. Thus I seek no primacy for Christianity but, rather, seek only to establish the legitimacy of religion as a source of values useful to the progressive liberal project.[2] Unfortunately, the secular humanism of the modern era holds the proper province of law and social justice to be a public realm in which formally equal persons compete for the scarcities of life within fairly neutral and determinate legal boundaries regulating the behavior of each for the average benefit of all.[3] The province of love is seen as a private realm of soft and mushy sentimentality. It is an emotion whose utility for law and justice, if it has one at all, is in ameliorating the harshness and cruelty sometimes characteristic of public life.

My understanding of the relevance of Christianity for issues of social justice rejects this separation of love from law and justice and adopts a much broader view of Christianity's supreme commandments. A love-based justice that is rooted in my understanding of the synthesis of pragmatic and prophetic strands of Christianity developed by King into a theory of the Beloved Community embodies these commandments of love. The first commandment is: "Love the Lord your God with all your heart and with all your soul and with all your mind and with all your strength."[4] The second is: "Love your neighbor as yourself."[5]

Although Nietzsche and others have read these laws as an ideology of self-denial and even self-flagellation[6]—leading to weak and self-sacrificial personalities ill-suited for the great possibilities of modernity— I will argue that the prophetic Christianity on which the commandments of love are based is vitally concerned with the individual's self-love and empowerment, though not of a Nietzschean or Deweyan stripe. Indeed, the commandments to love one's neighbor and to love God hold promise only when the conditions of self-love and empowerment are satisfied.

What, then, are the guiding principles of a love-based conception of justice? The answer lies in my earlier elaboration of King's Beloved Community, in his understanding of the overlapping duties owed to God, self and others.[7] First, to love God with all of our being requires a suitable conception of God that allows those from different traditions and with different orientations to see a common cause. Both Rauschenbusch's Social Gospel and King's Beloved Community develop an understanding of God that is compatible with democratic principles of diversity and equality.[8] In Rauschenbusch's and King's theologies, a love for God is no longer disconnected from a love for self and humanity. A unity is achieved that sees the interconnectedness of creation, while appreciating the diversity through which that interconnectedness is expressed. To love God completely is to open one's body, heart, mind and soul to the wonders and possibilities of this oneness through diversity. Far from being lost in a state of transcendent bliss that disconnects the faithful from the affairs of this world, one sees the world with a renewed sense of possibility and responsibility.

God, then, is love, the ideal toward which our feeble efforts incline. With all of our heart, soul, mind and strength we seek the way of love, knowing our paths are darkened by the shadows of human frailty and sin. Yet God, whose unconditional love brightens but never fully illuminates the paths we take, is with us even to the end of time. In this lies both the comfort and the challenge of the human condition, for we walk by faith and not by sight alone. With this faith that permeates body, heart, soul and mind, we fix the ear of our inner being to the call, faint though it sometimes may be, of God's eternal love.

Second, because we are to love our neighbor as we love ourselves, self-love is a condition for loving our neighbor, which, as I have noted, is also the only true measure of our love for God.[9] For it is written that "anyone who does not love his brother, whom he has seen, cannot love God, whom he has not seen."[10] That is, we must conceive and know God through our love for our fellow creatures. My contention, then, is that when self-love looks toward the higher love of other-love, and other-love toward the higher love of God-love, we can avoid the trap of narcissistic self-interest that has been the downfall of so much liberal thought. By linking each dimension of love to another, we define a set of duties and powers that provide both limits and possibilities for the individual and community. This analysis, appropriately begins, then, with an understanding of the duty of self-love.

A. The Law of Self-Love

The duty of self-love is not an explicit one in Christian theology; it is only implied by the higher duty to love one's neighbor as oneself. It is, nevertheless, a crucial duty, for we often project onto others our own self-obsession, doubt and contempt. The reflection blinds us to the divine in others because we fail first to acknowledge it in ourselves. The great tragedy of modern Western culture is that it seeks to sever self-love from its higher purpose by exalting it as an end rather than the means it should rightly be. Taken as the end rather than the beginning of human duty, self-love often leads to self-worship and an institutionalized narcissism that rationalizes the most hideous of practices against those whom we are obligated to love.

In his work, *Christian Love and Self-Denial*, Stephen Post recounts an important debate within early American Protestantism over the form and meaning of Christian love, focusing on the thought of Jonathan Edwards and Samuel Hopkins. These theologians differed markedly on the question of whether all self-love is prohibited by Christian ethics. On the one hand, Post argues that through Samuel Hopkins's theory of "disinterested benevolence," American Protestantism was bequeathed a doctrine of radically self-denying love. Edwards, on the other hand, imposed limits on self-denial, thereby permitting the individual's love for self to participate in communion with the individual's love for God and others. Edwards believed, as do I, that when the three dimensions of love are in true communion, the excesses of self-love as well as those of self-denial are avoided.[11]

What, then, is proper self-love? At first glance, self-love appears to require total self-denial, as Hopkins argued in his debate with Edwards above. We are compelled to love God with all our being—all of our heart, soul, mind, and strength. If total love must be given God, what is left for self? Yet, as we have seen with the Social Gospel, the mystery lies in our conception of the God to whom such uncompromising love is rendered.[12] If that conception is an exclusively transcendent and otherworldly Being, then love becomes transcendent, otherworldly, and an implicit denial of the particular and temporal manifestations of self and others. But, if one's conception of God keeps the transcendent and immanent, otherworldly and temporal, ideal and practical in constructive tension—denying neither and embracing both—self-love is at once given possibility as well as limit in human affairs.

Committing our heart, soul, mind and strength to a God who measures our devotion to Him by our love for humanity—itself inspired, as we shall see, by our love for the "least of these"—means that our all-encompassing love for God is never exclusively an abstract, intellectual or otherworldly love. Instead, it is concerned with the natural and not exclusively the supernatural other, as Dewey supposed. This focus on humanity as the window to God also suggests a more promising role for self-love, for if we are genuinely to love others as God intended, we must first prepare ourselves to love.

The duty of self-love commands that we prepare ourselves to love, that we cultivate our gifts, skills and interests so as to serve God better by serving humanity. This general requirement of self-love carries with it three instrumental commands. The first is to satisfy our basic physical needs. The second is to protect our fundamental freedoms. The third is to affirm our self-worth. Our ability to love our neighbor and thus God through the cultivation of our gifts, skills and interests is compromised by our failure to attend to these three basic concerns. These commands of self-love require further elaboration.[13]

First, we are obligated to satisfy our basic physical needs for food, shelter, clothing and all that is vital to an individual's basic physical functioning. The satisfaction of these physical needs is not without limit, for we must always ask ourselves whether the attainment of greater satisfaction is compatible with our larger purpose to love God through our love for humanity. Thus, Hobbes' account of the driving force in human beings for self-preservation captures a partial truth. God has so constituted the species to encourage its survival. We are given the natural appetites to seek sustenance, sleep, sex and shelter. Hobbes's mistake was to see this struggle for self-preservation as an end in itself and to predicate a theory of civil society on it alone.[14]

Second, because the satisfaction of basic needs under conditions of natural and artificial scarcity inevitably results in conflict, it follows that self-love requires us to protect the fundamental freedoms necessary to secure basic physical needs. These consist primarily of freedom from arbitrary death and invasions of bodily integrity, freedom from the seizure of one's possessions, and freedom of conscience and association. Again, these negative liberties, spheres of individual autonomy, do not exist as independent abstract rights to be consumed in unlimited fashion. Their purpose is to secure to the individual the space needed to fulfill a higher purpose.

Locke's emphasis on the acquisition of property and the drive to make that acquisition secure from arbitrary seizure captures a partial truth. Satisfaction of basic needs through the acquisition and security of private property is important, but it must be viewed as a means to a higher end if we are to observe vital limits. If, however, the acquisition and security of private property is elevated to the status of an end, Locke's glorification of the individual's unlimited appetite for acquiring property and power is the natural result.[15]

Third, the duty of self-love requires that we do what is necessary to affirm self-worth. A proper sense of self-worth is a precondition for vindicating fundamental freedoms, and also a precondition for satisfying fundamental needs under conditions of scarcity. Without a proper sense of self-worth, individuals may feel that they have no rights to protect and that they must satisfy their basic needs on terms far more restrictive than those actually warranted.[16]

The affirmation of self-worth is of critical importance in a culture that elevates the self-worth of some at the expense of others. My earlier discussion of the Social Gospel's conception of sin indicated how some individuals exploit collective power to perpetuate the subordination of others on the basis of class, race and other forms of identity. Self-love may require the individual to develop rhetorical, discursive and counterhegemonic practices to challenge the systematic evisceration of self-worth perpetuated by these systems.[17]

The duty of self-love commands, then, that we prepare ourselves to love, that we cultivate our gifts, skills and interests so as to serve God better by serving humanity. The quality of this self-cultivation will depend largely on our ability to satisfy basic physical needs, protect fundamental freedoms, and affirm self-worth. This understanding of individualism unleashes the great possibilities of creative intelligence and imagination, but does so within limits that protect us from ourselves. Love, properly understood, provides humanity with both possibility and limit, giving us simultaneously something to strive for and boundaries to strive within.

B. The Law of Love for Others

If love commands that we love others as we love ourselves, it stands to reason that we should desire for others what self-love requires of us. That is, we should strive to satisfy the basic needs, protect the fundamental freedoms, and affirm the self-worth of others. As with ourselves, this permits others to cultivate their gifts, skills and interests to serve God better through service to humanity.

A proper love for others provides a normative vision for majoritarian democracy. Although its underlying maxim, do unto others as you would have others do unto you, resonates with a political philosophy of enlightened self-interest, it goes far beyond this. We are to act not with reference to how others actually treat us, but with reference to how we would have them treat us.

This aspirational, and some would say utopian, dimension of love gives it its prophetic and transformative power. That is, our present endeavors must always be filled with the hope borne of faith in the possibilities of love. Sobered, to be sure, by a sense of human finiteness and frailty, we must transform the present by our hope for the future, teasing out of existing structures and processes an unknown potential. The projection of present values into a world not yet experienced is what I call the aspirational pull of God, the lure of the divine. With each act of love, we testify to its present reality and power.

To be sure, this love is to be cultivated by all for all, but with special attention to the "least of these"—a focus which reminds us of the indelible worth of all humanity. In one of his parables of the final judgment, Jesus told his disciples that the son of man would return to judge the nations, dividing them into the sheep on his right and the goats on his left. To those on his left he will say, "depart from me," for when I was hungry you fed me not, when I was thirsty, you gave me nothing to drink. When I needed shelter and clothes, you gave me neither, and when sick and in prison, you visited me not. Those on the left will then ask, when did we fail to do these things, and the King will answer, inasmuch as you did it to one of the least of these, you did it to Me.[18]

Few will question Jesus' commitment to the poorest and most marginalized segments of the community. He set his priorities when announcing the commencement of his ministry: "The Spirit of the Lord is upon Me. He has anointed Me to preach the gospel to the poor; He has sent Me to heal the brokenhearted, to proclaim liberty to the captives . . . to set at liberty those who are oppressed."[19] "Blessed are the poor in spirit," he later preached, "for theirs is the kingdom of heaven."[20] What does this normative commitment to the "least of these" mean for the restoration of a progressive liberal vision in America? A commitment to the "least of these," as King understood, has spiritual, social and strategic implications.

Spiritually, this normative commitment challenges us to see in others a reflection of ourselves. When we see some remnant of ourselves in those we deem "the least of these," that is, those we perceive as most unlike ourselves, we build bridges to each other's world and lay claim to a wonderful gift of spirit—the gift of unconditional love. No longer would one say of even the most wretched of the earth, "but for the grace of God, there go I." Rather, one would say, simply but profoundly, "there am I." Inasmuch as I think, say and do to the "least of these," I think, say and do unto God and myself.

The beauty of this gift is that by transforming our orientation towards "the least," it transforms our orientation towards all. That is, our acceptance of this gift liberates us from the sickness that weakens all relationships—the need to judge, control and manipulate. When we find in our own hearts an acceptance of those we find most reprehensible and unworthy of our love, our relationship to all of humanity is transformed. Suddenly, quite miraculously perhaps, the great divide between I and thou and us and them is bridged. We see for the brief moment in which spirit speaks to spirit a oneness our finiteness cannot long sustain.

We learn to love others more fully because in learning to love "the least," love of others is made easier. When once we reckon "the least" to be part of us and see ourselves as part of them, what demons can overcome our quest to love others whom we deem more like us than the least. Furthermore, through our practice of loving the least, we learn better to love ourselves, for we cannot truly love unless we ourselves feel loved. This is why Jesus said you shall know them by the fruits that they bear.[21] Our ability to love the least is a measure of our own self-love and spiritual growth, for that which we see in the lives of the least that makes them undeserving of our love is often a reflection of what we see in ourselves. Do we not most see hope when we ourselves are hopeful? Are we not more inclined to see despair when our lives are consumed by despair? Conversely, does not love cover a multitude of faults, frailty and failure? What sorrow cannot be transfigured by the joy that stirs a soul to rapture?

When we have conditioned ourselves to see in those we deem most unlike ourselves—the despised, downtrodden and degraded—something worthy of love, it can be only because we now know and feel our own worth and love. To feel our own worth and love, that is, to feel it unconditionally, is to surrender the judgment, condescension and pride that blinds us to human interdependency.

When our eyes are opened to this fundamental truth, the command of other-love, discussed above, seems not so onerous. We can desire for others what we desire for ourselves, for we know that, given our interdependency, we cannot be free unless all are free. We know that, as King put it, we all are woven into a single garment of destiny.

It is important, I believe, to talk about this spiritual dimension of love at the individual level, for we have little hope of institutionalizing the value of love and the normative commitment to the "least of these" at the social level if we do not simultaneously cultivate a temperament of love at the individual level. Just as Dewey came to see that democratic institutions were no substitute for democratic individuals, I understand that love-based institutions are no substitute for loving individuals.

"Soul work" that no laws or institutions can do must be initiated and diligently pursued by the individual. My hope, however, is that soul work done by the individual who is in the process of becoming more love- rather than fear-centered will shape social institutions that come to reflect the same, and that social institutions in the process of institutionalizing love will simultaneously shape the individuals who comprise them. In this way, individuals and institutions will simultaneously undergo spiritual and social conversion necessary to move toward a Beloved Community here on earth.

What, then, are the social implications of this normative commitment? Socially, a commitment to the "least of these" means that we must institutionalize our love for the least. We must desire for others, as we desire for ourselves, a fulfillment of their gifts, talents and skills in preparation for service to others. As developed above, this requires that we satisfy their basic physical needs, protect their fundamental freedoms, and affirm their self-worth. But who constitutes "the least of these" for purposes of our social and institutionalized love?

Those who constitute the least of these will differ depending on the society, culture and setting. Various criteria are employed to relegate various groups to the lowest rung of the community in question. The social commitment requires that we become cognizant of the overt and subtle ways communities construct their "least of these." It also requires that we attempt to transform those institutions and practices to reflect the spiritual understanding of love and interdependency discussed above. As I said, who constitutes the least will depend on the context in which one is operating. It could easily shift from African-Americans to women, gays and lesbians, Indians, immigrants, foreigners or some combination of these and others, depending on the particular community and context in question.

I am particularly interested, however, in the ways economic subordination interplays with these other forms of oppression. Because I believe the American context has largely been one where the pursuit of material wealth has necessitated the construction of inferior identities deserving of oppression and exclusion from the bounty of America's meteoric rise to economic supremacy, I will use economic stratification as a preliminary measure of who constitutes the least in terms of the distribution of American income and wealth.

When one cross-references information about the general distribution of income and wealth in America against the disproportionality of income and wealth among certain groups relative to their numbers in the population, it becomes clear that some groups are impacted more than others in terms of relative economic marginality. When one cross-references this information against the severity and longevity of American legal and extralegal modes of excluding groups from the economic bounty of America, the picture becomes even clearer.

Under my two-pronged approach, economic stratification is the first indicator of who constitutes the least in the American context. As King envisioned, then, certain interventions are needed to address the problems of the poor. I follow this broad categorization with further inquiries into which groups are disproportionately represented among the poor, and which have been subjected to the most intense histories of legal and extralegal exclusion. Knowledge gathered from this inquiry would require that the social intervention be designed to respond adequately to this history of disproportionality, its causes and cures.

For instance, while African-Americans constitute only 12 percent of the national population, they comprise over 30 percent of those in poverty. Institutionalizing a normative commitment to the least of these, then, means simultaneously alleviating poverty among all races and groups, and responding to the historic racism that has disproportionately located some groups, such as African-Americans, among the poor.

One can safely assume that it is racism that accounts for this disproportionate representation of African-Americans among the poor for two reasons. First, African-Americans are the only group in American society forced to directly bear the cultural, political and economic legacy of racism in such magnitude. This racism and its legacy have legitimated over 200 years of slavery and more than fifty years of Jim Crow segregation, and are presently subverting a scant thirty years of post-1965 freedom.

Second, there can be little doubt that racism continues to be a pervasive force in American culture, even after a "second" civil rights movement purporting to give equal rights to African-Americans. The most comprehensive national opinion poll on racial attitudes administered in 25 years was given in 1990. It revealed that a majority of whites surveyed still believed African-Americans were lazier, less patriotic, more violent and less intelligent than whites. Charles Murray's recent book, entitled *The Bell Curve*, is only one link in a chain of works dating back to the eighteenth century that purport to produce "scientific proof" of the intellectual inferiority of African-Americans.

In other words, along the mixed spectrum of poor Whites, Indians, Hispanics, Asians, women and children who make up the "American least," African-Americans constitute the extreme case, with poor African-Americans occupying the most vulnerable position.

Finally, there are strategic implications for the commitment to the least of these that must be considered. As we can see from the outline of its social dimensions, such a commitment entails an appreciation of the particularity of cultural identity, the specific ways in which rhetoric, ideologies and practices have constructed particular groups as "the least."

As King understood so well, however, if an appreciation of our inter-dependency is the spiritual goal, our rhetoric, ideologies, practices and the strategies we adopt to realize our spiritual and social aspirations should reflect this goal as well. We cannot divorce means from ends in our struggle for a Beloved Community. In other words, strategically, a commitment to the least of these should bring us all into a greater understanding of our interconnection with and mutual dependence on others. The normative commitment should aspire to make all of us more loving and just individuals. Our relationships to all and not just to "the least" should be transfigured by this normative commitment.

What this means specifically for an interrogation of the impact of race and class on the status of African-Americans is that we should try to shape our interventions to respond both to the particularity of the African-American experience and to the experiences of those sharing a common destiny. That is, strategies should shun an insularity and par-ticularism that further fragment and divide humanity. We should always preserve the possibilities of broad-based alliances that reflect the goals of true interdependency. Grasping what we share in common through an understanding and appreciation of our particular experiences is to be preferred over an abstract embrace of what we share in common that is blind to particular histories and realities.

In conclusion, this is the normative role that a commitment to the least of these can play in the revival of a progressive liberal vision in American politics. Its spiritual, social and strategic dimensions respond to serious problems faced by progressive liberals today. As I stated from the outset, the first problem is the need to develop a religiospiritual basis for the progressive liberal agenda, one that speaks to the profound spiritual need of individuals to live meaningful existences. The second is the need to engage directly the ways racism, particularly against African-Americans, is deployed to limit the progressive agenda of the years following World War II.

The next two chapters elaborate the more sophisticated understand-ing of racism that I believe progressive liberals must master in order to resurrect a progressive vision. The final chapter integrates this more subtle understanding of racism into the normative framework just developed and applies that framework to a fallen progressive program—affirmative action. I will suggest how my framework would have constructed and justified the program of affirmative action and perhaps safeguarded it from such an early demise.

Chapter 7

Racism and the Price of Denial

Where Progressive Liberalism Went Wrong

If progressives are to move toward the normative vision of a Beloved Community, with its spiritual, social and strategic commitments, they must understand where and how the progressive liberal vision got off track. How was it separated from a religiospiritual understanding of its underlying tenets, an understanding this work seeks to restore? How did it become obsessed with an empty bureaucratic functionalism, a preoccupation this work hopes to reorient? How was its vision of a community progressively realizing the inherent worth and dignity of all individuals subverted, a vision this work aspires to revive? This chapter attempts to answer these questions.

I will suggest that progressive liberalism has paid a hefty price for its refusal to remedy aggressively the legacy of American racism. This liberal denial of the pervasiveness of racism was the window of opportunity through which the counterrevolutionary forces of the fifties and sixties came like thieves in the night to steal a noble vision. By claiming it already existed, conservatives corrupted the ideal of the Beloved Community, a community whose splendor would reveal itself slowly as centuries-old institutions, behaviors and thought patterns succumbed to the spiritual, social and strategic commitments normatively guiding the social process of becoming. In the end, this corruption of a progressive ideal succeeded in widening the racial divide by blindfolding the progressive vision with a distorted ideology of color-blind law and justice.

In his provocative book entitled *The Culture of Disbelief: How American Law and Politics Trivializes Religious Devotion*, Stephen Carter provides overlapping explanations for why contemporary American liberal culture trivializes religious faith.[1] Carter believes this liberal trivialization of religious faith is at the core of the quandary in which liberal politics presently finds itself. I believe he is correct in this, but he ascribes the problem to the wrong causes.

The first cause is conceptual and the second is political. Conceptually, liberalism—given its emphasis on the rational, empirical and factual—sees questions of religious faith as a set of speculative assertions incapable of rational verification or disproof. Liberalism has, then, a structural bias against religious knowledge. The empirical orientation of the former has deemed the transempirical faith of the latter irrational from the start.

This raises an important question that is ultimately left unanswered by Carter's work. What is the compatibility, if any, between religious and liberal democratic discourses, given the constraints of liberal ideology? Parts I and II have provided a set of answers to this question that I will not repeat here. Suffice it to say that both Raushenbusch and King have demonstrated the compatibility of God and democracy, when both are liberated from dogmatic and traditional understandings.

It is Carter's political explanation of why progressive liberalism has failed to take religious faith seriously that I find more problematic. According to Carter, the religious right's condemnation of *Roe v. Wade*[2] in 1973 and the subsequent mobilization against abortion rights frightened many liberals into a reactionary resistance to religious justifications in public deliberation and policy. Individual autonomy has always been the cornerstone of liberal thought. In practice this translates into an understanding of law as a bundle of personal rights that protect the sphere of personal autonomy. To "right-thinking" liberals, nothing could be more "personal" than the decision about whether to carry a

pregnancy to term. Any notion of the rights of the unborn is too speculative for an empirically oriented modern liberal. Thus, when the religious right organized so vehemently against the Supreme Court decision that many liberals thought was the right decision, liberals felt their
vision of community was diametrically opposed to the vision of religionists who were willing to allow the state to intervene onto this most
sacred of liberal grounds, freedom of choice and the newfound constitutional right to privacy.

I believe that the rift between religion and progressive politics originated in two related historical developments preceding the 1973 decision by the Supreme Court. Had progressive liberals responded appropriately to these developments, the 1973 rift would not have been
nearly so earth-shattering. The first was the disintegration of the old
civil rights coalition in the mid-1960s, prompted primarily by an
unwillingness on the part of white liberals to address the unfinished
business of the black freedom struggle. The second was a conservative
white backlash that started in the 1950s after *Brown v. Board of Education*[3] in 1954 and was consummated by the election of Ronald Reagan
as president in 1980. This rising reactionary force exploited the breakdown of the left-liberal coalition. *Roe v. Wade* was merely a stepping-
stone for this conservative white backlash, which struggled at first but
surged to prominence when conservative Republicans joined forces
with conservative white Southerners, many of whom were Christian
fundamentalists and conservative evangelicals, to support a national
Republican platform that was anti-civil-rights, anticommunism, pro-
states'-rights, and after 1973, antiabortion.

The history of the relationship between religion, politics and race
over the last forty years, therefore, shows that a rapprochement
between religion and liberalism will require a fresh look at the role of
race in the split between religious and liberal discourse. If there is to be
a reunification of progressive politics and religion in particular and a
greater acceptance of religious discourse in public space in general, liberals will have to recommit themselves to the unfinished business of
racial equality that challenges the use of race to divide and conquer
potential allies and to subvert the progressive vision. Disagreement
over this issue prompted the splintering of the liberal coalition, which

then created the political vacuum exploited by the reactionary forces of the Christian and Republican right.

A. The Splintering of the Liberal Coalition

My basic argument is that when the liberal civil rights coalition splintered in the mid-1960s, the political/moral vacuum it left in its wake was filled by powerful and savvy counterrevolutionary forces. These forces were energized by *Roe v. Wade*, to be sure, just as they had been energized earlier by *Engel v. Vitale*, which held to be unconstitutional the recitation of school prayers. But the shaping and channeling of these forces had long been underway.

Roe cannot fully explain the shift in religious rhetoric from left to right for one simple reason; religious justifications of the decision were readily available to liberals in the abortion debate. The left had always competed against the right for divine sanction. Why did they cave in on this issue? During the abolitionist movement, for example, there were conservative religionists who believed and acted on the premise that slavery was a divinely ordained institution. This did not deter the left from constructing its own religious justifications. During the period of the antilynching crusade and the Social Gospel, there was no shortage of conservative clergy who saw God as a political conservative mandating believers to embrace the political and economic ideologies of states' rights and laissez-faire.[4] Nevertheless, many on the left continued to stamp their progressive and radical programs with the blessings of God. Finally, during the 1960s, King battled conservative clergy who joined in the chorus of detractors contending that his campaign of nonviolent direct action was either against God's will altogether or at least untimely.[5] This did not dissuade King, however, as his letter from the Birmingham jail makes clear.

No, something else has to account for why liberals did not construct a religious justification to counter the right's religious condemnation of *Roe*. The answer becomes more apparent when we realize that by 1973 there was no progressive liberal coalition to respond. It had already disintegrated, primarily because of an inability to reckon with the legacy of racism in America. The liberal coalition of the civil rights movement consisted of a precarious alliance of black, Jewish and Christian progressives, and the progressive wings of labor, white women's groups, young white college students and intellectuals. After the victory of the Voting Rights Act of 1965, all of these groups were posing the pressing question: "Where do we go from here?"[6] The answer was not apparent, and even some blacks in the movement, considering the era of protest over, looked to ordinary electoral politics for the answer.[7] Meanwhile, other answers were offered: white students joined the antiwar protests on their college campuses; white women became increasingly absorbed by a women's movement that would be catapulted to new heights by the prowoman decision of *Roe*; workers were concerned about job security in an economy of highly mobile multinational corporations; Jewish leaders turned inward, fearful of the implications for their own struggles of the race-conscious rhetoric of the young, militant, black groups; intellectuals returned to their universities to write their histories, thereby certifying the movement's dead-on-arrival status in 1965. In other words, the liberal civil rights coalition was fracturing, even disintegrating, and in its weakened state stood little chance of surviving the conservative forces preparing to take it by storm. By 1973 the coalition was truly dead. There was no response from the left, because there was no cohesive left to respond. The one thing that could have held it together—agreement on how best to deal with the legacy of race and class in American society—seemed beyond its grasp.

One might argue, in other words, that the liberal coalition reached its philosophical limits with the signing of the 1965 Voting Rights Act. The left-liberal coalition was held together by a core belief that African-Americans should be, as King captured it in his most revered public address, "judged not by the color of their skin, but by the content of their character."[8] In other words, most whites, and many blacks, saw the movement as a means of securing the formal rights of equality for blacks—their right to be treated like anyone else in the American democracy.[9]

Thus when, on August 6, 1965, President Johnson signed the Voting Rights Act into law, many thought they had witnessed the culmination of a second Reconstruction. It had started in 1954 with *Brown*, a case which tacitly repudiated the fundamental assumption that the Thirteenth Amendment's abolition of slavery had meant little; it continued through the 1964 Civil Rights legislation that restored black citizenship rights under the Fourteenth Amendment, and was thought to be complete when Congress passed a law restoring black voting rights under the Fifteenth Amendment. What more was there to be done? At least formally, blacks had all the rights of whites. Wasn't the agenda complete? Wasn't that all they wanted?[10]

"No!" came the defiant answer of blacks in Watts, Los Angeles, five days after the signing of the Act. The uprising left 35 dead, 28 of whom were Black. Invariably, many whites in the coalition found this reaction difficult to understand. Some were confused and others intimidated by the subsequent cries of blacks who claimed unfinished business. Still others rejected the cries on the grounds that blacks were being unreasonable and should channel their grievances through the proper political channels to which they now all had access.[11] The response failed to account for the one thing that blacks in Watts, who had always had the right to vote, knew all too well—the right to vote did not necessarily include the right to be heard or the right to power and control over one's community.

King, of course, never thought that the attainment of formal rights was the end of the struggle.[12] He properly understood formal liberal rights as an important step towards America's socioeconomic restructuring and spiritual regeneration. To that end, in February of 1966, he rented an apartment in a black ghetto of Chicago to draw attention to the nature of this unfinished business, and, in May of that year, he protested against America's involvement in Vietnam at a large antiwar rally in Washington, D.C. This shift to a multiple-front strategy represented King's attempt to answer the nagging question, "Where do we go from here?" His answer was to link the struggle against the evils of racism, symbolized by the civil rights movement, to the struggle against the evils of classism, symbolized by his move into a Chicago slum, to the struggle against military imperialism, symbolized by his increasing militancy against the Johnson administration's war in Vietnam.[13] This was a brilliant political move. Had it worked, it would have brought back into one fold students in the antiwar movement, white workers in the labor movement, moderate blacks in voter registration movements and radical blacks in various forms of black nationalist movements.

Why did King's vision of a new coalition not work? One is tempted to state the obvious. It did not have time to work, given the brevity of his life. I believe this accounts for much of the answer. If anybody in American history could have pulled it off, it was King and the black church that supported him.[14] Given his untimely assassination, this is, of course, quite speculative. There are arguments on the other side, particularly given the increasing ability of conservatives to discredit progressive leadership through smear campaigns. Indeed, Hoover had launched the first stage of such a campaign—the selective leaking of surveillance information—before King's assassination.[15]

The more immediate answer to why the new coalition did not congeal is found in the events of late 1966 and early 1967. In June of 1966 James Meredith was shot soon after he began his 220-mile March Against Fear from Memphis, Tennessee to Jackson, Mississippi. King, the Southern Christian Leadership Conference (SCLC), the Student Nonviolent Coordinating Committee (SNCC), and other segments of the interracial coalition decided to resume Meredith's march. Near Greenwood, Mississippi, SNCC leaders Stokely Carmichael and Willie Ricks used the slogan "Black Power" for the first time in public, in the presence of reporters who made it front page news the next day.[16]

The controversy between King and SNCC represented some fundamental differences in the movement's ideology and programmatic objectives.[17] Black Power raised questions about whether the nonviolent commitment of the SCLC-dominated movement was justified in an atmosphere fraught with violence against blacks, a dilemma whose stark reality was typified by the assassination of Medgar Evers and by reports of snipers lying in wait for marchers on their way to Jackson.

Black Power advocates raised unsettling questions about the role of whites in the movement, contending that white liberal funding and activism had co-opted much of the movement's potential to bring about real shifts in political and economic power for blacks. Many in SNCC found it impossible to continue to preach a gospel of nonviolence and racial harmony. They had been for too long on the front line of the white South's violence, suffering the pain of cattle prods and other abuses in Southern jails during the Freedom Rides and bearing the burden of verbal and physical abuse during the early sit-ins.[18] Their bruised bodies and heavy hearts now resonated to a different beat—

Black Power—the only thing they could see as affectively battling white power in white America.[19]

The rebellions of 1967 sent a clear and unequivocal message that, at least as far as many blacks in urban areas were concerned, the social justice agenda was not completed by the signing of the 1965 Voting Rights Act. Twenty-three deaths and 725 injuries in Newark, New Jersey from July 12 to 17 and 43 deaths and 324 injuries in Detroit, Michigan from July 23 to 30 sent that message. There were other uprisings as well in 1967 that seemed to carry the same message: Jackson State, Mississippi on May 10; the Roxbury district of Boston, Massachusetts on June 2; Tampa, Florida on June 11; Cincinnati, Ohio on June 12; Buffalo, New York on June 27; Cairo, Illinois on July 17; Durham, North Carolina on July 19; Memphis, Tennessee on July 20; Cambridge, Maryland on July 24; and Milwaukee, Wisconsin on July 30. According to a report of the Senate Permanent Investigating Committee, there were 75 major uprisings in 1967, killing 83 people, compared to 36 killed in uprisings in 1965 and 11 in 1966.[20] The Republican candidate, Richard Nixon, was elected president the following year on a platform that promised, among other things, to restore law and order to America.

The frustrations and anxieties vented during these uprisings prompted congressional investigation. In February of 1968, the National Advisory Commission on Civil Disorder (the Kerner Commission) said that white racism was the primary cause of the riots in American cities. In prophetic language not unlike Daniel of the Old Testament, who prophesied against Babylonian exploitation and corruption, the commission read the handwriting on the American wall. The message was clear: America was "moving toward two societies, one Black, one white—separate and unequal."[21] Four days later, in Washington, D.C., King announced plans for the Poor People's Campaign, a multiracial movement designed to engage in massive civil disobedience to demand jobs and income for all poor people. Meanwhile, the more radical H. Rap Brown had replaced Stokely Carmichael as chairman of SNCC and was developing alternative understandings of the events of 1967. The remedy was couched in race conscious language and focused on the attainment of black power, increasingly defined in separatist terms that called for independent political, economic and cultural self-determination for blacks.

The understandable anger and justifiable rage that carried the cry of Black Power to white ears was misunderstood, even resented, by many liberal allies in the movement.[22] King's genius was that he understood these dynamics and tried, with great love and dexterity, to mediate the rift between Black Power advocates and others in order to hold together his coalition.[23] The Poor People's Campaign that King spearheaded in 1968 was a last ditch effort at accomplishing this realignment. As I stated earlier, this was part of a larger design to galvanize a broadly based, multiracial coalition against the triple evils of racism, classism and imperialism. But King was assassinated before his labor could bear fruit, and his death set off a wave of black unrest in inner cities that brought the era of the black-led movement for social justice to an end. The coalition that appeared dead in 1965 certainly died in 1968 with the assassination of the one person on the American scene whose vision, determination and charismatic genius might have resuscitated it.

In summary, the liberal left was in no position to present a religious counter to the Christian right when *Roe* was decided, primarily because the liberal left was in a state of utter disarray. Its ideological cohesiveness was dissipated and its politics splintered by the three interrelated dynamics discussed above. First, many believed that the movement's struggle for black equality before the law had been won, and that liberalism had delivered its promise. They were prepared to go no further for blacks. Second, groups comprising the coalition turned inward to their own concerns and became absorbed by their own separate causes. Finally, the Black Power movement and violent uprisings throughout the North and West confused, intimidated and repulsed many onlookers, creating ever-deepening rifts among former movement supporters. King attempted to bridge these chasms at the end of his life, but had he lived, they might have proved too formidable even for a man of his temperament and vision.

B. The New Conservative Coalition

I want to argue here that the conservative and counterrevolutionary forces that filled the vacuum created by the disintegration of the liberal coalition were in play and flexing their political muscle long before the 1973 decision of *Roe*.[24] More importantly, the same political and cultural developments that precipitated the disintegration of the liberal coalition provided favorable conditions for the rise of the new conservative coalition. When the liberal coalition was divided over the issues of America's involvement in Vietnam, urban unrest and allegations of continued racism, conservative Christians and Republicans showed great unity. Playing off each other in impromptu fashion, conservative Christians and Republicans eventually harmonized on certain themes. The tune was antiblack, anti-civil-rights, anti-Jewish, anti-women's-rights, anti-student-protest and anti-intellectual. It was the antiblack/anti-civil-rights chord, however, that resonated most powerfully with conservative Southerners and largely accounts for the strength of the conservative coalition in the South. Thus racial fear and antagonism explain not only the breakdown of the liberal coalition but the formation of a conservative coalition as well.[25] This is best understood by briefly examining the dynamics of race and politics in the American South and the ways Republicans masterfully exploited these dynamics to their advantage.

To begin with, it is important to remember that, as blacks were registering to vote by the thousands in the late 1960s, they overwhelmingly joined the party whose leaders had supported their cause—the party of Roosevelt, Truman, Johnson and the Kennedy boys—just as they had joined, during the first Reconstruction of the 1860s, the party of Lincoln, Sumner and Stevens. This prompted a major political realignment among the Southern white population, from the Democratic Party to the Republican Party. The Old South had been, on the whole, a one-party region. The South saw the Democratic Party in the nineteenth century as a bastion of resistance and defiance against Yankee imperialism. Democrats were determined never to forget that shameful period when white men stood with Negroes against other white men in what radical Republicans called a Reconstruction.[26]

Even before the Reconstruction, the Democratic Party under Jackson was pro-states'-rights and pro-slavery. The Whig Party, which eventually became the Republican Party, was opposed to the spread of slavery into the new and free territories of the Northwest. After the end of Reconstruction in 1877, prompted by the Hayes/Tilden Compromise in which Democrats allowed Rutherford B. Hayes to become president in a close and disputed election in exchange for a

Republican promise to withdraw troops from the South, blacks remained in the Republican Party. The legal persecution and extralegal terror that pervaded the South in the wake of Reconstruction's fall effectively disenfranchised black Republican votes in the South, and without black support, the Northern Republican party was forced to retreat from the South, as the iron curtain was dropped and the region became a one-party confederacy.

The endless lynchings and persecution of blacks in the South, along with the attraction of better lives in the North, pushed and pulled blacks from the rural South in what began as a trickle but ended as a flood of migrations to urban centers in the South and North between the turn of the century and the close of World War II. This demographic shift prompted significant political changes at the national level that would once again reconfigure the matrix of politics and race in America.

Indications that Democratic presidents Roosevelt and particularly Truman were attempting to attract the Northern black vote prompted many Southern white Democrats to continue to vote Democratic at the state and local levels, where their party could be kept lily-white, but not at the national level, where blacks were beginning to play the role of "swing-vote" in national elections.

As the Democratic Party got blacker, then, the Republican Party got whiter, attracting disaffected white voters in the South who had broken or threatened to break with the Democratic Party and join the Dixiecrats, a prosegregation party again resisting Northern "imperialism".[27] Throughout a region often referred to as the Bible Belt, many of these converts to the Republican Party were also religious conservatives who possessed the kind of evangelical zeal that, if harnessed by politicians, could put the South even more firmly in the Republican back pocket. The creation by conservative whites in the South of their own racially exclusive parties to oppose an increasingly integrated Democratic Party sent a clear message to the politically ambitious hoping to displace Democrats from power. Republicans heard this message loud and clear in the late 1950s, and capitalized on it to their great benefit, controlling the White House for five of the next seven presidential terms. They realized the potential of controlling the House and Senate as well. As early as 1964, a year after the Birmingham civil rights demonstrations, Birmingham's congressional district elected John Buchanan to the House of Representatives as part of the Goldwater faction of Republicans seeking office throughout the country.[28] Buchanan was thought to be part of an "emerging new Republican majority sweeping the Old South in the mid 1960s . . . white, conservative, and part of the backlash against the civil rights movement."[29]

Buchanan was a Baptist minister who had a consistently conservative record. He voted to remove the restrictions on bombing targets in North Vietnam, proposed a constitutional amendment to permit voluntary prayers in school, and stood by Nixon to the very end. By 1980 he showed some signs of changing with the times, moderating his views both on women—by supporting the Equal Rights Amendment—and on Blacks, who comprised a third of his district and who demanded accountability. In 1980, however, he lost the primary to a candidate backed by the Moral Majority. Ironically, the Goldwater conservative was too liberal to pass the litmus test of the Moral Majority, who by 1980 was a key player in the new coalition of conservative Christians and Republicans.

At the same time that Buchanan was campaigning for office in 1964 in the deep South as part of the anti-civil-rights backlash, there were political developments taking shape out West that were of no less consequence for the imminent merger of the Republican and Christian right. In 1966, only one year after the passage of the Voting Rights Act and the black uprising in Watts, Los Angeles, a retired Hollywood actor was elected governor of California. His masterful use of the media had made him a star, first in the world of entertainment, then in the world of corporate promotions, and finally in the world of politics. Ronald Wilson Reagan campaigned on a political platform that was antibusing, antitax, anticommunism and pro-law-and-order, positions that resonated with significant segments of the voting public in the wake of the Watts uprising and the antiwar protests of students at Berkeley, California. This would be Reagan's experimental laboratory for putting together a package of reactionary programs neatly wrapped in God, country and family. With the guidance of his image-making consultants, Spencer-Roberts and Associates, he made a reactionary agenda appear moderate and a liberal agenda appear radical. Reagan's apparently affable, genteel and grandfatherly demeanor was the perfect bow to sit atop the package that would, in November, 1980, be triumphantly presented to the American public, just in time for Christmas.

The emerging conservative backlash was thus evident everywhere by the time King was assassinated in 1968. Two months later, while the nation was still mourning King's death, Bobby Kennedy was gunned down during his presidential campaign. Vice President Hubert Humphrey went on to lose to Nixon, who had quickly shed his old skin of moderate Republicanism in order to appease conservative Southerners, without whom Republicans stood little chance of recapturing the White House. Nixon's opposition to forced busing, forced integration, quotas, welfare recipients and rioters, sent a clear message that the counterrevolution was in full stride.[30]

So then, by 1973, the racial backlash against the gains of the civil rights movement was in place, the lines drawn, and the Republican road map to success on the national political front well established. Much of the Southern religious right had already crossed over to the Southern political right, the Republican Party, by the time *Roe* was decided in 1973. When conservative Christians reacted to the case, the Republican Party gladly supported the position, lest they lose a pivotal region of voters they needed to reclaim the White House after the disaster of Watergate. It is important to note that conservative Christians were on the whole anti-*Roe*, anti-civil-rights and, by implication, anti-black-progress as well. After all, they started voting for Republicans like Buchanan, Goldwater and Nixon for that very reason.

In summary, the merger between conservative Republicans and conservative Christians was already underway before the 1973 decision of *Roe*. Given the sentiment against blacks, civil rights and federal government among conservative whites in the South, the merger made perfect sense. Republicans needed a strong South to inaugurate a counterrevolution against the redistributive agenda of the Democratic Party. Religion was merely a way of mobilizing those needed voters who had given up on politics and were patiently awaiting Jesus' return. They did not get Jesus, but they got what many considered the next best thing, a long succession of Republican candidates and officials who pampered them and quoted their manifesto, the Bible. These politicians invented a Republican identity that gave Southern conservatives a political home and tapped their human yearning for community. Unfortunately, the conception of community manufactured by Republican image-makers was a far cry from the Beloved Community King had envisioned. Like all reactionary community rhetorics and ideologies, it reflected the hopes, fears and phobias of the community.

The election of Ronald Reagan in 1980 must have seemed like the Second Coming, the Kingdom of God brought finally to earth by a counterrevolutionary movement that had been steadily building since the Supreme Court's decision in *Brown*, twenty-six years earlier. Ironically, the kingdom turned out to be a Calvinistic kingdom of the elect, excluding many who had, with great faith, labored in the vineyard and believed they too would be saved. These outcasts were the conservative white supporters of low and moderate income who had helped bring Reagan into office but who were hurt by a counterrevolutionary agenda that took money from the poor and gave it to the rich through a trickle-down, supply-side economics that promised to lower taxes, increase defense spending and balance the budget, but ended up dangerously deregulating the economy and tripling the federal debt.

Conclusion

The historical relationship of religion, politics and race over the last forty years demonstrates that Stephen Carter's emphasis on *Roe* is overstated. This history reveals his inability to see that the reunion of religion and liberalism necessitates a fresh look at the role of race in the historic split between religious and liberal discourse. Such a fresh look requires a reconceptualization of liberalism's understanding of race as much as its understanding of religion.

If liberals are to negotiate a rapprochement with religion, they must admit two crucial points. First, an important factor accounting for the disintegration of the civil rights movement was the unwillingness of white progressive liberals to struggle beyond the limits of formal equality to secure a radically different conception of community—such as the one envisioned by either Black Power advocates or King.

The liberal ideology that accommodated the freedom struggle up to the signing of the Voting Rights Act could not accommodate, for many white liberals, some of the answers that Black Power advocates were giving to the question: "Where do we go from here?" Black consciousness, as opposed to colorblind consciousness, violence, as opposed to nonviolent protest and reasoned deliberation, and agendas of cultural, political and economic independence, as opposed to integration, struck many white and black liberals as retrograde and illiberal.

Nor could these liberals support the direction in which King was moving at the end of his life. Many of these liberals were faithful supporters of Johnson, and thus King's stand against American involvement in Vietnam alienated them. Many favored free market, unfettered capitalism, and thus his stand on wealth redistribution and democratic control over the means of production alienated them. Finally, while many liberals would fight for a colorblind society, they abhorred race-conscious remedies—such as racial quotas and preferential treatment—to the unfinished agenda of poverty and lack of opportunity. Thus King's concessions to the demands of Black Power advocates alienated many white liberals as well.

This, rather than a subsequent abortion opinion, is why liberals distanced themselves from and came to trivialize religious discourse. They could support neither King nor those white religious conservatives who had always opposed him and now were gaining the upper hand. Instead they chose to stand in the middle, precariously negotiating the tension between the two groups, watching the more radical black nationalists, whose views they certainly could not embrace, out of the corner of their eye.

The marriage of conservative Republicans and conservative Christians was a lasting one because they were committed to a counter-revolutionary political agenda that brought people together, giving them something for which to live and for which to fight. Unfortunately, much of this sense of community was based on a legacy of American racism, with its attending fears, hostilities and brutalities. Yet, King attempted to do the same toward the end of his life by creating a broad progressive coalition to address the problems of continued racism that plagued the black community, the uneven distribution of wealth and power that afflicted the poor of all races, and American imperialism's drain on economic and spiritual resources that affected all of every race and class.

The trivialization of religion in American culture is a problem of the limits of moral conviction and political will to face the unfinished work of the struggle for racial justice. If that work is ever taken seriously, the integrity of the struggle will build a bridge between secularists and religionists, blacks and whites, who, while they may speak different languages, will experience those rarest of moments when one sees into the soul of another and knows truth.

Progressive liberals have not seriously reckoned with the extent to which America's legacy of racism continues to undermine the progressive agenda. This requires, I believe, a more sophisticated understanding of racism than liberalism has produced. The next chapter responds to this deficiency.

Toward a Progressive Liberal Understanding of Racism

This chapter develops a multidimensional understanding of racism based on an analysis of the Rodney King beating, the trial of his assailants and the acquittal of the defendants by an all-white Simi Valley jury. After defining racism, I move on to discuss four kinds of racism that I believe progressive liberalism must understand and develop responses to. They consist of conscious overt and covert racism and unconscious institutional and cultural racism. I then go on to explore the implications of each within a framework that makes the concepts more assessable—the racial implications of the Rodney King saga. Many saw the episode as a blatant act of racism akin to the dark period of American history in which public mobs routinely lynched blacks. It also provided a bird's-eye view of the complex development and intricate configuration of American racism. For several reasons, I believe the Rodney King incident, more than the O.J. Simpson trial, provides a helpful framework for understanding the multilayered reality of American racism.

First, most of us are still too emotionally invested in and torn by the

Simpson trial to analyze the race, class and gender dynamics of that saga with any degree of objectivity. In many ways the events surrounding that trial pose some of the most difficult challenges to the spiritual, social and strategic dimensions of the love-based conception of community I am urging progressive liberals to adopt. The race, class and gender questions associated with the O.J. Simpson trial are obfuscated by opinions of whether he committed the heinous murders of which he was accused. People find it difficult to separate the two sets of inquiry. Some believe he did it, others, that he did not. Some believe he did it but was rightly acquitted, the prosecution failing to establish its case beyond a reasonable doubt. Others believe the evidence overwhelmingly confirmed his guilt. There is a greater consensus, at least among liberals, that the acquittal of the police officers in the Rodney King trial was a wrong decision, and that the claim of "reasonable force" made by the gang of police officers who surrounded and beat him on that fateful night to near-unconsciousness was ludicrous.

The Rodney King case provides, then, a better lens through which to understand the intricacies of American racism, because most liberals, I would surmise, are more willing to entertain the proposition that racism was involved in the beating and/or verdict in that case. If my assumption is correct, it will be easier to convince liberals of the reality of the four forms of racism I think it imperative for them to take seriously in order to revive progressive liberal politics in America. Thus the King case, rather than the Simpson case, is the better window through which to see the relationship between overt and covert forms of conscious racism and the institutional and cultural forms of unconscious racism this chapter elaborates. The progressive liberal failure to aggressively combat these four dimensions of racism has resulted in much of the racial division we see in this country today, and a continued denial of its pervasiveness is no longer an option.

Second, we can better understand certain aspects of the Simpson trial—for instance, the drastically different responses by blacks and whites to the verdict—by exploring the Simi Valley acquittal. African-Americans who cheered the Simpson verdict were largely reacting to a history of biased justice which caused many to doubt the legitimacy of a criminal justice system that made their pain and suffering invisible, particularly when that pain and suffering was inflicted, as was the case in the Rodney King trial, by white perpetrators. That is, a long history of Rodney King type abuses by both policemen and sham proceedings by courts was the backdrop for many of those cheers. The King trial may be a clearer and more compelling example of the different worlds perceived and occupied by whites and African-Americans. African-Americans could not understand how white Simi Valley jurors could look at the vicious beating of Rodney King and "reasonably" conclude that excessive force was not used. In light of a long history of police harassment, brutality and wrongful death, the verdict could be understood by them only as yet another instance of white racism's "genocidal treatment" of African-Americans. On the other hand, whites could not understand how African-American jurors could look at the "flood of blood evidence" and conclude that the case against Simpson was not proven beyond "reasonable" doubt. The decision could be understood only in terms of irrationality, the racial connotations of which have deep roots in the history of Western racism, or in terms of a reverse racism provoked by Johnny Cochran's race-baiting and card-playing courtroom antics.

The most important question is missed by these name-calling characterizations of the two verdicts. That question is: How is "reasonableness" constructed differently by the different experiences of African-Americans and whites. A history of abuse, pain and suffering inflicted by the police and criminal justice system may have constructed a different standard of "reasonable doubt" for African-American jurors. Similarly, a different set of experiences and understandings of the police, courts and black men, particularly, may have constructed a different standard of what constituted "excessive force" in the minds of Simi Valley jurors.

A. Defining Racism

Defining racism is extremely difficult in light of the often-conflicting understandings of the term bandied about in both popular and academic circles. Some see racism as the use of any classification that ascribes qualities to any one individual based on generalizations about the class of individuals to which the one individual belongs. Thus, it is racist to assume that any given African-American is more likely than some other person of a different race to be more violent, to like basketball, to be a good dancer or an eloquent orator, or that a Jew is more likely than members of other groups to be cunning or intelligent. The sin against which this view of racism rebels is the use of general classifications to define individual persons. We call this stereotyping. Whether the claim is invidious—blacks are more violent and Jews more cunning—or benign—blacks are eloquent orators and Jews are intelligent—individuals should not be placed into such categories based on their arbitrary membership in a racial or ethnic group. The generalization may not hold true as to the particular individual, and even if it did, one should not see race or ethnicity, but rather, personal choice and background as accounting for the occurrence of the disdained or honored quality. We should see and evaluate each person as a unique and autonomous individual and not as a member of a particular group whose general or average qualities, real or invented, serve as a proxy for the evaluation of the particular individual.

Others refuse to see the sin of racism as merely the use of race-based generalizations to distribute honor and contempt. For them, racism occurs only when racial stereotypes are coupled to a power to dominate groups on the basis of those stereotypes. Thus, an analysis of race is inextricably connected to a use of power to dominate on the basis of race. This means two things. First, one must distinguish between invidious and benign racial classifications. The generalization that blacks are violent should not be viewed as the moral equivalent of the generalization that Jews are intelligent. The first generalization is invidious because it is predicated on assumptions of black inferiority that stigmatize, demean and perpetuate domination of blacks in the society. This generalization devalues any given black who may be industrious but who is diminished by the shadow cast on the group as a whole. The second generalization is benign, assuming intelligence is a desirable quality in the culture. This generalization empowers and enhances the prestige of any individual Jew who may not satisfy the particular understanding of intelligence used but who benefits vicariously from the prestige accorded the group.

The second point suggested by the coupling of race to power is that the generalization by whites that blacks are more violent than whites is not to be viewed in the same light as the generalization by blacks that whites are more violent than blacks. This is so because whites, not blacks, are in a position of dominance in the culture, with the power to use the generalization as either a conscious or an unconscious basis for persecution—building more prisons, reinstituting chain gangs, intensifying police harassment and brutality, selectively prosecuting offenders, administering biased judicial proceedings, and imposing discriminatory sentencing. Thus, the concept of reverse racism is a misnomer according to the advocates of this view. Black people lack any real power in the American society to be racists in reverse.

The two views are mirror images of the other. The first is too idealistic. It sees racism as the failure to think about individuals in the right way. This failure is a deviation from the liberal ideal of rational individualism that sees the individual as separate and detached from history and culture. If the first theory of racism is too abstract, the second is too empirical, too wedded to a historical/cultural understanding of existing power relations. Its assumption that, given the asymmetry of racial power relations in this country, blacks could never be racists seems dangerously one-sided.

The appropriate middle ground is a view that ties the definition of racism to either a consciously or an unconsciously held belief in the inherent inferiority of a group, ascribing to individual members of the group a presumption of inferiority based solely on their membership in the group. This definition admits, of course, of the possibility of black racists. More importantly, it allows us to address the complexities of racism suggested by the comparison of the King and Simpson trials above. Under this definition of racism, one cannot be called a racist for merely using a racial generalization. The relevant question is whether that racial generalization is tied to some set of assumptions about the inherent inferiority of the group classified. Thus, this theory of racism acknowledges the useful distinction between benign and invidious forms of domination. The statement "Blacks really are eloquent orators" is not racist, then, unless being an eloquent orator somehow presupposes the inferiority of blacks.

Now, a belief in the "inferiority" of a group is a belief that members of the group are less worthy of love, respect and dignity than others. They are less worthy than others by virtue of certain negative or undesirable qualities that are "inherent" to the group, that is, by virtue of qualities that are inborn in or innate to the group of which they are members. Thus, the "unworthies," "the least of these," must be marked off in some way by the dominant group. Some fixed and empirical difference must be made the marker or sign of inferiority. Skin color, the full range of supposed biological differences, intelligence, moral behavior and a full range of cultural differences have all been made the empirical markers of this alleged "inherent" inferiority from time to time in American history. We will discuss a few of them shortly. For now, however, suffice it to say that my working definition of racism assumes a belief system, variously operationalized by individuals, institutions and cultures, that consciously or unconsciously presupposes the inherent inferiority of another group.

Having settled on a suitable definition of racism, I will argue that there are four dimensions to racism that progressive liberals need to recognize and challenge more aggressively than they have in the past. The four dimensions consist of consciously overt and covert racism and unconscious institutional and cultural racism. Progressive liberal ideology has done an excellent job in remedying consciously overt racism, has a mixed record at remedying consciously covert and unconscious institutional racism, and has done a shamefully poor job at addressing the unconscious cultural racism that lies at the root of most of America's racial strife. I will now elaborate each type of racism, suggesting why I believe progressive liberalism has responded to each in the way that it has, and suggesting how it should respond to each in light of the normative framework of a Beloved Community outlined earlier.

1. Consciously Overt Racism

Conscious racism is a consciously held belief in the inherent inferiority of another group that becomes the basis for either overt or covert behavior against that group. Overt racism is the most easily discerned and vehemently condemned form of racism. It occurs when individuals publicize their racist beliefs in advance of or contemporaneous with their behavior. Overt racists consist of such diverse figures as Thomas Jefferson, Abraham Lincoln, Senator Bo Bilbo, Dr. Shockley, Al Campanis and, of course, organizations like the Ku Klux Klan and the many white-supremacy groups that have proliferated over the past twenty years.[1] Both Jefferson and Lincoln present interesting cases because, in the prevailing folklore, they are seldom thought of as racists. While Jefferson authored the Declaration of Independence, which proclaims all men equal and endowed with inalienable rights of life, liberty and the pursuit of happiness, and while he championed an antislavery clause that was ultimately negotiated out of the document by Southern slaveholding interests, his views of blacks were those of an overt racist.[2] In his comparison of blacks and whites, Jefferson noted that:

> The first difference which strikes us is that of colour. Whether the black of the negro resides in the reticular membrane between the skin and scarf-skin, or in the scarf-skin itself; whether it proceeds from the colour of the blood, the colour of the bile, or from that of some other secretion, the difference is fixed in nature, and is as real as if its seat and cause were better known to us. And is this difference of no importance? Is it not the foundation of a greater or less share of beauty in the two races? Are not the fine mixtures of red and white, the expressions of every passion by greater or less suffusions of colour in the one, preferable to that eternal monotony, which reigns in the countenances, that immoveable veil of black which covers all the emotions of the other race? Add to these, flowing hair, a more elegant symmetry of form, their own judgment in favour of the whites, declared by their preference of them, as uniformly as is the preference of the Oran-ootan for the black women over those of his own species. The circumstance of superior beauty is thought worthy attention in the propagation of our horses, dogs, and other domestic animals; why not in that of man?[3]

Similarly, Lincoln is warmly remembered in history as the Great Emancipator of black people, as if his decision to free black slaves during the Civil War in 1863 indicated his willingness to see them as equals. Lincoln made it clear that it did not:

> I am not, nor ever have been, in favor of bringing about in any way the social and political equality of the white and black races. . . . I am not nor ever have been in favor of making voters or jurors of negroes, nor of qualifying them to hold office. . . . I will say in addition to this that there is a physical difference between the white and black races which will ever

forbid the two races living together on terms of social and political equality. And inasmuch as they cannot so live, while they do remain together, there must be the position of superior and inferior, and I, as much as any other man, am in favor of having the superior position assigned to the white race.[4]

It is almost inconceivable that individuals of the stature of Jefferson or Lincoln could get away with such overt racism today. This is not to say that such beliefs are not widely held. To the contrary, covert racists hold similar beliefs about the natural inferiority of blacks, but simply respond in ways that elicit greater approbation than that given overt racists.

It is a true measure of the accomplishments of progressive liberalism that such racism is morally condemned in our society today. The public record of the American experiment in democracy for most of American history is regrettably tainted by the dehumanizing language of otherwise honorable public figures such as Benjamin Franklin, Thomas Jefferson, Abraham Lincoln and Woodrow Wilson, to name but a few. For most of the history of this country, the law has been an inviting forum for the expression of this native racism and the consummate tool for the cultural reenforcement of racist norms. From Justice Taney's majority opinion in *Dred Scott*, where he boldly proclaimed that because of the widely accepted belief in black inferiority, blacks had no rights that whites were bound to respect, to the dissenting opinion of Justice Brown in *Plessy v. Ferguson*, who, even in arguing on behalf of the black plaintiff, could not doubt the belief of the white majority in its own superiority, American jurisprudence is not without blemish.

Both contemporary liberal law and morality condemn overt racism. Overt racism violates central tenets of liberal dogma, foremost of which is the belief that persons should not be judged on the basis of an immutable or fixed characteristic such as race over which they have no control. One of the traditions within the modern liberal paradigm permits to be "known" only those things that can be empirically proven. Thus, overt racism is particularly troubling because one has empirical proof, the racial epithet or verbal expression of racist intent, that the liberal tenet is being violated. In the absence of empirical proof, one might say that other things more plausibly account for the questionable treatment.

Take our comparison of the King and Simpson cases again. Had Mark Fuhrman, the detective who found key pieces of incriminating evidence against Simpson and who was later proven to be a racist, been one of the policemen accused of beating Rodney King, the allegation that the incident was racially motivated would be quite compelling under the liberal paradigm. In such a case, one would have the smoking gun, the strongest of empirical proof of the perpetrator's racist mental state—taped conversations of Furhman not only using the "N" word but also stating that, if he had his way, he would tie all the "N———s" together and burn them.

But what happens when a racial epithet is not used, when language that has both racist and nonracist connotations is used? This creates, under the liberal paradigm, epistemological doubt, since one cannot "really know" which of the possible connotations the perpetrator intended or had in mind. This was the argument made in the Rodney King case in response to the allegation by some that his beating and the acquittal of the officers were racially motivated. At various stages in the Rodney King saga, language was used by defendant officers and by their lawyers in appeals to the jury that suggested to many that certain parties possessed a belief in the inherent inferiority of African-Americans. References like "gorillas in the midst," "raging bull" and policemen being the "thin blue line separating us from the jungle," are examples of empirical referents from which some might reasonably infer a racist mental state that accounts for the seemingly excessive beating of King and the acquittal of the defendant police officers. But this assumption becomes "reasonable" only when characterizations like gorilla, raging bull and jungle are connected to a long history of racism in which blacks are deemed subhuman and their communities only slightly higher than the wild kingdom of the jungle. Without that connection to history and culture, one might argue that the disputed characterizations were about a particular personality and situation and only coincidentally about blacks. The use of the language, the argument goes, may have been unfortunate, perhaps even insensitive, but certainly not racist.

Now what happens when you move from the clear case of a Fuhrman who repeatedly uses the "N" word and spouts genocidal rhetoric to a more ambiguous case in which perpetrators characterize the victim as "a raging bull," to the still more ambiguous case where no such aspersions are cast at all but the behavior is just as reprehensible. That is, take the same videotaped scene of Rodney King being beaten, but without any of the statements about gorillas and raging bulls that later surfaced. If the liberal paradigm that requires empirical evidence of racial animus has difficulty dealing with the second scenario, one can see how it would have even greater difficulty dealing with the third. This is precisely the challenge faced by liberalism's limited understanding of racism as intentional and its concomitant difficulty in dealing with forms of covert, institutional and cultural racism. As we will see, progressive liberalism flirted with the idea of using other empirical referents as a measure of racial animus or racist intent. But these efforts were always in tension with a more dominant and conservative conception of liberalism that, when supported by the reactionary forces that organized in the wake of the civil rights revolution, eventually reclaimed its interpretive throne.

2. *Consciously Covert Racism*

Consciously covert racism is once again predicated on a belief in the inherent inferiority of another group. Like overt racists, covert racists have an aversion to members of a group deemed inferior. This aversion manifests itself in efforts to avoid contact or competition with the group in employment, residential and educational arrangements.[5] The difference is that exclusion of the group is routinely achieved through the use of nonracial criteria. Covert racists are not likely to base their unwillingness to live in the same neighborhood as blacks on a belief that blacks are inferior. They veil their racism with an ostensibly race-neutral justification such as the fear of declining property values offered by the logic of market dynamics. Similarly, it is not that whites attain greater positions of authority and status because blacks are intellectually inferior, as suggested by Al Campanis who contended that the reason there were so few black coaches and administrators in major league baseball was because they lacked the intellectual capacity for such jobs.[6] Rather, blacks are simply not qualified by some ostensibly objective and race-neutral criterion, again, generally market-related in our times. While invisible to many, this form of racism is often visible to members of the dominated group who, in order to survive, learn to interpret the meaning of the complicated maze of unspoken but clearly communicated language that effectively excludes them from the opportunities open to whites.

Covert racism, then, is racism that has gone underground. The actual beliefs held by the overt and covert racist are the same. The latter, however, has chosen to window-dress the outward appearance of those beliefs in order to avoid criticism by the larger society. As social norms shift to make the public racism of a Jefferson or a Lincoln and the extralegal racism of a KKK member unacceptable, two things happen. In some cases individuals are resocialized by a culture that now has different expectations about the propriety of certain beliefs, statements and behavior. In other words, society reorients its citizens, and fewer racists are produced. But, many studies reveal that racist attitudes are still very prevalent in American culture and have shifted very little over time. This means that the critical difference between the times of Jefferson, Lincoln, Wilson, Kennedy and our own is that people have become more sophisticated in their ability to conceal racist beliefs.

Those beliefs surface not as virulent genocidal racism: "blacks should be gathered together and burned," or as racial epithets: "blacks are lazy." Neither are they expressed in the more ambiguous language that "coincidentally" analogizes blacks and situations they are in to "gorillas" and "raging bulls." The covert racist is generally too clever or too cowardly for this. Instead, the covert racist finds other justifications unrelated to race to justify his negative treatment of a group deemed inferior.

Now let us assume that an employer, similar to the employer in the Supreme Court case of *Griggs v. Duke Power*, has traditionally excluded blacks from certain prestigious and higher-paying jobs and relegated them to a category of menial labor designated "Negro jobs." Let us further assume that this was no mere tacit understanding, but that the employer disclosed on applications and in the application process that blacks could apply only for certain positions. What happens when there is a shift in the racial paradigm like that inaugurated by the civil rights movement, the Civil Rights Act of 1964 and the Voting Rights Act of

1965? All of a sudden, it is illegal for the company and its managers to engage in an overtly racist hiring policy. If the assumptions about black inferiority are not changed, however, the racist sentiment formerly expressed through company policy must now find a different avenue of expression to achieve the same result of excluding blacks from the more desirable and higher-paying jobs.

That alternative avenue may very well be the arbitrary attachment of qualifications to the desired jobs that one is certain black applicants cannot satisfy because of the discrimination to which the company and the general society have subjected them. For instance, the company might say now that those who wish to apply for the better jobs must have a certain number of years of experience in working in those jobs. Of course, it would be impossible for blacks to qualify, since they were excluded from the jobs before. The company might say that such positions are to be filled by union members, when blacks were excluded from unions because white workers were attempting to preserve the best jobs for themselves. The company might say that such positions must be filled only by those who pass a certain test, knowing that either their subjective evaluation or the lower education levels of black workers will result in the continued exclusion of blacks from those positions. My point is that with proper window dressing, the company's racism simply finds another way of achieving its earlier objectives.

Progressive liberalism understood that if one made overt racism, that is, intentional or invidious racism, the only legally actionable basis of redress, the impact of *Brown* would be short-lived. In education, politics and employment, a more sophisticated covert racism would preserve the hierarchies of privilege and subjugation put in place by years of overt racism. There was a need, then, to develop another measure of conscious racist intent to complement the classical liberal test that required an empirically verifiable expression of racist intent through unambiguous language. What was that test to be? In Title VII employment discrimination cases, courts required employers to show that the race-neutral criteria they used to hire and promote employees was truly job-related when the use of that race-neutral criteria was shown to have a discriminatory impact on African-Americans. If, for instance, having a high school diploma or a certain score on a test administered to measure qualifications for the position was not really necessary to perform the job competently, and the use of the criterion disproportionately excluded African-Americans from those jobs, one could reasonably assume that covert racism was in play. In other words, this use of an employment criterion unrelated to the competent performance of the job itself became, under the progressive variant of the liberal paradigm, sufficient empirical evidence of invidious intent or conscious racism.

In Fourteenth Amendment equal protection law that covered the practices of the public sector in, among other things, employment, education, housing and voting, progressive liberalism attempted a similar feat. Relief was to be granted when a plaintiff could establish that the race-neutral criterion employed by government had a discriminatory effect against African-Americans and was not essential to the fulfillment of some other compelling objective. The progressive liberal shift in the understanding of what constituted sufficient evidence of invidious intent or conscious racism was eventually rejected altogether in equal protection law and severely circumscribed in Title VII law.

The reasons for the short-lived success of the progressive liberal intervention had to do with both the counterrevolutionary political developments discussed in the previous chapter and the nature of the progressive liberal intervention itself. That intervention never really questioned the liberal paradigm directly but, rather, tried to modify slightly its test of what counted as sufficient empirical proof of invidious intent or conscious racism within that paradigm. This left progressive liberals vulnerable to an attack from the right, claiming that it was betraying fundamental liberal tenets through its embrace of an effects-based test of discriminatory intent. It was betraying these tenets because, if employers and others were not verifiably using race as a criterion for distributing benefits and burdens, it was illiberal to assume that they were racists simply because their practices impacted African-Americans more adversely than whites. To assume racism on such scant empirical evidence was tantamount to assuming that all whites making decisions adverse to African-Americans were no better than those who overtly practiced racism. To place the two groups of whites—overt racists and those whose decisions coincidentally excluded blacks from distributed benefits—into the same category was a type of generalizing and stereotyping that was at the very source of racist attitudes and practices. This was racism in reverse.

The relevance of the above analysis to the King beating is clear. Perhaps some or all of the officers involved in the incident were covert racists who had thoughts about African-Americans similar to those of Mark Fuhrman in the Simpson case. Perhaps the only difference between Fuhrman and those policemen was that they did a better job of concealing their racist sentiment, having avoided, for instance, taped interviews with aspiring screenplay writers.

African-American history is certainly replete with stories of policemen and other public figures who covertly use their positions of authority as a way of facilitating KKK or white-supremacist agendas. It is this history that constructs the African-American understanding of what it is "reasonable" to believe in those instances where police behavior is called into question. Perhaps it is the absence of such a history that constructs the white American understanding of the same.

The problem, of course, is that the liberal paradigm's approach to covert racism tries to play both ends against the middle. Unless one is to be accused of reverse racism, one must find an empirical reference point that reflects the police officer's covert racism. But what is the liberal paradigm willing to accept as sufficient empirical proof? For the conservative liberal, the beating itself is not sufficient, because it may be "reasonably" explained as a necessary restraint. Even the use of language like "gorillas" and "raging bulls" can be explained in "race-neutral" ways that divorce the language from any racist motivations.

Progressive liberalism attempted to expand the scope of acceptable proof by, for instance, permitting an inference of racist intent from certain empirical referents, such as whether African-Americans are disproportionately impacted by police brutality, or whether African-Americans have been the victims in a disproportionate number of cases in which police officers were accused of police harassment or brutality. Conservative liberals soon accused progressive liberals of the same racism they were attempting to remedy. If the policemen who beat King were deemed racists simply because others had overstepped boundaries in the past, conservative liberals argued, this was an instance of judging the individual on the basis of attributes ascribed to the group. In this deft sleight of hand, the police officers in the Rodney King case could then become the "victims" of reverse racism.

Progressive liberalism got into this contradiction because it wanted to have the best of both worlds, getting better results out of the liberal paradigm without questioning the legitimacy of that paradigm's treatment of racism. That is, even when progressives sought to get better results out of the paradigm by expanding the permissible scope of empirical evidence from which one could infer invidious purpose, the analysis remained oriented toward a proof of "the individual's" bad motives or racist state of mind. This was the problem. Even progressive liberalism could not give up the need to link these inquiries to some moral judgment of the individual as a bad person whose sufficiently verified racism justified the legal action in question.

Progressive liberalism clearly needed a way of questioning much more thoroughly than it did the individualist orientation of the liberal paradigm. Two theories of racism were offered by the Black Power movement of the sixties that would have given progressive liberals a way of breaking out of the liberal paradigm that limited social reform. Progressive liberals refused to embrace these understandings, because their implications for not only understanding racism but restructuring American society seemed much too radical. The theories explained racism in terms of American institutions and culture. While Black Power advocates tended to focus on the conscious use of institutions and culture to perpetuate a racist society, more sophisticated versions focused on the unconscious reproduction of racial hierarchy. It is this understanding of unconscious institutional and cultural racism that I want to explore as responses to the dilemma of progressive liberals elaborated above.

3. Unconscious Institutional Racism

As discussed earlier, racism is the consciously or unconsciously held belief in the inherent inferiority of another group. Institutional racism offers an account of how these beliefs may not be consciously held by individuals when they make decisions but may be the unseen backdrop against which race-neutral decisions are made. The Skolnick Report to the National Commission on the Causes and Prevention of Violence summarized the problem in this way:

Because of the influence of historical circumstances, it is theoretically possible to have a racist society in which most of the individual members of that society do not express racist attitudes. A society in which most of the good jobs are held by one race, and the dirty jobs by people of another color, is a society in which racism is institutionalized, no matter what the beliefs of its members are.[7]

Unconscious institutional racism occurs through the application of ostensibly neutral institutional norms. These norms are not racist on their face, nor necessarily administered by individuals with conscious racist motives, but they may have racist effects nevertheless.[8] How, then, can these norms be characterized as racist, if they do not embody an explicit belief in the inherent inferiority of blacks? The answer lies in an understanding of how individuals who apply these race-neutral institutional norms are often unconscious of how the norms perpetuate a history of overt and covert racism, that is, how racial desparities of income, wealth and opportunity have been institutionalized by economic, political and cultural practices.

We might better understand what is meant by institutional racism if we explore the application of a popular race-neutral institutional norm. A prevailing norm in American institutional life is the norm of meritocracy, the assumption that membership and mobility within institutions are contingent on individual qualification and merit. Membership or mobility even partially contingent on race is deemed an undesirable deviation from this central norm. Thus affirmative action has come under increasing scrutiny and criticism in education, employment and politics. While progressive liberals try to justify the deviation of affirmative action from meritocratic norms by reference to the history of institutional exclusion of blacks or the need to diversify their institutions, conservative liberals tolerate race-based remedies only in the most egregious and unmistakable instances of intentional exclusion of blacks.[9] Both progressive and conservative liberals, then, view the remedial inclusion of blacks as a deviation from an unquestionably acceptable meritocratic norm. Progressive liberals are simply more willing to tolerate the deviation for historical and policy reasons. Ironically, whether blacks are the beneficiaries of progressive liberal paternalism or the victims of conservative liberal exclusion, they are unqualified to be in the institution in any event.

Most liberals never question the legitimacy of the meritocratic norm itself; they only bicker about the proper scope of its application. They seldom interrogate how the norm does not embody a unitary standard and why only certain deviations are problematic. Many liberals either deny or do not wish to elaborate fully the relationship between the exclusion of certain groups by the institutional norm and the history of overt societal racism that has resulted in the absence of qualities now deemed fundamental to meritocratic consideration. They are even less inclined to inquire whether the so called meritocratic standard itself is a measure of merit or rather a set of preferences perpetuating race, class and gender privilege in American society. They prefer, instead, to talk about the need for diversity which critics quickly disparage as a too costly deviation from merit. Only by bringing the concept of merit itself under scrutiny and demonstrating its shifting, plural and socially constructed meaning can progressive liberals challenge the conservative use of merit. This critique brings to the forefront the plural criteria that have always constituted our understanding of merit. By democratizing the concept of merit, progressive liberals could undermine the conservative argument that diversity and restitutional concerns were too costly deviations from the otherwise neutral and efficient norm of merit. When progressive liberals fail to make this analysis, institutions willingly participate in the perpetuation of racist perceptions and domination that find their genesis in forms of conscious racism.

Ostensibly neutral institutional norms blind many whites to the insidious racism that continues to plague the society and influence the administration of justice in America. Thus the race-neutral institutional norms legitimate oppressive racial hierarchies. Institutional racism consists of continuing to embrace these norms while knowing the effects of doing so is to perpetuate beliefs in the inherent inferiority of African-Americans, for example, that blacks are inherently less intelligent than whites. According to the theory of institutional racism, the past and present racism of the outside world serves as a filter, doing the dirty work of disqualifying many Blacks from the pool of possible beneficiaries. The race-neutral norm, educational attainment, seniority and performance tests then do the relatively clean work of determining which individuals in the restricted pool of candidates should be given the benefits. No attention is paid to how the pool of potential candidates is constructed, that is, how racism has systematically benefited some and diminished others in the attainment of qualifications necessary to be included in the pool in the first place. No attention is paid to how the performance test might not be an accurate prediction of performance as a worker or a student and might simply be used to mask the continued privilege of others.

From the perspective of the institution, however, concerns of so-called societal discrimination stand beyond the pale of institutional consideration. Institutional administrators cannot redress every social imbalance and inequity supported by history and social science. They owe their fiduciary duties to the institutions they govern. The institution is best served by hiring and promoting the most qualified individuals to do the job.

The problem necessitating a theory of institutional racism is, then, twofold. First, the institutional norms may be the by-product of covert racists who have subordinated the disfavored group by ostensibly neutral criteria and deflected criticism of the consequences resulting from the norm's application. Second, even if the institutional norms are developed and applied in good faith, the theory of institutional racism recognizes the interrelationship among various spheres of social organization. It appreciates the ways and extent to which a history of consciously overt and covert racism reinforces and perpetuates itself by ostensibly neutral norms that build on the uneven playing field created by that history.

Both the difficulty of assessing present state of mind and/or historical intent and an awareness of the role ostensibly neutral norms play in a context of past and present racism necessitate a way of thinking about racism that avoids the irony of those liberals who feel bad about the past but deny responsibility for the present. The concept of institutional racism responds to this dilemma by focusing on the effects as well as the intent of institutional practices.

In the Rodney King trial, one wonders how jurors could have sat there and watched the brutal beating of King on that fateful night and concluded that the force used was "reasonable" rather than "excessive."

One reason is that the institutional mechanism through which the tape was analyzed permitted its fragmentation by lawyers, who drained from it any sense of historical significance and urgency, any sense of brutality and pain. By showing bits and pieces, rather than the full tape, lawyers managed to transform the viewing of the tape from a potentially riveting and traumatic human experience into a dry, technical exploration of physical mechanics.

The jurors in Simi Valley operated within an institutional culture whose norms of law urged them to put aside all personal feelings and understandings of history and culture in order to render an objective and fair verdict. This is at the very core of institutional racism, which divorces the individual from any memory of a racist world by requiring that the incident be viewed through the lens of ostensibly race-neutral institutional norms.

One is not permitted to consider the implications of the incident for the perpetuation of black subordination. That is, one is not permitted to question the connection of this incident of beating to a history of such incidents and their collective role in monitoring the racial hierarchy in American society. These questions are outside the purview of one's institutional role as juror. Defense lawyers showed the videotape over and over again, and urged the separation of law from moral understanding and intuition. Cloaked in a dispassionate and quasi-scientific detailing of frame-by-frame blows, accounting for and justifying each by reference to arcane police policy and procedure, the jurors were desensitized and eventually internalized the institutional norms that encouraged a separation of their consideration of "the law" from their "visceral feeling" of injustice and inhumanity.

Institutional racism, then, requires individuals to discard personal subjectivity and cloak themselves with institutional objectivity. Through this process, the jurors believe that their institutional duty requires a verdict very different from their own subjective feelings and beliefs. Thus, by diminishing individual responsibility for the decision, the institutional process might, ironically, encourage the very racism its impartiality is designed to overcome. Excessive force was not found because the defense attorneys succeeded in convincing the jurors that the visual images of abuse were other than they appeared.

The institutional mechanisms through which the real and deadly

192| *Anthony E. Cook*

were reconstructed as illusory and harmless are an everyday part of courtroom tactics. The norms of the courtroom are defined by rules of evidence and procedure that determine what can be known by the jurors and the process by which it can be made known by the lawyers. These norms are race-neutral, yet allegations by African-Americans of a racist criminal justice system persist. This is so because many African-Americans have understood from direct experience that justice is not blind, at least not color-blind. Rules of evidence and procedure do not permit certain stories to be told. They are deemed immaterial and irrelevant, failing to qualify as *evidence* in the neutral dispensation of justice. Thus, ostensibly neutral rules are regularly deployed to achieve biased results. The Rodney King verdict was simply another instance of this history, and many blacks feared the Simpson trial would constitute more of the same, notwithstanding Simpson's celebrity and wealth. In other words, many African-Americans had long been suspicious of a criminal justice system that professed impartiality but was shot through with the politics of race.

Many African-Americans found the negative response of whites to the Simpson verdict puzzling and infuriating. Cochran was accused of pandering to racist loyalties, black jurors were accused of irrationality, racism and intimidation, and white jurors were accused of being browbeaten into submission by overbearing African-American jurors. All of a sudden the system was broken, in need of substantial reform, and a black lawyer and jurors were accused of setting race relations back decades. The response sickened many African-Americans who for so long had decried the system's injustices and who could offer as testimony the broken bodies and spirits of millions past and present. This disproportionate response by whites to the verdict and the inability by most even to entertain the motivation of black jubilation struck many African-Americans as yet another instance of black invisibility and the inability of whites to see problems that did not directly impact them. More importantly, the white response was further evidence to many blacks of the pervasiveness of institutional racism. Whites were so accustomed to seeing the so-called neutral process of the criminal justice system work in their favor that they could not tolerate a verdict that no longer privileged their world view.

African-Americans were frustrated by a society whose institutions perpetuated, long after the civil rights movement, their histories of abuse and exclusion under a different name. Thus cheers that welcomed the Simpson verdict in much of the African-American community were more a collective sigh of relief that there was some small slice of the criminal justice system where African-Americans could expect to be treated equally to commonly situated whites than a belief that Simpson was innocent of the crimes with which he was charged. That is, the Simpson verdict proved that at least in those situations where blacks could combine the elements of a skillful black attorney with a wealthy black defendant and a majority of black jurors, they might be able to get out of the system what whites had long grown accustomed to expect from that same system.

What are the problems associated with this theory of institutional racism? As we noted above, the liberal paradigm was ambivalent about how to handle covert racism. The deep-seated psychological resistance to remedying the problem was, I believe, rooted in an unwillingness to falsely accuse individuals of being racists when their actions adversely affected blacks but were not predicated on an invidious or racist intent to harm them. Progressive liberalism flirted with an effects-based test, but the tension was always apparent precisely because the implications of the effects-based test was that the decision-makers found to have violated the law were no better than overt racists.

From this perspective, then, institutional racism has the same problem as the progressive liberal attempt to ameliorate the effects of covert racism. The problem, it is argued, is that it blames individual whites for something they did not cause and for which they should bear no personal responsiblity. Again, it is illiberal, the argument goes, to taint every white involved in the defense and trial of the white police officers in the King case or the investigation and prosecution of Simpson as racist, merely because the history of criminal justice has disproportionately disadvantaged blacks. It is illiberal because the approach ascribes to the white jurors in Simi Valley, for instance, attributes shared by a particular group of whites who are "verifiably racist." The approach fails to treat people as individuals rather than as members of some identifiable group.

Alternatively, institutional racism could be viewed as an attempt to move beyond this individualist dilemma. It is no longer necessary, under this approach, to characterize individuals as racists. In other words, it is no longer necessary to find some empirical reference point from which we can infer a corresponding racist mentality, as the liberal paradigm requires. Disparate racial impact, racial inequality in American institutional life, is itself the wrong, and not its real or supposed connection to a racist mind-set. It is only necessary to concede that a racist past has created an uneven playing field for blacks and to understand that institutions transmit that past into the present and future. Thus institutional redress need not be either an explicit or an implicit condemnation of those who live today. It need only recognize the ways in which we are inextricably connected to past and future through our present institutional ordering of communal life.

Yet the unwillingness to take the idea of institutional racism seriously is precisely what led many to probe the American psyche even further, in search of an explanation of the resistance to racial justice. The answer to many was to be found in an understanding of unconscious cultural racism.

4. Unconscious Cultural Racism

The understanding of institutional racism with which I ended the above section seeks to reorient the liberal obsession with individual consciousness and redirect it toward institutional power. But when liberalism rejects both a progressive effects-based test that permits an inference of racist intent consistent with the individualist paradigm of liberalism and the attempt to move outside that paradigm through a more radical group-oriented understanding of institutional racism, what avenue is left the advocate of racial justice?

Many have concluded that the resistance is rooted in a nascent white supremacy that pervades the culture, producing individuals inclined to see blacks as inherently inferior and unworthy of equal status in the society. Much of the work that is variously called, among other things, cultural criticism, critical theory and hermeneutics, is focused on unpacking how both our unconscious and our conscious minds are shaped and constructed by systems of thought such as liberalism and Christianity, and identities such as race, class and gender. Out of this construction flows the system of privileging and subordination that is, among other things, the racism of which we are presently inquiring.

Therefore, the argument goes, we need to demonstrate how these systems of belief and identities have conditioned us to think about the problem in a certain way. We entertain only certain understandings of the problem and interventions to redress the problem as "reasonable" possibilities or as plausible. When we have demonstrated the arbitrariness of the worldviews assumed by these systems of thought and identities, perhaps individuals will experience a greater degree of freedom, even a greater sense of duty, to construct worlds different from those they inherited.

Unlike the understanding of institutional racism with which I ended the last section—an understanding that made it unnecessary to characterize individuals as racist—cultural racism suggests that racism is a cancer that consumes the body politic. No one has escaped its malignancy. In some way it has touched us all, instilling in some an arrogance of supremacy and in others a deep-seated self-hate. The critique of cultural racism demands that all engage in an almost spiritual interrogation of our innermost thoughts and beliefs, ferreting out all fears and insecurities rooted in the racist soil of our psyches.

Cultural racism is a process of social comparison that results in the subordination of an out-group by an in-group that uses its own group as the positive point of reference to measure the worth or merit of the out-group members. Its proponents suggest that cultural racism is the true foundation of racism in our society. On it rest the histories of institutional and individual racism, and because of it the pervasive problems of black subordination remain intractable. Cultural racism socializes and conditions the individuals comprising the institutions whose norms, though neutral on their face, contain the countless assumptions of white superiority that countenance an insensitivity to the plight of the oppressed.

The following is an account of how a racist discourse of white supremacy infuses a culture's thinking and is transmitted from one generation to the next. After centuries of life predicated on the assumptions of white supremacy, society finally reaches a point at which the assumptions no longer need stating. They provide the backdrop for conversations, interactions and encounters that never utter a racist word, but yet reproduce the racial hierarchies that perpetuate the subordination of blacks in the society.

The Historical Sources of Anglo-American Racism

The problem of cultural racism in American race relations finds its genesis in the earliest contacts between English explorers and the African peoples they encountered on their voyages.[10] The values that emerged were conditioned by a Anglo cultural orientation that glorified whiteness, the Greco-Roman aesthetic, and the lifestyles and behavior of the familiar. As long as this orientation remained quartered within the mental constructs of prejudicial reflection, it was guilty of no more than an extreme ethnocentricism.

When extreme ethnocentricism linked itself to the domination of African peoples through the slave trade, however, it became cultural racism—the support system for the institutional, overt and covert racism discussed above. The English chronicled on their travels the physical and cultural differences between the African and the English. These distinctions were heavily laced with an English ethnocentrism that implied the superiority of English people and culture in all such social encounters and comparisons.[11] These accounts of difference provided the basis for what Winthrop Jordan perspicaciously called the history of white over black.[12]

The impact of African color on the English mind cannot be understated. Before the first substantive contacts by England with West Africa in the middle of the sixteenth century, there was little actual knowledge of the people who inhabited these lands. By contrast, both the Spanish and Portuguese had made contact with North Africa centuries earlier. Indeed, both countries experienced invasion by "people both darker and more highly civilized than themselves."[13] By contrast, the voyages of British ships to West Africa brought some of the palest and darkest shades of the human color spectrum face to face for the first time. Given the limited nature of prior English contact with people of color, the shock was probably greater for the English. "Travelers rarely failed to comment upon it; indeed when describing Negroes they frequently began with complexion and then moved on to dress . . . and manners."[14]

Initial shock does not account, however, for the contempt and disdain accompanying the reality of difference. Jordan notes the importance of the fact that the "English discovery of black Africans came at a time when the accepted standard of ideal beauty was a fair complexion of rose and white. Negroes not only failed to fit this ideal but seemed the very picture of perverse negation."[15] The general disdain for the appearance of Africans was not limited to pigmentation but encompassed the entire African physiology. In contrast to the white ideal, blacks were deemed inferior by reason of their "color . . . [their] 'horrid curls' and 'disfigured' lips and nose[s]."[16] Indeed, we have noted how Jefferson was influenced by the assumption of these times as well.

African sexuality was another source of English fascination and ultimate disdain, and was seen as further proof of African inferiority. Jordan observed that:

[d]epiction of the Negro as a lustful creature was not radically new . . . when Englishmen first met Negroes face to face. Seizing upon and reconfirming . . . long-standing and apparently common notions about Africa, Elizabethan travelers and literati spoke very explicitly of Negroes as being especially sexual.[17]

As early as 1566, Jean Bodin studied the writings of the ancients on Africa and concluded that "heat and lust went hand in hand and that 'in Ethiopia . . . the race of men is very keen and lustful'."[18] The obsession over male African genitalia provided a constant source of condescension. African men, reported a seventeenth-century traveler, "sported large Propagators"[19] and the Mandingo men were "furnisht with such members as are after a sort burthensome unto them."[20]

It was common in the commentary of the day to compare African sexuality to that of apes and thus always to perceive the African male as a beastly threat to the norms of white purity and chastity.[21] During the same period, however, African women were cast as "hot constitution'd Ladies[22] possessed of a 'temper hot and lascivious, making no scruple to prostitute themselves to the Europeans for a very slender profit, so great [was] their inclination to white men.[23] Even in these early encounters, the sexual jealousies and obsessions that would be central components of the psychosexual dynamics of American race relations for centuries manifested themselves as a justification for the domination of black males and the subjugation of black females.

In addition to reckoning with the differences of black physiology and sexuality, the entire cultural ethos of West Africa around the middle of the sixteenth century was strikingly different from Elizabethan

England. James Jones catalogued many of these differences in an attempt to illustrate the many points on which the English felt compelled to assert their cultural superiority and thereby justify their domination of Africans.[24] According to Jones, African culture differed significantly from English culture on matters of religion, social organization, the role of property, education, sense of time, nature of music and view of the world.[25]

The meaning attributed to these cultural differences by white Europeans and the high value associated with Eurocentric norms left no doubt about the superiority of white culture. Few saw the question of biological and cultural difference between Africans and Europeans as did Captain Thomas Phillips, a master of a 1694 slave vessel. He wrote of the difference of color:

> I can't think there is any intrinsic value in one colour more than another, nor that white is better than black, only we think it so because we are so, and are prone to judge favourably in our own case, as well as the blacks, who in odium of the colour, say, the devil is white, and so paint him.[26]

As is clear from the subsequent history of slavery and racism, most rejected Phillips's biological relativism and were quite prepared to hold, as they were in the sphere of cultural differences generally, that the difference was profoundly important. Religious, scientific and quasi-scientific justifications were marshalled in support of prejudices and racism.

The Religious and Scientific Sources of Cultural Racism

Religious and scientific discourses help legitimize practices of racial domination. Common sense is no more than the way a given culture organizes its understanding of the world. That organization is profoundly shaped, among other things, by religious and scientific stories that give its members a sense of identity and purpose. Thus, when life and the realities of domination are explained and tacitly sanctioned by religion and science, socially constructed oppression takes on a mystique of naturalness and inevitability, an appearance that things were always meant to be just so. The transformation of the socially constructed into the naturally constituted is facilitated, then, by religious and scientific discourses that tap into the commonsense notions of those expected to acquiesce in the practices of racist domination.

Therefore many sought to explain the inherent inferiority of Africans and their culture in terms of religious and scientific discourses.

Religious Influences

The Judeo-Christian account of black inferiority begins with the Old Testament story of Noah who, in his drunkenness, unclothed himself and fell asleep in his tent.[27] One son, Ham, looked upon his father's nakedness, while the other sons, Shem and Japheth, covered their father without looking.[28] Noah later awoke and cursed one of Ham's sons, Canaan, denouncing him as a "servant of servants" unto his brothers.[29] Distorted scriptural exegesis over the years somehow managed to turn this curse into an explanation of African skin color and a justification for the domination of Africans by the supposed progeny of Shem and Japheth.

One could see the Old Testament story as motivated by the same concerns that have motivated many of the myths of Christianity; the need to show that one's power and status comes from God, and thus are authorized by one higher than those who threaten to take them away.[30] In this case, God approved of the Hebrew conquest of Canaan, a land predestined for conquest by a "convenient" curse upon its inhabitants. That this story survived so many centuries as a plausible account of why black people have been subjected to such oppression is a testimony to the power of religious ideology. While the curse quite clearly envisions the servitude of Canaan, there is no mention of skin color. Thus the curse may have just as logically or illogically condemned the nation of Canaan to a skin color lighter than the already-dark Noah. Only social convention and European ethnocentrism assumed the curse involved color, and that darkness rather than paleness constituted the distortion of purity. Second, the curse was put on only one of Ham's children, Canaan. If one follows biblical genealogy and geography, most of Africa and all of West Africa were peopled by Ham's remaining children, on whom no curse befell.[31]

Much of the tolerance of inconsistency may be attributed to the willingness of racists to rely on inconsistent and speculative accounts to justify their practices. A good deal of the tolerance may also be attributed to an oral and written tradition that explicitly altered scriptural text and meaning. For instance, Jordan contends that Talmudic and Midrashic sources suggested that "'Ham was smitten in his skin', that Noah told Ham 'your seed will be ugly and dark-skinned', and that Ham was father 'of Canaan who brought curses into the world, of Canaan who was cursed, of Canaan who darkened the faces of mankind', of Canaan 'the notorious world darkener'."[32] The authority of historic Hebrew sources provided a veneer of authenticity to subsequent Christian interpretations in the seventeenth century that the enslavement and subjugation of Africans was scripturally predestined. Christian nations combined this with the New Testament's seeming approval of slavery, and concluded that the black people of the earth were predestined to serve the superior white race through the institution of slavery.

The story of Ham played a dual role in the subjugation of Africa. Not only did it explain the quandary of color in a way that privileged the status of whiteness, but it also explained the strange sexuality of African peoples. The infraction that resulted in the curse was one of sexual impropriety. Black men were thus accursed or "burdened" with large penises, and because of their size could not, as Adam did in the Garden of Eden, conceal their shame.[33] The curse eternally subjected black men to the invasion of privacy inflicted upon Noah. In addition, African men and women were cursed with an animal-like, lascivious and promiscuous sexuality, lacking the capacity for shame and constraint, qualities found among the more civilized races. Taken together, the myths manifested themselves throughout history in countless acts of white sexual jealousy, insecurity and aggressiveness that often resulted in the aversion to and punishment by castration of black males and the desire for and exploitation of "hot constitution'd" black females.[34]

Scientific Influences

If religious discourse played an important role in the transmission of cultural racism, the discourse of science figured prominently as well. Although anthropology and psychology are younger disciplines than theology and history, their impact on the study of race has been monumental. Both disciplines developed on the coattails of a sweeping European cultural secularization that heralded the powers of Man and Reason and embraced an ever-growing skepticism toward religious and theological accounts of natural phenomena. Newtonian science and the Enlightenment nurtured an insatiable appetite for exploration, explanation and the domination of mind over matter. The study of man and the consternation over physiological and cultural human diversity provided an irresistible forum for empirical research, measurement and classification of natural phenomena. It was anthropology that first directed its Enlightenment-inspired energies toward the study of race and the perpetuation of mythologies of racial inferiority.

While Johann Friederich Blumenbach is credited as the founder of anthropology,[35] Carolus Linnaeus, the eighteenth-century Swedish botanist, was the first to attempt a comprehensive classification of humans according to physiognomy, temperament and culture. Thus, Linnaeus's *Systema Naturae*[36] provided an imprimatur of objectivity and truth to the casual comparisons and speculations that were by that time commonplace in European and American cultures. Blumenbach advanced the work of Linnaeus and purported to prove that the original type of man was Caucasian.[37]

The studies implied the supposed superiority of white Europeans, even though neither system of classification explicitly ranked humans in terms of superior and inferior races and claimed only to be descriptive.[38] For instance, while Linnaeus described the European as gentle, acute, inventive, covered with vestments and governed by customs, he described the African as crafty, indolent, negligent, covered with grease and governed by caprice.[39] Similarly, Blumenbach situated the Caucasian type at the center of his horizontal scale of comparison and situated the Ethiopian and Mongolian types at opposite ends of the spectrum.[40] The clear implication was that value, beauty and worth were a function of ones' proximity to the central white norm, thought to represent the point of perfection.

The implicit hierarchy of supposedly value-free scientific observation and classification developed into explicit hierarchical rankings by race. These scientific studies always situated whites at the very top of the human species on the Chain of Being and blacks at the very bottom, practically on par with the ape. Physiognomy, craniology, cultural anthropology and evolutionary biology were all used between the eighteenth and nineteenth centuries intentionally and unintentionally to justify the increasing pillage and domination of Africa, its people and descendants.

In 1883, Francis Galton, Charles Darwin's cousin, founded the science of eugenics as "'the study of the agencies under social control that may improve or impair the racial qualities of future generations either physically or mentally'."[41] Galton suggested that "'it would be quite practical to produce a highly gifted race of men by judicious marriages during several consecutive generations'."[42] The science of eugenics received a devastating blow during World War II when used by Hitler and the Nazi regime to justify the barbaric treatment and extermination of Jews in death camps. It has proved resilient, however, as attested by the more recent work of William Shockley, suggesting the genetic inferiority of blacks.[43]

Psychology gained acceptance as a field of science in 1883, around the same time as eugenics appeared on the scene. The former immediately charted a course purporting to measure mental processes or intelligence. It was not long before tests purporting to measure a so-called intelligence quotient provided their contribution to the science of racism, conclusive proof that, as had been conjectured for centuries, blacks were inferior to whites. Charles Murray's *Bell Curve* is but another chapter in an endless chain of quasi-scientific attempts to prove the inherent intellectual inferiority of those of African descent.

B. Cultural Racism and the Rodney King Trial

How does all of this relate to our analysis of race and law in general and the verdict in the Rodney King case in particular? The jurors in Simi Valley may have consciously desired to acquit the white police officers because they believed the race of the latter entitled them to absolution for beating a black man. Such an explanation, however, appears too simplistic. If the jurors in the Rodney King trial were covert racists, we will never know. Indeed, we hardly have a language that allows us to explore such possibilities legitimately. Institutional ideology often provides convenient window dressing for covert racists, and the institutional framework for presenting and analyzing the videotape in the King case could have provided such a cover for covert racists. But even the possibility of covert racism does not seem to be the likeliest understanding of the verdict. Let us assume that the jurors harbored no conscious beliefs in the inherent inferiority of African-Americans and thus were neither overtly or covertly racist. The question remains: How can we account for a jury that could examine the apparent brutality of police officers on that film and conclude that this was a "reasonable" exercise of force?

Although it is unlikely that the jurors consciously held racist beliefs as individuals or a group, their commonsense frame for viewing the tape, hearing the arguments, and understanding the world was shaped by racist forces. Deeply socialized into the myths of white supremacy, the Simi Valley jurors were predisposed to embrace their institutional role and to view the officers' brutality as a "reasonable" response to the threat posed by King. Neither the change of venue nor the detailed instructions on the institutional role and duty of jurors could neutralize this process of acculturation. Even in the absence of conscious racist beliefs, this socialization provided a commonsense frame through which discrete facts, such as the frame-by-frame analysis of the film, took on new meaning, and the language comparing King to "a raging bull" and the police to "the thin blue line standing between us and the jungle" was decoded and acted upon.

Both the theological and scientific paradigms discussed earlier embrace a process of social comparison resulting in the subordination of an out-group by an in-group using its own group as the positive point of reference in measuring the worth or merit of out-group members. In the story of Ham, therefore, blackness represents a curse and deviation from the unquestionable purity of whiteness. In science, the curse and norm are disguised by the detailed descriptions of natural phenomena that pass as objective study. Cultural racism is the unreflective acceptance of the norm and its consequential curse on black people. It is a failure of progressive liberalism to understand that norms and curses are socially constructed meanings, and that in a social context characterized by pervasive racism, they are likely to perpetuate the domination of blacks.

In many ways the Simi Valley jurors inherited this cultural tradition. History conditioned them as it conditions us all. The way they viewed the world is unquestionably influenced by the way racism shaped the world. When an officer testified that King appeared as a "raging bull," the imagery of animal-like appearance and behavior connected with a long history, supported by religious and scientific doctrine, asserting that black men were more like animals than men. The dehumanization of King diminished the empathy that one human being feels for another who is suffering unjustifiably. Viewed not as human but as standing somewhere between human and beast, Rodney King was a threat and deserved his suffering. If he could not hear and heed the call of human reason to "not move" and "stay down," perhaps he could not feel the human pain inflicted by over ninety blows to his body and head. In describing the relationship between the image of black men and animals in the minds of whites, Winthrop Jordan states:

> Castration of Negroes clearly indicated a desperate, generalized need in white men to persuade themselves that they were really masters and in all ways masterful, and it illustrated dramatically the ease with which white men slipped over into treating their Negroes like their bulls and stallions whose "spirit" could be subdued by emasculation. In some colonies, moreover, the specifically sexual aspect of castration was so obvious as to underline how much of the white man's insecurity vis–a–vis the Negro was fundamentally sexual.[44]

The defense attorneys' plea to the jury that policemen must receive the benefit of the doubt because they constitute the "thin blue line separating us from the jungle" connected with centuries of racist imagery that pictured black life as mysterious, uncivilized and ghastly. These are but contemporary versions of the images constructed by Anglo culture in its earliest contacts with Africans and perpetuated by religion, science, and art over the centuries. The defense attorneys' plea described a place where reason succumbs to passion and, if unleashed, destroys civilized life. These influences had to be contained, at all costs, lest they infiltrated the pristine suburbs of Simi Valley in which many, perhaps like the jurors, had sought refuge from the evils of the inner-city jungle. The thin blue line transformed in this imagery to both hero and victim. How could a criminal justice system have victimized these heroes who daily put their lives on the line to make the community safe from the forces of darkness that lurked in the asphalt jungles beyond?

American culture teaches these lessons in countless ways, and the morals are neatly tucked away into the subconscious and surface when needed. They vent themselves in a myriad of ways that span the gamut between conscious and unconscious racism, convincing the mind of the juror that the eyes see something other than a prone, unarmed man, writhing in pain as he is beaten unmercifully by three police officers while twelve other officers look on in a conspiracy of silence and tacit approval and do nothing. The socialized and acculturated mind convinces the juror, instead, that the eyes view a threat, one that justifies this "reasonable" use of force by heroes now victimized by a criminal justice system that does not appreciate what is really at stake.

In conclusion, the problem is that the liberal understanding of racism views racism as an instance of deviant consciousness, a bad mental state to which all must be traced. It fails to realize that racism manifests itself on four interrelated levels and may be neither deviant nor conscious in its operation. Both institutional and cultural racism operate at the unconscious level, and given the pervasiveness of cultural racism and its influence on how we view and understand the world, racism is as American as apple pie.

The implications of such a view of racism for American progressive liberalism seems clear. The view calls for a far-reaching, progressive, liberal agenda geared toward the transformation of a society whose educational, economic and political systems all perpetuate the reproduction of sociopsychological frameworks that continue to produce the kind of brutality, inhumanity and injustice depicted in the Rodney King saga and the myriad of responses to that injustice that surfaced during the Simpson trial and its aftermath. The crucial question is whether progressive liberals are ready for this more sophisticated critique of racism and are prepared to see its implications through to the end. It is this question to which our final chapter will venture some response.

Chapter 9

Where Progressive Liberalism Went Wrong in the Affirmative Action Debate

I have urged from the outset that the resurrection of a progressive liberal vision in American politics requires two things. First, progressives must construct a religiospiritual framework for advancing their vision and must develop the rhetorical skills and confidence needed to communicate that vision effectively to the American people. Second, it is imperative that they develop a sophisticated understanding of how conservatives have used racism to undermine the progressive liberal agenda in American politics and dare to counter that phenomenon with a vision of a truly multiracial and multicultural democracy.

This chapter suggests how progressives might have incorporated both of these objectives in justification of a now-fallen progressive program—affirmative action. The progressive liberal understanding of affirmative action developed below integrates the history of race and politics explored in Chapter 7, along with the multidimensional understanding of racism developed in Chapter 8, into the new religiospiritual framework I am suggesting progressive liberalism adopt. That framework embraces a love-based conception of community, developed in chapter 6, that I have extrapolated from King's spiritual, social and strategic understanding of the Beloved Community, discussed in chapter 5, which was itself drawn from the pragmatic and prophetic strands of the African-American religious tradition, explored in chapter 4.

My hope is that by examining where progressive liberalism went wrong in the affirmative action debate and how the new framework I am developing might have prevented this result, progressive liberals will be better prepared for future battles. The analysis proceeds in four parts. First, I define affirmative action as a progressive liberal attempt to respond to some of the deficiencies associated with the liberal paradigm's approach to race, discussed in the previous chapter. Second, I elaborate the centerpiece of the conservative assault against affirmative action as a commitment to abstract individualism, or color blindness. I then explore how the progressive liberal justifications of affirmative action did not adequately respond to this restrictive understanding of liberalism. Finally, I explore how progressive liberals could have effectively challenged the conservative appropriation of color-blind ideology by embracing the spiritual, social and strategic dimensions of the love-based conception of community developed in this work.

A. Racism, Affirmative Action and the Paradox of the Progressive Liberal Vision

Affirmative action has many faces. It sometimes appears as a way of facilitating equality of opportunity and sometimes as a way of securing equality of results. It is sometimes involuntarily imposed by courts, and at other times voluntarily adopted by institutions. Involuntary affirmative action came on the heels of Title VII and equal protection suits, as judicially imposed remedies for illegal discrimination by private and public institutions. Courts required violators, for instance, to hire and/or promote African-Americans within prescribed time periods as a good-faith showing of their intent to prohibit racial discrimination in their recruitment, hiring, promotion and termination practices.

In cases of voluntary affirmative action, institutions voluntarily acted to modify their recruitment, hiring, promotion and/or termination practices to achieve greater racial and gender diversity in the workplace.

The nature of the voluntary changes differed greatly. Some institutions merely rectified the manner in which they advertised for available positions and modified their recruitment strategies accordingly. Others modified their employment criteria to create a more diverse pool of qualified candidates. Others adopted flexible goals and timetables as to what employment goals they desired to accomplish within the prescribed time, and outlined strategies they believed would best secure those objectives. In some instances, but not nearly as many as the critics alleged, flexible goals and timetables turned into rigid quotas that reserved a certain number of slots and opportunities for women and minorities.

Affirmative action was the progressive liberal response to the problems of covert and institutional racism discussed in the previous chapter. The civil rights laws of 1964 prohibited discrimination on the basis of race. But institutions might remain impervious to any substantive redistribution of power and opportunity by making decisions on the basis of some race-neutral criterion that accomplished the same exclusion as a decision based on race.

Progressive liberalism took the position that if an employer or any institution used a race-neutral criterion that had a disparate impact on the hiring, promotion and retention of blacks, and the employer could not offer a convincing justification for using that criterion, the courts should require the employer to take affirmative steps to remedy its presumptively racist practices. Progressive liberalism understood, in other words, that reading minds and hearts was, at best, an imperfect art. One could know whether the employer was acting on the basis of illicit motives, that is, had an invidious purpose or racist mind-set, only by examining the fruit of the decision-making process. By their fruits ye shall know them.

Meanwhile, inside various institutions, progressives adopted voluntary affirmative action programs intended to achieve greater inclusion of previously excluded groups. Progressives understood the difficulty in discerning and legally challenging covert racism. Many understood how the race-neutral norms of meritocracy masked the perpetuation of racial domination. So they attempted to reform these institutions through goals, timetables and sometimes quotas designed to facilitate racial and gender equality.

But I believe affirmative action always posed certain paradoxes for the progressive liberal that, because they remained unresolved, always made the affirmative action initiative vulnerable to attack. The central parodox was this: the progressive liberal dependence on discriminatory effects remained a prisoner of the individualist orientation of the liberal paradigm. The presence of discriminatory effects allowed one "reasonably" to infer that decision-makers had an invidious purpose. This need to track backwards to a smoking gun or bad individual mind-set would eventually undermine progressive liberalism's defense of affirmative action. Below I examine how the conservative assault on affirmative action exploited this very weakness.

B. The Conservative Assault and Liberal Defense

The conservative assault on affirmative action adopted many rhetorical techniques to justify the dismantling of these programs. The most critical one for our purposes, however, was a moral vision of a color-blind society and a jurisprudential conception of color-blind law and adjudication. Ironically, many conservatives cited Dr. King's "I Have A Dream" speech of 1963 in defense of their fundamentally reactionary agenda.

In a nutshell, color blindness prohibited progressive liberals from using race to solve racial problems put in place by centuries of Anglo-American racism. Race was a permissible classification only in that narrow set of cases where it could be proven that the perpetrator used race to harm the victim intentionally. Since conservatives had become increasingly unwilling to permit the inference from effects to intent, this meant that the only way of establishing such a violation was by finding the smoking gun of invidious intent. Since racists very seldom left paper trails, the remedy was more form than substance.

Conservatives argued that race-conscious affirmative action programs violated the individual rights of those "more qualified" whites passed over in preference for "less qualified" African-Americans. Since the rhetoric of color blindness evinced an aversion to thinking in terms of group injuries and rights, it complemented the ideology of individual rights quite nicely. The Constitution was color-blind and protective of personal rights, decision after decision from the Supreme Court reminded us. It did not recognize group rights and could not redress alleged group injuries. The importance of this commitment to individual rights becomes apparent when we examine the justifications given by progressives for affirmative action.

Progressives marshalled three justifications for affirmative action. None really answered the conservative criticisms, because progressives were unwilling to let go of or reconceptualize the individualist commitments of the liberal paradigm. The first defense of affirmative action viewed it as restitution for past and present societal discrimination. But within the paradigm of individual rights, a "more qualified" white could not be forced to give up or forego a benefit because of a preference for a "less qualified" African-American alleged to be the victim of an amorphous "societal discrimination." The "less qualified" African-American had to establish a specific injury. A specific injury could be established only if it were shown that a specific perpetrator intended to cause the injury in question. A general claim of societal discrimination was insufficient, because this was a vague abstraction incapable of satisfying the standard of an empirically verifiable causation. The "more qualified" white forced to give up the benefit in question to remedy societal discrimination became the "innocent victim" whose "personal rights" the Court was sworn to uphold.

The second defense of affirmative action justified it as a way of providing role models for previously excluded groups. The problem with this theory, the conservatives argued, was that it assumed some essential link between race and being a good role model. Whites were capable of being good role models to African-Americans just as blacks were capable of being good role models to whites. All of the essentials of integrity, professionalism and compassion transcended race. People were to be measured not by the color of their skin but by the content of their character.

The third justification saw affirmative action as a way of securing diverse institutions. Progressives contended that, particularly in the field of education, it was important to have a mix of viewpoints and perspectives represented in environments that valued the free exchange of ideas as a vehicle to personal growth and development. Indeed, progressives in the corporate world talked about the value of diversity and the need to have the racial and gender representation inside the firm reflect the labor market. Shortly after his election, President Clinton talked about the need to have a cabinet that looked like America.

The objection to the diversity justification was that, like the role-model justification, it assumed some essential link between race and perspective. This was the kind of racialism that ascribed to individuals certain attributes and views based on their membership in a racial group. There was no monolithic African-American, white or Asian community or perspective. Each group had within it the full range of perspectives, experiences and orientations. Thus race was not a sufficient proxy for viewpoint and experience diversity. If viewpoint or experience diversity was what universities and businesses wanted, race was not a sufficiently tailored means to achieve that end.

Therefore all of these justifications have gone by the wayside in the affirmative action debate. They have fallen because progressive liberalism could not fully defend them while refusing to question the basic presuppositions of the liberal paradigm, its commitment to an abstract individualism reincarnated as color-blind ideology. So long as liberals agreed that the chief aspiration of law and justice was to protect the rights of the autonomous individual, any notion of the society's duty to blacks that infringed on personal rights was automatically suspect.

Progressive liberalism needed a way of reorienting the understanding of individualism embraced by liberal theory. It is precisely such an orientation that this book seeks to develop. Thus I offer below a different justification based on the conception of a love-based community outlined earlier. This framework frees us from the limitations of too individualistic a liberal paradigm by developing an understanding of how the individual's mutual interdependency with others creates a set of overlapping duties to self, others and God that fulfill the spiritual, social and strategic goals of a Beloved Community.

C. Rethinking Liberal Individualism: Affirmative Action and the Spiritual Dimension of the Beloved Community

The liberal approach to remedying racism is problematic for one central reason. Its underlying commitment to an abstract individualism that refuses to see the individual as constructed by race and other "group" identities that shape and orient perspective, experience and possibility undermines any attempt to redress "group" wrongs. Progressive liberalism has, at times, through its embrace of an effects-based test for remedying covert and institutional racism, glimpsed the possibility of a different paradigm. But it always recoiled from the light, retreating, instead, into the familiar havens of abstract individualism.

Progressive liberals always felt compelled to link the empirically verifiable occurrence of bad effects and disparate impact back to the individual's bad or racist motives. This liberal preoccupation with individual mind-set and consciousness, this understanding of the individual as an autonomous being disconnected from culture, history and community, is the source of the problem. Institutional change always comes at the expense of finger-pointing and blaming someone else's "racism" as the cause of the disproportionate impact. As I said before, this creates unneeded psychological resistance to needed change.

If the progressive vision is to move forward, it must free itself from this outmoded and overly restrictive understanding of the relationship between the individual and the community. It is precisely this different understanding that I have suggested Rauschenbusch's Social Gospel and King's Beloved Community provide. The love-based conception of community, rather than the fear-based conception pervading liberal thought, envisions a community in which life is interrelated and interdependent. Unlike the liberal I of autonomous individualism, there is no I without thou in the normative vision of a Beloved Community. We all are woven into a single garment of destiny. This alternative vision captures the best of liberalism. It embraces a healthy concern for self and reorients it away from an obsession with personal blame, guilt and causation, redirecting it toward a service to God and humanity that symbolizes the interdependency and sacredness of life. When self-love is linked to other-love that is linked to higher love, both humility and possibility are nurtured. We understand, as never before, the spiritual, social and strategic dimensions of holistic community.

At the very core of our love for others is an abiding compassion for the least of these that spiritually transforms our understanding of ourselves and, ultimately, all humanity. An orientation towards the least, then, becomes a gateway through which we are challenged to become better persons, persons capable of constructing and preserving better communities.

As developed earlier, the law of love requires that we nurture a proper self-love enabling us to love others more fully. If we are to desire for others what we desire for ourselves, our attention should focus on satisfying their basic physical needs, protecting their fundamental freedoms, and enhancing their self-worth. These instrumental commands of love obligate us to cultivate the gifts, skills and interests of ourselves and others. This self-cultivation or self-empowerment, then, is not an end in itself, but rather, a means to the end of love for and service to others. Thus liberalism's motif of self-empowerment is incorporated into this framework but directed toward the nobler ends of helping others and building a community based on love and justice.

The practical import of this approach is to empower others to empower themselves who, having been touched themselves by love, are moved to love and empower others. Subsistence charity, then, may at times be all that is possible, but love that enables others to love is greater still. Furthermore, because love remains focused on the empowerment of others, we ensure that self-possibilities are developed while self-serving behavior is limited. When extended to the sphere of collective action, this formulation both encourages the possibilities and defines the limits of democracy. Would it not be wonderful if government were a vehicle through which people empowered people to love others who find in that other-love the elusive self-love for which their souls do long?

This love for others is a social love, a truly democratic love. To assure that our love is not focused on an overly narrow conception of neighbor, we must measure it by a commitment central to the religious tradition on which this framework is based, a commitment to "the least of these." Any assessment of who constitutes "the least of these" is, of course, contingent on time and place. In our personal lives "the least" are those whom we most despise, those in our hearts for whom we have the greatest disdain and desire most to avoid, those who through our eyes are unworthy of equal respect and concern. We all have a "least," and spiritual growth is about learning to find and appreciate the inherent worth of those we perceive to be most unlike ourselves.

D. Rethinking Liberal Individualism: Affirmative Action and the Social Dimension of the Beloved Community

Just as we all have our own "least of these" in our personal lives, society produces a "least of these" within the body politic. The social "least" may sometimes be the same as the personal "least," but not necessarily so. The social "least" will be a function of the particular culture of a community; that culture is itself a product of historical conflicts and struggle. A community is an arrangement of interdependent living that expands to encompass broader and broader networks of people bound by reciprocal duties. This ever-expanding network moves out from family through civic, social and religious organizations to town, state and nation, and finally to the world community itself.

Each of these communities produces a conception of "the least" based on the unique histories and culture of the community. Many of these histories and cultures will, of course, overlap and produce overlapping conceptions of "the least" as well. Sometimes certain experiences are so pervasive throughout the broadest possible community, here the international community, that they become formative experiences in the development of plural communities within that larger community. I believe that the particular intersection of capitalist development and the international slave trade that produced a class-based and race-based international culture was one such formative experience that shaped the plural development of communities throughout society. In other words, the impact of these international experiences was so great that it transformed communities as different as the family and the nation state.

Modern slavery and mercantile capitalism were sixteenth-century developments that accompanied yet another phenomenon, the conquest and pillage of America. Racism, classism and imperialism, then, have long marked the course of Western and American development. Thus when King, in the 1960s, claimed that these were the three evils that needed to be challenged by progressives, he was calling into question the very foundation of Western society. This was a truly revolutionary insight that, I believe, necessitated his assassination by forces that understood the threat posed by his analysis.

As demonstrated by my discussion of cultural racism above, understandings of black inferiority developed during this modern period to rationalize the slave trade and the conquest of indigenous people. Thus much that has passed under the name of "racism" is rooted in the desire to exploit African and African-American labor during this period of capitalist growth through colonial expansion. Racism continues today, even when it appears that cheap black labor is obsolete, because there is now a need to justify the inequitable distributions of wealth, opportunity and privilege created by this long history. Racism plays the role of legitimating the distribution of material and psychic benefits to the "haves" and defeating the redistribution of the same to the "have-nots."

So any understanding of the "least of these" will have to take this defining moment of modernity into consideration when pondering the social dimensions of a Beloved Community. In other words the understanding of the "least of these" would need to take class, race and the imperialistic conquest of indigenous peoples into consideration.

In keeping with King's analysis of class, I want initially to understand "the least" in economic terms. King's life ended while he was defending striking garbage workers in Memphis, Tennessee. Against the recommendation of his advisers, he postponed his planning of the Poor People's Movement to be in solidarity with garbage workers struggling for a better existence. In speech after speech, he called for a national redistribution of wealth and income and a Marshall Plan for the poor. As Christians, he would say, we are called upon to feed the forty million poor people of this land. But soon we must question the structure of a society that produces forty million beggars. We must start to ask who owns the iron ore and the oil, and question why people should pay for water in a world that is two-thirds water. King planned to bring the plight of America's poor and his vision of wealth redistribution to the attention of the American public through a massive Poor People's Movement that would shut down the national government in a wave of nonviolent mass protest.

We need, then, social programs that take affirmative steps toward eliminating poverty and facilitating the mobility of those in poverty to a better existence. All individuals meeting certain economic measures would qualify for such uplift. Reforms should focus on meeting the basic needs, protecting the fundamental rights and enhancing the self-worth of such persons so as to permit a fuller development of their gifts, talents and interests. These nutritional, housing, health care, child care, educational, job training and entrepreneurial programs would try to empower persons and communities to empower themselves. The focus would not be on the delivery of cash and services from some bureaucracy external to the community of beneficiaries. Instead, those beneficiaries would take greater responsibility for their lives and the lives of those around them.

Such an approach would provide progressive liberals with an opportunity to develop a truly transracial politics and social welfare policy reminiscent of the best of progressive populism in this century. By emphasizing the spiritual orientation of interdependency discussed above and adopting a rhetorical strategy informed by that spiritual understanding, progressive liberals will go far in reviving the progressive liberal vision in American politics.

In keeping with King's analysis of race and imperialism I want to further understand "the least" in terms of group identity, particularly racial and indigenous groups dominated through racism and imperialism. Special attention should be paid to those disproportionately represented among the poor and retained there, in part, by a pervasive societal disdain of them perpetuated by legitimating rhetorics of inferiority. In keeping with King I want to take the particular histories and experiences of these identity groups seriously, while maintaining the possibilities of transgroup understanding and coalition.

As explored earlier, King's dialogue with the black nationalists of his day demonstrated his understanding of the seriousness of racism in American society. He understood the need to take this history and legacy seriously by affirming the self-worth of blacks who had been victimized by white supremacy's "cultural homicide" of black culture. He understood the need to educate white Americans out of the false sense of superiority that imposed serious limits on the possibility even of class-based reform of American society.

If group identity is to be taken seriously, we must examine the ranks of the poor to see which groups are disproportionately represented therein. When that disproportionality is accompanied by a history of societal attitudes and behavior that presupposes the inherent inferiority of such groups, a presumption is created. That is, if there is a prolonged history of legal and extralegal discrimination against the groups, the presumption is that the disproportionate representation of the group among the poor is not just class-based but identity-based as well. Let me take one example.

Because of their disproportionate representation among the poor and the accompanying history of public and private racism against them, African-Americans constitute the clearest, although not the only, case in need of attention. In many ways, 200 years of slavery, over fifty years of segregation and only thirty years of formal freedom have made blacks the paradigm case for the study of injustice and oppression in American society. Thus, when one examines the ranks of the American poor, one discovers there are 39,265,000 poor people in America, representing 15.1 percent of the American population. But while blacks constitute only 12 percent of the nation's population, they constitute 33.1 percent of the nation's poor, while whites, who are 83.9 percent of the national population, constitute 12.2 percent of the poor. More than one-third of all blacks live in poverty, while only 11 percent of all whites are poor. Looking even closer at the ranks of the black poor, we see that 25.7 percent of them are black men, 32.4 percent black women and 41.9 percent black children.

There are three implications of this layered approach of class and identity. The first implication of this approach is that it expands the conception of affirmative action to make it more inclusive and a natural extension of other social policies. The truth of the matter is that our country has always engaged in affirmative action for many groups. We have given subsidies to farmers for not planting their fields and to businesses for investing in certain industries and technologies. We give benefits to veterans of wars and tax breaks to those who buy rather than rent their homes. The children of alumni and major donors have always benefitted from preferential treatment. Slavery and segregation were comprehensive affirmative action programs for whites who were benefited in varying degrees. For most of our history, true access to power and opportunity has been limited to a core of elite white males who still account for over 95 percent of all the managers of corporate America. Under the approach proposed, we would see affirmative action policy as ranging from policies governing community-based welfare, education and training to job placement and business development at every level. The entire system would be one of preferences based on the needs made manifest by an intersectional analysis of class and identity.

The second implication of this class and identity approach to affirmative action is that affirmative action programs seeking to empower the poor must anticipate the ways in which racism against African-Americans might complicate the delivery and diminish the advantages of goals and opportunities distributed to the poor. Progressives must make sure that racism and other forms of ingrained bigotry do not result in certain sectors of the poor benefiting at the expense of others. Thus, programs would need to document a rough correlation between the demographics of poverty and the benefits and opportunities allocated on the basis of those demographics.

Third, the disproportionate impact that disadvantages African-Americans is not exclusively a function of class bias that makes their problems indistinguishable from the problems of the white poor. On the contrary, we can assume that the reason blacks are disproportionately located among the poor is because they bear the additional burden of racism. Studies have proven that blacks are not poor simply because they happen to fall into demographic categories that happen to have high rates of economic deprivation, categories such as female-headed households, residents of inner cities and people with low educational attainment. In each of these categories, poverty rates are two to three times higher for blacks than whites. Thus race is a factor.

Therefore affirmative action is needed to correct for the societal imposition of this burden of race on blacks. This means that blacks who are not poor but are presumed, like the black poor, to be burdened by past and present racism, are entitled to a form of affirmative action tailored to their needs. Three additional observations justify this conclusion.

First, racism impacts the African-American middle class as much and arguably more directly than the African-American poor, since the former directly seeks access to, and mobility within, recalcitrant mainstream institutions. Studies on racial attitudes suggest that, while whites are comfortable with token integration, they become increasingly resistant when the numbers of proposed blacks to be integrated increases beyond a certain point. Sociologists have referred to this point as the "tipping point."

Second, affirmative action for the African-American middle class is essential for fully securing the empowerment of the poor. Without it, the glass ceilings and barriers confronted by the middle class will perpetuate the subordination of African-Americans in general at other levels of American society. Allowing these limitations to stay in place will defeat what should be the aim of affirmative action, which is to secure the full development of a group's talents, skills and interests by bolstering their self-worth, promoting their basic freedoms, and satisfying their basic physical needs.

Finally, there is too much empirical evidence suggesting the persistence of racist attitudes that limit black access and mobility—housing discrimination test studies, opinion surveys, qualitative analyses such as Ellis Cose's *Rage of a Privileged Class*, and volumes of anecdotal evidence of persistent bigotry in every walk of life as illustrated by Studs Terkel's masterful work on race.[1]

As applied to blacks, then, affirmative action would include both a class-based social welfare dimension that deals with the specific problems of the black poor and a race-based dimension that deals with the legacy of American racism. This approach would change considerably the largely discredited and dismantled affirmative action we know today.

First, I would permit blacks and other qualifying groups to bring class action suits to remedy their exclusion from public and private institutions that satisfy certain size criteria. I would take these matters out of the courts as much as possible and require that they be handled by mediation councils drawn from the respective communities represented by the parties. Of course, some interim and all final decisions can be appealed to a court of law, but one needs a more communal vehicle to facilitate more communal outcomes for these potentially divisive suits. Within these mediation councils, a showing by the plaintiffs that the percentage of blacks in the institution is less than their percentage in the relevant workforce or market would be all that was required of the plaintiff. There would be no need to trace such a disparity or even to suggest that such a disparity was somehow connected to a racist mind-set. Thus the new legal structure and new standards of review would not be designed to blame, finger-point or create a sense of guilt and resentment. They would simply be a form of truly communal remedies to supplement political remedies designed to restructure American institutions.

The institution would have an opportunity, however, to give an account for the disparity or to offer reasons why the institution is in no financial position to alter the disparity. Depending on the credibility of the institution's account, the council would then have several remedies at its disposal. First, the council could order the immediate inclusion of qualified candidates. Second, it could require the reformulation of the institution's acceptance criteria, so as to facilitate the closing of the disparity. Third, it could require that certain monies be escrowed for special programs designed to recruit, train, hire, retain and promote "qualified" candidates.

That is, if the council believed that the acceptance criteria used by the institution were legitimate, the institution should not be required to accept individuals failing to satisfy the criteria. Instead, the council would direct the institution to escrow an amount of money necessary to get qualified candidates up to that standard. This could require internship programs as early as junior high school, scholarships, summer work and other creative interventions. Standards of good faith would have to be established to make sure the institutions were attempting, in earnest, to correct the proven disparity. The council and court would maintain jurisdiction to make sure the institution was following through on its plans. The institution should be permitted a tax credit from the federal government equal to any amount escrowed for purposes of rectifying the disparities in the future. Given a progressive tax structure this will assure that the costs associated with deinstitutionalizing racism, sexism, and classism in this society will be equitably distributed. Such an approach breaks out of the individualist model of liberalism on the ideological, structural and operational levels. It effectively reckons with the history and legacy of racism, but without the guilt, blame and pain that customarily permeate the discourse on race in America.

None of this is to say that only the poor and those groups disproportionately located among the poor should benefit from affirmative action. Diversity should be a legitimate goal of institutions in a multicultural and pluralist society. Other historically excluded groups may not be disproportionately located among the poor, but may be under-represented at higher economic levels. Institutions may, of course, voluntarily act to include such groups. Such groups would have standing to bring legal actions against institutions in which they did not have proportional representation. But the burden of proof would be on groups to show that their under-representation was connected to a history of prejudice and bigotry which more likely than not continues to influence the decision making process of the institution in question.

E. Rethinking Liberal Individualism: Affirmative Action and the Strategic Dimension of the Beloved Community

The guidelines discussed above can facilitate the development of affirmative action programs that walk the political tightrope between demands for diverse beneficiaries and sensitivity to particular histories of oppression like that experienced by African-Americans. Yet a substantive reconceptualization is only part of the solution. We must link this reconceptualization to a new orientation, a reborn spirit, no less, that affects the way we talk and write about affirmative action and race in America. This new spirit must foster a new sense of interdependency among those divided by our tragic history of race.

In other words, the social dimension of our love-based conception of community is only part of the solution. As King understood, the Beloved Community has a strategic dimension as well. The social focus on the least of these is but a path to the ultimate spiritual truth of human interdependence. Our attitude towards and efforts to liberate the least of these should inform and embellish our love for others. The hope is that when we understand that we and the other are inextricably connected in a single garment of destiny, we can clear the channels of communication of the refuse of age-old distortions and hostilities.

In our feeble efforts to aid the destitute and downtrodden, then, we strengthen our capacity for love. By making their cause our own, however briefly, we discover links and causations of which we were unaware. By the always-presumptuous and ill-fated projection of ourselves into their world, we apprehend the otherness of ourselves and the interdependent context of our being. Our love for the least of these is, then, excellent training for our love of others, for it should instill in us a new spirit, a new orientation toward the world and its problems. This new spirit should seek to strengthen the bonds of interdependency while challenging abject forms of dependence and isolationist forms of independence.

This new spirituality should certainly be reflected in the rhetorical strategies of public officials whose decisions define and clarify our public values. In this regard, one of the most important functions of the judge, mediator or administrator is to edify, to call us to something more than we think ourselves capable of becoming.

The act of judging, then, the art of making the difficult choices that life requires of us, must have a certain strategic as well as substantive quality, instilling in those who read and hear these decisions a sense of beauty and good, allowing us always to glimpse the possibilities and not just the dangers of our interdependence. The current discourse on affirmative action unfortunately negates this spirit. That discourse must be reinvented to promote the spirit of interdependence, which, as we have seen, is a genuine love for others founded on a proper love for self that connects to a purpose higher still. In the future, the progressive liberals will need to concern themselves with not just the social dimension of their vision but the ways that social vision is communicated to others as well. For, through our words, we will shape the possibilities and limits of community.

Edifying decisions, then, should salvage and affirm the self-worth of those to whom its principles and rules apply. This requires a critical historical consciousness that the judicial philosophies of originalism, plain meaning, and fidelity to precedent do not possess.

One view of affirmative action's potential is that it breaks the cycle of cultural reproduction that perpetuates the myth of black inferiority and white superiority. If affirmative action were implemented on the scale explored above and achieved rough proportional representation of blacks at all income and wealth levels throughout society, the cultural impact alone would quickly dissipate the vestiges of slavery and segregation. That is, the identities of young white children would develop in a social context in which their sense of what is proper, good, just, natural or in accordance with common sense would not be predicated on the accumulated inequities of slavery and segregation. They would see blacks occupying positions in every walk of life in rough proportion to their numbers in society, rather than disproportionately represented among the economically and symbolically subservient positions of maids, janitors, shoe shiners and the unemployed.

Affirmative action that went far beyond its present tokenism would also directly enhance the self-worth of blacks, who could then visualize and pursue possibilities previously foreclosed to them. Young black children born in the wastelands of many inner cities would grow up in a world radically different from the one known by their parents. Hard work and diligence would be rewarded with real opportunity rather than the early death, cycle of pain and dead ends that presently define the lives of too many. The grounds on which racial interaction take place for these future generations would be quite different from the grounds on which they generally now take place. At least this effort would weaken the pervasive and socially conditioned reflex that blacks are unworthy to do certain things because they have not done them before.

Yet our impoverished jurisprudence of race has itself diminished the possibilities of using affirmative action to affirm self-worth. Our talk of affirmative action, even when we approve of its use, is akin to a bitter-tasting medicine we are forced to take but believe we have been wrongly prescribed. Our resentment grows with every dose, and we are unlikely to admit our improvement, even if it is so.

Our rhetoric has turned affirmative action into a spoiler of what we deem more just and acceptable preferences. Far from affirming self-worth, affirmative action has taken up arms against it, aiding the very racism that it might otherwise challenge. Failing really to challenge the multidimensional understanding of racism this work develops, the rhetoric of affirmative action often drains the wellspring of self-worth and raids the inner sanctuary of human dignity, robbing its supposed beneficiaries of life-affirming and life-protecting powers, leaving blacks and whites alike bitter, fractured and disempowered.

The rhetoric of affirmative action sends clear yet subtle messages to blacks that, notwithstanding their formal acceptance by institutions which have historically excluded them, they still do not belong. They are not truly worthy, their presence constituting an exception to otherwise objective meritocratic standards, nothing more than a forced concession or act of charity.

The rhetoric of affirmative action also sends clear messages to whites. The understanding of affirmative action as a just restitution for slavery and segregation suggests that the reason blacks are not better off is because of this history. What, then, accounts for why some whites are not better off? The implication, which many whites complaining of affirmative action cannot concede, is that they may simply be inferior to those whites to whom they have regularly lost out.

The above view complements another view that is, I believe, more prevalent. If complaining whites understand affirmative action as a deviation from fair meritocratic norms, the suggestion that blacks are the undeserved beneficiaries of societal benefits is a kind of existential capital that compensates whites for losing out in the competition for scarce resources. Their subordination or feelings of alienation in our culture, the job or promotion they fail to secure, the educational program from which they are excluded and their feelings of inadequacy over status and success in other facets of life are often made more tolerable by the castigation of affirmative action, a scapegoat offered in atonement for perceived shortcomings. When those who are socialized to believe they are superior to others can extract such ideological and existential sustenance from affirmative action, the shriveled and ineffectual condition of this progressive liberal program is not surprising.

In summary, the jurisprudence of love is concerned not merely with the bottom-line result of policy and law, but with the rhetorical garb in which the result is dressed. Love realizes that it is often the dress, how something is said, that is of greatest consequence, sending signals that foster resentment or acceptance, jealousy or admiration, rage or understanding. We must promote not only the end of love, but the way of love as well. What should this new way of talking about affirmative action be? What rhetoric would be most consistent with the spritual and social dimensions of affirmative action just discussed?

The rhetorical strategy that progressive liberals should adopt requires them to reclaim the ideology of color blindness. Progressive liberals should provide a different understanding of the color blindness that conservatives have enslaved in the service of a dutiless individualism. This alternative understanding would reject the conservative distortion of King's 1963 "I Have A Dream" speech and restore that speech to its rightful place in a progressive moral vision of a community that is in the process of becoming.

1. Color Blindness: A New Critique of an Old Idea

Simply put, the narrative of color blindness suggests that the lesson we should draw from centuries of race-based laws, traditions and customs designed to subordinate blacks is that race should seldom be used as a criterion for decision making, even when its use purports to make restitution for the present effects of a racist past. Proponents of color blindness contend that, precisely because this past denigrated the worth and dignity of blacks relative to whites, we must maintain a fidelity to color blindness. In effect, it is argued, blacks have the most to lose when race is recognized in law, for even so-called benign uses are based on demeaning stereotypes, and will ultimately foment resentment and hostility against blacks, exacting a cost elsewhere. For those acting in good faith, color blindness is thought to elevate blacks to the status of equals before the law, giving them a dignity past laws seldom acknowledged. Judges can assure themselves that this commitment is being honored when, in the distribution of burdens and benefits to citizens, laws do not formally recognize race without compelling justification. This assures that individuals will be judged not by the color of their skin, but by the content of their character.

What this defense of color blindness fails to grasp is that racial recognition is necessary precisely because the domination of blacks was achieved through race-specific means. It is because the domination of blacks in American society was predicated on their subhuman nature, lack of intelligence and general unworthiness to associate with those of the superior race that race-based affirmative action is essential. It is needed to reeducate a society whose formative years were steeped in racist demagoguery and domination.

Our contemporary jurisprudence confuses the ontological category of race with its functional role in the American society. The recognition of racial difference has not been the cause of, but the occasion for, black exclusion and subordination. That is, the badge of color provides a visible distinction to which socially constructed derogatory meaning is attached. This negative meaning is then used as a justification for the group's persecution. Race, then, was the occasion for such subordination because of the larger cultural meaning associated with it and with color. That cultural meaning imbued race with preexisting beliefs in black inferiority and white superiority, justifying the subordination of blacks by whites. Thus the recognition of race is not problematic in and of itself; the problem is that it has often been used as a way of achieving the larger purpose of black subordination.

Our contemporary jurisprudence of race has missed the point. The outlawing of race as a criterion for determining who gets limited positions and goods does not solve the problem. Indeed, it exacerbates the problem, for the cultural significance of race continues to thrive, notwithstanding the color-blind protestations of our laws and judicial interpretations. Race's cultural significance—the perpetuation of beliefs in black inferiority—is reinforced by economic and social realities, and transmitted through the cultural conventions of jokes, stories, art and religion. Prejudice is nurtured by the mass of information that we consciously and subconsciously consume. It periodically surfaces for air, venting itself in the form of a spontaneous laugh to a racist joke, an "inadvertent" use of a racial epithet, a prolonged stare, an unwarranted assumption, a blatant act of discrimination or a discriminatory impact ushering from an inarticulate aversion to associating with "them" at work, home and play.

Racism finds its outlet in many forms and, ironically, accomplishes its evil in ways more devastating than before. For if blacks are no longer the victims of racism in an ostensibly color-blind world governed by antidiscrimination laws, they have only themselves to blame for their continued subordination. The accumulated assessment of their lack of worth is vindicated after all. Given every opportunity to excel, they are still unable to compete, their absence from the upper echelons of American society itself evidence of their inferiority.

The rhetoric of color blindness, then, wields a two-edged sword, protecting the status quo through its disempowerment of blacks, and reconciling many poorer whites to positions of subordination by inducing them to believe that they are privileged participants in a social structure which, in reality, oppresses them as well. It is in this respect that the Supreme Court's conception of color blindness is most tragic, for the conception rationalizes oppression and forces into different channels the deep-seated racism no culture with our history could have already expected to overcome.

The equality undergirding the conception of color blindness just discussed is a formal one akin to the traditional Christian version discussed earlier. Just as all within the community of believers are considered equals before God, with no concern for their material relations, here all within the community of citizens are deemed equal before the law, again with no concern for their material relations. Both conceptions of formal equality attempt to grasp the universality of our experience by ignoring the particularity and diversity of that experience. I propose just the opposite, that we seek to capture what is universal through the particularity of experience guided by the normative commands of love.

2. Color Blindness: A New Conception of an Old Idea

At its core, the spirit of love is animated by a faith in the equal dignity of human life, the interdependence of human existence, and the hope for cooperative struggle. Yet this unifying impulse does not require blindness to difference. Indeed, it is not the recognition of difference but the interpretation of difference that is crucial. Some interpretations transgress the commands of love. These we should avoid. Others follow those commands and thus satisfy the basic needs, protect the fundamental freedoms, and affirm the self-worth of others whom we are commanded to love as ourselves. These we should embrace.

Within my framework, the universalism to which distorted conceptions of color blindness can only allude is that experience which comes from our genuine love for others and the human interdependence affirmed by that love. While I have attempted above to give some concrete meaning to an otherwise sentimental subject, a discussion about the spirit of love is essential precisely because there is no formula for its unequivocal attainment and no quasi-scientific test by which we can discern its indefatigable presence. But of this we can be certain: its attainment will require that we grapple with an existential and not just an abstract conception of being. For it is through the variegated existence of life that we experience the reality of commonality, a reality reaching beyond our partial selves to grasp some sense of the whole.

The identity-based particularism required by the use of racial classifications in affirmative action should be seen, then, as a necessary step toward this larger spiritual awareness. For only when stark oppressive differences are diminished can individuals begin to see and appreciate common links, needs and outlooks. Therefore, more than just formal freedom of choice and action are needed to give individuals this capacity to grasp that which is universal about their particularism.

Unfortunately, abstract conceptions of color blindness fail to acknowledge the extent to which individuals are constituted as individuals. We are constituted not simply by the universalism of our moral capacity to choose, but by the complex network of social relations that creates and sustains our identities and conditions our choices. It would seem incontrovertible that institutions like family, school, church and work significantly shape who we are, our outlooks and orientations, fears and hopes, and blindnesses and visions—in short, our so-called freedom to choose. We draw from these institutional relations the stuff of life. They provide the filters through which we sift the valuable from the worthless, the right from the wrong, and the good from the bad. We are ever producing ourselves, consciously and subconsciously, from the countless affiliations that give human existence its richness. Even when we most distance ourselves from others by our supposed individuality, we are close to them because, together, unknowingly perhaps, we have built the bridges that divide and bind.

Race, it seems, is one such bridge that divides and binds. Slavery, segregation and the common experiences of oppression and suffering have provided for black people what the institutions of family, church, school and work provided for all—points of psychological and cultural convergence. That a people forced to live, sleep, eat, learn, worship and die together would not, as a result, develop certain commonalities of outlook and perspective would be remarkable indeed. Yet the very fact of coerced black existence has profoundly affected the coercers and their progeny as well. For much of this country's jurisprudence, public values, music, art, technology and politics is directly attributable to the presence, struggles and contributions of black people.

Understood in this way, race-based affirmative action can be seen as a path to the truth of human equality and interdependence. For, as oxymoronic as it sounds, we are different and yet the same in our difference, independent and yet dependent in our independence. Thus in following the historical paths of our particular experiences, we ineluctably traverse and shadow the paths of others. And if we are discerning and outward-looking in our introspection, we will on occasion see the forest that defines both the limits and the possibilities of our common plights.

The masterful storyteller—judge, mediator, legislator or layperson—should tell the story of racial oppression in a way that captures this truth and nurtures tolerance and respect for those whose self-worth has been systematically ravaged by a despicable past to which all are heir and for which all must accept responsibility. Through the spirit of love, we should meet the oppressed where they are, with all their richness, diversity, hopes and fears. In the complicated matrix of that interaction, something remarkable, even mystical, often happens. We experience the other not as other, but as self. Their possibilities and limits become our own as we struggle together to find a common way. A proper spirit of love is crucial, for the application of the theories elaborated above depends on a proper spirit. Without it, our applications will ossify, turn oppressive and self-serving, and defeat the very concerns that love is sworn to uphold.

Thus, to some extent, we too must hold high the banner of color blindness and universality, though it be quite different from the one flaunted within the contemporary rhetoric of race. By a normatively guided immersion into the particularities of racial experience, we struggle for the commonality and oneness for which the best interpretation of color blindness reaches. When guided by the norm of love, as I have understood and presented it in this book, we become something more than ethical relativists, though something less than moral absolutists. We embrace the modern project of individual emancipation and the full development of our protean powers, but within a framework where belief in a common good and our overlapping duties to God, self and the least of these is both possible and essential.

Notes

Introduction

1. ROBERT L. ALLEN, RELUCTANT REFORMERS: THE IMPACT OF RACISM ON AMERICAN SOCIAL REFORM MOVEMENTS (1974).
2. STEPHEN L. CARTER, THE CULTURE OF DISBELIEF: HOW AMERICAN LAW AND POLITICS TRIVIALIZE RELIGIOUS DEVOTION 58 (1993).

Chapter 1

1. JOHN DEWEY, HUMAN NATURE AND CONDUCT: AN INTRODUCTION TO SOCIAL PSYCHOLOGY 331–32 (1922).
2. *Biography of John Dewey*, in 2 THE PHILOSOPHY OF JOHN DEWEY 21 (Paul Arthur Schlipp ed., 2d ed. 1951).
3. GEORGE DYKHUIZEN, THE LIFE AND MIND OF JOHN DEWEY (1973).
4. JOHN DEWEY, THE QUEST FOR CERTAINTY: A STUDY OF THE RELATION OF KNOWLEDGE AND ACTION (1929) [hereinafter DEWEY, QUEST]; DEWEY, *supra* note 1.
5. JOHN DEWEY, A COMMON FAITH 80–81 (1934).
6. *Id.* at 80.
7. JOHN DEWEY, FREEDOM AND CULTURE 18–19 (1939).
8. *Id.* at 21.
9. JOHN DEWEY, EXPERIENCE AND NATURE 420 (1925).
10. JOHN DEWEY, *The Need for a Recovery of Philosophy*, in CREATIVE INTELLIGENCE 3, 69 (Octagon Books 1970) (1917).
11. DEWEY, QUEST, *supra* note 4, at 272.
12. *Id.*
13. *Id.*
14. *Id.*; JOHN DEWEY, ESSAYS IN EXPERIMENTAL LOGIC 349–89 (1916).
15. DEWEY, QUEST, *supra* note 4, at 278.
16. *Id.*
17. JOHN DEWEY, THE DEVELOPMENT OF AMERICAN PRAGMATISM in PHILOSOPHY AND CIVILIZATION 56 (New York, Capricorn Books, 1963).
18. Brown v. Board of Educ., 349 U.S. 294 (1955).
19. BERTRAND RUSSELL, A HISTORY OF WESTERN PHILOSOPHY 851–52 (1945).
20. DEWEY, *supra* note 1. at 331–32.
21. DEWEY, *supra* note 10 at 69.
22. SOREN KIERKEGAARD, THE POINT OF VIEW FOR MY WORK AS AN AUTHOR 70 (Benjamin Nelson ed. & Walter Lowrie trans., 1962) (1939).
23. RUSSELL, *supra* note 19, at 828.
24. DEWEY, note 10 at 69.
25. JOHN DEWEY, *What I Believe*, in I BELIEVE 347 (Clifton Fadiman ed., 1939).
26. *Id.*

Chapter 2

1. Lochner v. New York, 198 U.S. 45 (1905).
2. JOHN DEWEY, *Logical Method and Law*, 10 CORNELL L. Q. 17 (1924).
3. OLIVER WENDELL HOLMES, THE COMMON LAW 5 (Mark Howe ed., 1968) (1881).
4. ROSCOE POUND, *Mechanical Jurisprudence*, 8 COLUM. L. REV. 605, 607 (1908).
5. DEWEY, *supra* note 2, at 22.
6. *Id.* at 22–23.
7. 198 U.S. 45 (1905).
8. FELIX COHEN, *Transcendental Nonsense and the Functional Approach*, 35 COLUM. L. REV. 809, 821 (1935).
9. *Id.* at 809.
10. *Id.* at 809.
11. *Id.* at 823.
12. *Id.* at 848–49.
13. *Lochner*, 198 U.S. at 75–76 (Holmes, J., dissenting).
14. EDWARD A. PURCELL, JR., *American Jurisprudence Between the Wars: Legal Realism and the Crisis of Democratic Theory*, 75 AM. HIST. REV. 424 (1969).
15. *See generally* KARL LLEWELLYN, THE COMMON LAW TRADITION (1960).
16. HERBERT WECHSLER, *Toward Neutral Principles of Constitutional Law*, 73 HARV. L. REV. 1, 19 (1959).
17. 321 U.S. 649 (1944).
18. 334 U.S. 1 (1948).
19. 347 U.S. 483 (1954).
20. Korematsu v. United States, 323 U.S. 214 (1944).

Chapter 3

1. For helpful commentary on the Social Gospel and its development, *see generally* AARON IGNATIUS ABELL, THE URBAN IMPACT ON AMERICAN PROTESTANTISM: 1865–1900 (1943): PAUL CARTER, THE DECLINE AND REVIVAL OF THE SOCIAL GOSPEL (1954); JAMES DOMBROWSKI, THE EARLY DAYS OF CHRISTIAN SOCIALISM IN AMERICA (1936); DONALD GORRELL, THE AGE OF SOCIAL RESPONSIBILITY (1988); ROBERT HANDY, THE SOCIAL GOSPEL IN AMERICA (1966); CHARLES HOWARD HOPKINS, THE RISE OF THE SOCIAL GOSPEL IN AMERICAN PROTESTANTISM: 1865–1915 (1960); RICHARD D. KNUDTEN, THE SYSTEMATIC THOUGHT OF WASHINGTON GLADDEN (1968); HENRY F. MAY, PROTESTANT CHURCHES AND INDUSTRIAL AMERICA (1949); DONALD B. MEYER, THE PROTESTANT SEARCH FOR POLITICAL REALISM, 1919–1941 (1960); ROBERT MILLER, AMERICAN PROTESTANTISM AND SOCIAL ISSUES, 1919–1939 (1958); RONALD WHITE, JR. & CHARLES HOWARD HOPKINS, THE SOCIAL GOSPEL (1976).
2. The same Social Darwinism confronted by Dewey also made its way into theological circles. William Graham Sumner was the most vocal advocate of Herbert Spencer's "social statics." Sumner contended that "even a

drunkard in the gutter is just where he ought to he. Nature is working away at him to get him out of the way, just as she gets up her processes of dissolution to remove whatever is a failure in its line. Gambling and less mentionable vices all cure themselves by the ruin and dissolution of their victims." WILLIAM GRAHAM SUMNER, SOCIAL DARWINISM: SELECTED ESSAYS OF WILLIAM GRAHAM SUMNER 24, 122–23 (William E. Leuchtenburg & Bernard Wishy eds., 1963).

3. *See generally* GORRELL, *supra* note 1 (locating the development of the Social Gospel within the full context of other events, movements, and trends in the United States during the Progressive era).

4. For an illuminating treatment of the effects of the European Enlightenment and the paradigm of modernity on the Social Gospel, see HARRY ANTONIDES, STONES FOR BREAD 1–7 (1985) (characterizing the Enlightenment as a commitment to autonomy, reason, melioristic optimism, progress, and toleration).

5. For a systematic examination of the principal founders of the Social Gospel and their works, *see* HANDY, *supra* note 1 (examining the work of the pillars of the Social Gospel: Washington Gladden, Richard T. Ely, and Walter Rauschenbusch); KNUDTEN, *supra* note 1 (exploring the thought of Social Gospel founder, Washington Gladden).

6. Rauschenbusch's major relevant works include: CHRISTIANITY AND THE SOCIAL CRISIS (1907); CHRISTIANIZING THE SOCIAL ORDER (1907) [hereinafter RAUSCHENBUSCH, SOCIAL ORDER]; FOR GOD AND THE PEOPLE: PRAYERS OF THE SOCIAL AWAKENING (1910); THE SOCIAL PRINCIPLES OF JESUS (1916) [hereinafter RAUSCHENBUSCH, JESUS]; A THEOLOGY FOR THE SOCIAL GOSPEL (1917) [hereinafter RAUSCHENBUSCH, THEOLOGY].

7. For sources exploring the effect of the social gospel on American secular culture, see PAUL BOASE, THE RHETORIC OF CHRISTIAN SOCIALISM 39 (1969) (tracing the development of the social gospel in original works from Joseph Cook in 1878 to Martin Luther King in 1968, contending that "the basic fundamental issue of church and individual involvement with social evil–moral, political, and economic–is as potent and explosive as ever"). *But see* CARTER, *supra* note 1, at 3 (suggesting that many Social Gospel advocates may have been seduced by the bureaucratic hopes of the New Deal: When Roosevelt in his inaugural on March 4, 1933 declared that "the money changers have fled from their high seats in the temple of our civilization," he spoke the language of the Social Gospel).

8. *See* WALTER RAUSCHENBUSCH, SELECTED WRITINGS 113 (Winthrop Hudson ed., 1984). Here, Rauschenbusch sought to remove the mystery associated with the traditional conception of God by reworking the understanding of Revelation by which humans come to know the will of God. Just as the Protestant Reformation returned the church to Paul's theology of justification by faith, Rauschenbusch's objective was to return Christianity to the historical Jesus in whose life revelation was made complete. "There is no higher revelation conceivable for us than this," Rauschenbusch proclaimed, "that a human life should become by nature

and experience the complete and clear expression of the will of God for men." *Id.*

9. RAUSCHENBUSCH, THEOLOGY, *supra* note 6, at 167.
10. *Id.* at 178–79.
11. *John* 3:16 (New Int'l).
12. *Romans* 3:23 (New Int'l).
13. RAUSCHENBUSCH, THEOLOGY, *supra* note 6, at 174–75.
14. *Galatians* 3:26 (New Int'l).
15. RAUSCHENBUSCH, THEOLOGY, *supra* note 6, at 186–87.
16. *Id.* at 187.
17. *Id.* at 186.
18. *Id.* at 143.
19. *Id.* at 186.
20. *Id.*
21. Some have noted that, on the whole, very little was said by Social Gospel proponents about the plight of black people and the problem of racism during the Progressive era, a time called by C. Vann Woodward the "nadir" of race relations in America. This view has been challenged, however. *See generally* RALPH E. LUKER, THE SOCIAL GOSPEL IN BLACK AND WHITE 268–311 (1991) (contending that Social Gospel proponents "were less indifferent to race relations than the historians suggest.... [T]he spectrum ranged from Josiah Strong's radical assimilationism to Josiah Royce's conservative assimilationism and from Edgar Gardner Murphy's conservative separatism to Thomas Dison, Jr.'s, radical separatism."); CALVIN S. MORRIS, REVERDY C. RANSOM: BLACK ADVOCATE FOR THE SOCIAL GOSPEL (1990) (describing the contributions of a black minister to the development of the Social Gospel): RONALD WHITE, JR., LIBERTY AND JUSTICE FOR ALL (1976) (demonstrating that many of the social gospelers did not ignore racial issues). Rauschenbusch was, indeed, reluctant to say much about racial matters in America and was basically silent until the 1920s. "For years," he acknowledged, "the problem of the two races in the South has seemed to me so tragic, so insoluble, that I have never yet ventured to discuss it in public." LUKER, *supra*, at 315 (quoting Rauschenbusch). Rauschenbusch's reluctance to speak of the problem in public was due, at least in part, to his hope that the amelioration of the class problem would substantially deal with the race problem. He observed:

> A solution of the labor question so thorough that it would be possible to hand over entire industries to the black race without evoking industrial hostility, would offer a solid hope to the Negro.

Id. at 317 (quoting speech made by Rauschenbusch at the Third Sagamore Sociological Conference in 1909).

The conflation of class and race is a problem common to much progressive and left wing thought and is one my jurisprudence of love outlined in subsequent chapters avoids. One of Rauschenbusch's most prophetic statements about race relations bears repeating, however, for it, directly implicates the command of love to be discussed shortly. He wrote:

> No resolution of race relations by Southern white men that failed to instill hope and self–respect in black men and women or pride and ambition in black communities was acceptable to the nation's Christian conscience. White Southerners who would deny black people's humanity or condemn them to a permanently servile caste might be a minority, but small, determined oligarchies with inherited prejudice and economic interest had imperiled national unity and progress in the past. We owe it to our brethren in the South to say that the solution of the problem does not lie that way and never will. The spirit of Pharaoh never works the will of God.

Id. at 320. For specific references to Rauschenbusch's reflections on race, see generally Walter Rauschenbusch, *The Negro and the Church Crisis*, 67 AM. MISSIONARY ASS'N 232 (Feb. 1914); Walter Rauschenbusch, *The Problem of the Black Man*, 68 AM. MISSIONARY ASS'N 732 (Mar. 1914).

22. RAUSCHENBUSCH, THEOLOGY, *supra* note 6, at 186.

23. *Id.*

24. *Id.* at 184.

25. *Id.* at 119.

26. *Id.* at 184.

27. Nearly one fourth of Rauschenbusch's A THEOLOGY FOR A SOCIAL GOSPEL is devoted to the topics of sin and evil. His awareness of the importance of sin and evil for human capabilities pervades an even greater portion. Critics have confused his appreciation for the limitations imposed by sin and evil with whether one should succumb to these forces. Rauschenbusch refused to succumb and encouraged his followers to take a similar position. *See* RAUSCHENBUSCH, THEOLOGY, *supra* note 6, at 69–76 (explaining how institutions designed for good often turn bad). But Rauschenbusch believed that an awareness of evil should not deter us from challenging it. This conviction was the role of faith. *Id.* at 102.

28. Rauschenbusch was forever guiding individuals away from an exclusively individualistic conception of sin and evil that pictured the individual in a personal tug of war with God on the one side, urging moral uprightness, and the Devil on the other, urging vice. Rauschenbusch wanted to see Satan in a more institutional and complex sense. Rauschenbusch approvingly cited the following passage: "Much as Satan glories in his power over an individual, how much greater must be his glorying over a nation embodying, in its laws and usages, disobedience to God, wrong to man, and contamination to morals!" RAUSCHENBUSCH, *supra* note 8, at 62.

29. RAUSCHENBUSCH, THEOLOGY, *supra* note 6, at 48.

30. *Id.* at 48.

31. *Id.* at 60.

32. *Id.* at 79.

33. RAUSCHENBUSCH, SOCIAL ORDER, *supra* note 6, at 420–21.

34. Just as Rauschenbusch attempted to maintain a constructive tension

between transcendental and contextual conceptions of Good and Evil, he desired to challenge the theological category of salvation and of the Kingdom of God. His challenge to abstracted conceptions of the Kingdom can be seen most vividly in his opposition to the millenarianism of his day. He argued for a conception of the coming Kingdom that inspired collective struggle for the present approximation of the Kingdom of God on earth. "The question is, which will do more to make our lives spiritual and to release us from the tyranny of the world, the thought that we may at any moment enter into the presence of the Lord, or the thought that every moment we are in the presence of the Lord?" Rauschenbusch sided clearly with the latter. RAUSCHENBUSCH, *supra* note 8, at 94.

35. RAUSCHENBUSCH, JESUS, *supra* note 6, at 197.
36. RAUSCHENBUSCH, THEOLOGY, *supra* note 6, at 130.
37. *Id.* at 146.
38. *Id.*
39. *Id.* at 145.
40. RAUSCHENBUSCH, *supra* note 8, at 76–79.
41. *Id.*
42. RAUSCHENBUSCH, THEOLOGY, *supra* note 6, at 145.
43. *Id.*
44. *Id.* at 142.
45. *Luke* 4:18–19 (New Int'l).
46. RAUSCHENBUSCH, THEOLOGY, *supra* note 6, at 142.
47. *Id.*
48. *Id.*
49. *Mark* 12:29–31 (New Int'l).
50. RAUSCHENBUSCH, THEOLOGY, *supra* note 6, at 143. *But see* SUSAN CURTIS, A CONSUMING FAITH 14 (1991) (claiming that the effect of the ideas and practices of the Social Gospel was to ease the transition to a secular consumer–based culture).
51. RAUSCHENBUSCH, THEOLOGY, *supra* note 6, at 143.
52. When the rich young man inquired of Jesus, "Teacher, what good thing must I do to get eternal life?" Jesus eventually replied, "If you want to be perfect, go, sell your possessions and give to the poor, and you will have treasure in heaven. Then come, follow me." *Matthew* 19:16, 21 (New Int'l). For a discussion of the influence of Christian Socialism on the Social Gospel, see generally WHITE, JR., & HOPKINS, *supra* note 1.
53. *John* 15:13 (New Int'l).

Chapter 4

1. ANNE C. LOVELAND, SOUTHERN EVANGELICALS AND THE SOCIAL ORDER, 1800–1860, at 206 (1980).
2. *Luke* 4:18 (King James).
3. *Matthew* 10:34 (King James).
4. Albert J. Raboteau, *The Black Experience in American Evangelicalism: The*

Meaning of Slavery, in THE EVANGELICAL TRADITION IN AMERICA 180, 190 (L. Sweet ed., 1984).

5. *Id.* (footnote omitted) (quoting Garnet, *An Address to the Slaves of the United States of America* (1843), reprinted in STERLING STUCKEY, THE IDEOLOGICAL ORIGINS OF BLACK NATIONALISM 165, 168–72 [1972]).

6. *Hush, Hush Somebody's Calling My Name, in* SONGS OF ZION 125 (Abbingdon 1981).

7. *Steal Away to Jesus*, in SONGS OF ZION, *supra* note 6, at 180.

8. Raboteau, *supra* note 4, at 193–94 (emphasis in original).

9. MARTIN LUTHER KING, JR., *Letter from Birmingham City Jail* (1963), reprinted in A TESTAMENT OF HOPE: THE ESSENTIAL WRITINGS OF MARTIN LUTHER KING, JR. 292–93 (James M. Washington ed. 1986) [hereinafter A TESTAMENT OF HOPE].

Chapter 5

1. MARTIN LUTHER KING, JR., *Pilgrimage to Nonviolence* (1960), reprinted in A TESTAMENT OF HOPE, *supra* chap. 4 note 9, at 35.

2. *Id.* at 36.

3. JOHN J. ANSBRO, MARTIN LUTHER KING, JR.: THE MAKING OF A MIND 189 (1982).

4. *Id.* at 293.

5. KING, *supra* chap. 4 note 9, at 295.

6. KENNETH L. SMITH & IRA G. ZEPP, JR., SEARCH FOR THE BELOVED COMMUNITY: THE THINKING OF MARTIN LUTHER KING, JR. 127 (1986).

7. *Id.* (quoting King, *Nobel Prize Acceptance Speech*, reprinted in NEGRO HIST. BULL., May 1968, at 21).

8. MARTIN LUTHER KING, JR., *The Time for Freedom Has Come* (1961), reprinted in A TESTAMENT OF HOPE, *supra* chap. 4 note 9, at 160, 165.

9. MARTIN LUTHER KING, JR., *The Ethical Demands for Integration* (1963), reprinted in A TESTAMENT OF HOPE, *supra* chap. 4 note 9, at 117, 124.

10. MARTIN LUTHER KING, JR., *The Trumpet of Conscience* (1967), reprinted in A TESTAMENT OF HOPE, *supra* chap. 4 note 9, at 634, 649.

11. MARTIN LUTHER KING, JR., WHERE DO WE GO FROM HERE: CHAOS OR COMMUNITY? 187 (1967).

12. KING, *supra* note 1, at 37.

13. MARTIN LUTHER KING, JR., *Where Do We Go From Here?* (1967), *reprinted in* A TESTAMENT OF HOPE, *supra* chap. 4 note 9, at 245, 250.

14. *John* 15:13 (King James).

15. KING, *supra* chap. 4 note 9, at 292.

16. *Id.*

17. KING, *supra* note 13, at 575.

18. *Id.* at 576.

19. *Id.* at 577.

20. *Id.* at 578.

21. *Id.* at 677.

22. *Id.* at 579.
23. *Id.*
24. *Id.* at 580.
25. *Id.*
26. *Id.* at 582.
27. *Id.* at 574.
28. *Id.* at 587.
29. *Id.* at 573.
30. *Id.* at 590.
31. *Id.* at 594–95.
32. *Id.*
33. *Id.* at 572.
34. *Id.*
35. *Id.* at 585.
36. *Id.* at 578.
37. *Id.* at 588.
38. *Id.* at 594.
39. *Id.* at 578.

Chapter 6

1. For a leading theological treatment of the implications of love for contemporary problems, see generally LOVE: THE FOUNDATION OF HOPE
(Frederic B. Burnham et. al. eds., 1988). Jürgen Moltmann is one of the
most influential theological voices of our day. The value of love assumes a
central place in his theology. Like the best advocates of the Social Gospel,
he attempts to carve out a position between a conception of God that is
totally transcendent and one that is totally immanent in the personal
struggles of humanity, a position preoccupied with individual salvation and
obsessed with the redemption of man's social existence.

> (S)alvation, *soteria*, must also be understood as *shalom* in the Old
> Testament sense; This does not mean merely salvation of the soul,
> invidual rescue from the evil world, comfort for the troubled con-
> science, but also the realization of the eschatological hope of justice,
> the humanizing of man, the socializing of humanity, peace for all cre-
> ation. This "other side" of reconciliation with God has always been
> given too little consideration in the history of Christianity.

JÜRGEN MOLTMANN, THEOLOGY OF HOPE 329 (1967) (footnote omitted).
2. Indeed, some believe that psychoanalysis is the field of knowledge most
likely to develop a theory of love. The editors of one pioneering treatment
point out that

> Love is a way of transcending the self and of participating in another's
> transformation as well. The force of love oscillates between the loss of
> the self in fusion with another, and the consolidation and emergence of

new aspects of self. Out of love, with its roots in the past, grow the possibilities for the future.

Judith F. Lasky & Helen W. Silverman, *Introduction* to PSYCHOANALYTIC PERSPECTIVES 12 (Judith F. Lasky & Helen W. Silverman eds., 1988).

3. The religion clauses of the First Amendment bar Congress from making laws "respecting an establishment of religion, or prohibiting the free exercise thereof." These clauses have been interpreted to require varying degrees of separation of church and state. See LAURENCE TRIBE, AMERICAN CONSTITUTIONAL LAW 1158–60 (2d ed. 1988) (describing three distinct schools of thought that influenced the drafters of the Bill of Rights: the evangelical view of strict separation of church and state needed to safeguard religion, the Jeffersonian view of strict separation needed to safeguard secular institutions, and the Madisonian view that both religious and secular interests were advanced by the diffusion and decentralization of power so as to assure competition among sects rather than dominance by any one).

4. *Mark* 12:30 (King James).

5. *Mark* 12:31 (King James).

6. FRIEDRICH NIETZSCHE, ON THE GENEALOGY OF MORALS 129 (Walter Kaufmann & R.J. Hollingdale trans., 1969); *see also* RUSSELL, *supra* chap. 1 note 17, at 766–67 (discussing Nietzsche's rejection of Christianity and Christian love in favor of the power embodied in the "noble" man). Nietzsche's invectives against Christianity are well known:

> What is it that we combat in Christianity? That it aims at destroying the strong, at breaking their spirit, at exploiting their moments of weariness and debility, at converting their proud assurance into anxiety and conscience–trouble; that it knows how to poison the noblest instincts and to infect them with disease, until their strength, their will to power, turns inward, against themselves—until the strong perish through their excessive self– contempt and self–immolation; that gruesome way of perishing...

Id. at 766 (quoting Friedrich Nietzsche's *Ecce Homo*).

7. Anthony E. Cook, *Beyond Critical Legal Studies: The Reconstructive Theology of Dr. Martin Luther King, Jr.*, 103 HARV. L. REV. 985 (1990).

8. See *supra* chap. 3, text accompanying notes 10–16.

9. *See* STEPHEN POST, CHRISTIAN LOVE AND SELF–DENIAL vii–viii (1987). Post details an important debate within early American Protestantism over the form and meaning of Christian love, focusing on the thought of Jonathan Edwards and Samuel Hopkins. These theologians differed markedly on the question of whether all self–love is prohibited by Christian ethics. Post argues that through Samuel Hopkins's theory of "disinterested benevolence," American Protestantism was bequeathed a doctrine of radically self–denying love. Edwards, on the other hand, imposed limits on self–denial, thereby permitting the individual's love for self to participate

in communion with the individual's love for God and others. Edwards believed, as do I, that when the three dimensions of love are in true communion, the excesses of self–love as well as those of self-denial are avoided.

10. *I John* 4:20 (New Int'l).

11. POST, *supra* note 9, at vii–viii.

12. See *supra* chap. 3, text accompanying notes 8–16.

13. See Konrad Brown, *Justice and the Law of Love* (New York: Contemporary Books, 1951).

14. *See generally* THOMAS HOBBES, LEVIATHAN (Crawford B. Macpherson ed., 1979) (1651).

15. Cook, *supra* note 7, at 993–1005.

16. *See* Thonnia Lee, *Black Liberation Theology: Activism Isn't Alien to Faith; Fight for Justice is Christian*, ATLANTA J. AND CONST., Mar. 23, 1991, at E6; *see also* H. R. Harris, *Black Church Renews Call to Social Action; Communities Can't Wait*, WASH. POST, Sept. 7, 1991, at G10 ("The National Baptist Convention U.S.A. Inc., the country's largest black denomination, convened its 111th session . . . with a call for its churches to help solve some of the social ills plaguing the black community.") Black theology holds that one cannot affirm the individual without affirming the group with which the individual strongly identifies. Systematic oppression experienced by the individual is inseparable from the oppression of a group based on an identity the individual shares in common and for which members of the group are castigated and subordinated by other groups. Under such circumstances, it is often important to resurrect the worth of the group as a way of resurrecting the worth of the individual. This dimension of black nationalism is acceptable, because this alone is not inconsistent with a unifying love for humanity. Black nationalism should challenge both the oppressed and oppressor to repent from those practices that rob groups of their self–worth and dignity. Cultural criticism as an element of social struggle is essential and noble because, to paraphrase Jesus, it removes the plank from one's own eye before taking the sawdust from our brother's. That is, such efforts correct the distortions that shackle victim and perpetrator alike, distortions based on irrationality, fear, and legitimation. *See* JAMES CONE, GOD OF THE OPPRESSED 15 (1975). *See generally* James Cone, *Black Theology and the Black Church: Where Do We Go from Here?*, 17 MID–STREAM 271 (1979).

17. I contend that this framework of love accommodates both nationalist and integrationist concerns. Under my approach, blacks are obligated to develop programs of self–help and community empowerment that satisfy basic needs, protect fundamental freedoms, and enhance self worth. As a duty of self–love, this responsibility lies first and foremost with the individual and extends outward through networks of association that give human life its purpose and meaning: family, community, ethnic or racial group, etc. Obviously, the duty of self–love will often require that we challenge racist ideological and material practices that destroy and limit the possibilities of self–love. These limitations constitute a breach of the duty of love owed to us by others. Our acceptance of those limitations consti-

tutes a breach of the duty of love owed to ourselves. Thus, both the self–help orientation of black nationalist strategies and the protest orientation of integrationist strategies are consistent with the commands of love. The choice between developing black–controlled institutions and vying for inclusion in white–controlled ones is a question of choosing the most effective means in any given context to promote the end of love.

18. *Matthew* 25:31–46 (King James).
19. *Luke* 4:18 (King James).
20. *Matthew* 5:3 (King James).
21. *Matthew* 7:16 (King James).

Chapter 7

1. CARTER, *supra* intro. note 1, at 130.
2. 410 U.S. 113 (1973).
3. 347 U.S. 403 (1954).
4. *See* LOUIS GASPER, THE FUNDAMENTALIST MOVEMENT (1963). Gasper discusses the relationship between the influence of Calvinist theology on Southern fundamentalism and the laissez–faire conception of politics and economy so prevalent throughout the region: Calvin's ideals for all Christians were "thrift, industry and sobriety, which permitted men to prosper economically without fear of being regarded as tainted by the sin of avarice." *Id.* at 4.
5. One white clergyman admonished King for his "untimely" Birmingham demonstrations by pointing out that "all Christians know that the colored people will receive equal rights eventually, but it is possible that you are in too great of a religious hurry. It has taken Christianity almost two thousand years to accomplish what it has. The teachings of Christ take time to come to earth." KING, *supra* chap. 4 note 9, at 296.
6. The splintering of the liberal consensus in the mid–sixties resulted from several factors, including the disaffection of white liberals from the movement as the campaign shifted its focus to class–based oppression in the North; the radicalization of the Student Nonviolent Coordinating Committee (SNCC) and its adoption of a more militant stance calling for Black Power; the shift in the federal government's attention from the domestic problems of race relations and the war on poverty to Cold War concerns; the mounting white backlash against what appeared to be rapid Black gains; and finally, the belief among many of King's own associates that with the attainment of the franchise in 1965, use of the democratic processes of the political system would secure the balance of the Movement's agenda. *See* RICHARD KLUGER, SIMPLE JUSTICE 761–62 (1977); FRANCES PIVEN & RICHARD CLOWARD, POOR PEOPLE'S MOVEMENTS: WHY THEY SUCCEED, HOW THEY FAIL 252–55 (1979).

The split within the African–American ranks of the movement over the viability of nonviolence as a strategy was of major importance. *See* LOUIS LOMAX, THE NEGRO REVOLT 246–47 (1962) (warning of impending violence unless whites responded to African–American demands for reform);

PIVEN & CLOWARD, *supra*, at 248 (describing Black masses joining the protest by rioting in the ghettos of several major cities).

7. KING, *supra* chap. 5 note 11.

8. MARTIN LUTHER KING, JR., *I Have a Dream* (Aug. 28, 1963), reprinted in A TESTAMENT OF HOPE, *supra* chap. 4 note 9, at 219.

9. For an excellent discussion of the limits of liberalism in addressing issues of racial domination, *see* Gary Peller, *Race Consciousness*, 1990 DUKE L.J. 758–83.

10. For an extensive historical treatment of the legal dimensions of the Second Reconstruction, *see* CARL M. BROWN, JOHN F. KENNEDY AND THE SECOND RECONSTRUCTION (1977); KLUGER, *supra* note 6.

11. A newspaper column by Rowland Evans and Robert Novak, one week after the Watts uprising put the problem this way: "The implied message of the Moynihan report is that ending discrimination is not nearly enough for the negro. But what is enough? The phrase 'preferential treatment' implies a solution far afield from the American dream. The white majority would never accept it." GODFREY HODGSON, AMERICA IN OUR TIME: FROM WORLD WAR II TO NIXON—WHAT HAPPENED AND WHY 67 (1978).

12. If King ever saw the achievement of formal rights as the end of his struggle, he did not see it this way for long. The realities of *de facto* segregation and the countless permutations of systematic disempowerment made it clear that the subordination of African–Americans was inextricably connected to the American class structure. Thus, true liberation was inseparable from a fundamental redistribution of wealth and power—inseparable, that is, from a sustained social struggle to transform the very foundations of the American capitalist system.

13. For King's analysis of these three evils, *see* Martin Luther King, Jr., The Three Evils of Society, Speech at the New Politics Convention (Aug. 31, 1967), at 7.

14. For a reading of the influence of the Black Church on King's vision, *see* Lewis Baldwin, *Martin Luther King, Jr., The Black Church and the Black Messianic Vision*, in MARTIN LUTHER KING, JR., CIVIL RIGHTS LEADER, THEOLOGIAN, ORATOR (David Garrow ed., 1989). Baldwin observes:

> It was King's conviction that what black people have to offer this country and the world in terms of values and a world view is grounded in their experience of suffering–a fresh and genuine spirituality, humanitarian spirit, a prophetic vision of democracy, an incurable optimism, and a way of viewing humanity as a whole.

Id. at 15.

15. *See* DAVID GARROW, BEARING THE CROSS: MARTIN LUTHER KING, JR. AND THE SOUTHERN CHRISTIAN LEADERSHIP CONFERENCE 475–527 (1988).

16. For an explanation of the meaning of Black Power and SNCC's involvement with the Black Power movement, *see* Charles Hamilton, *Black Power: An Alternative*, in SEVEN ON BLACK: REFLECTIONS ON THE NEGRO EXPERIENCE IN AMERICA 134 (William G. Shade & Roy C. Hanenkohl eds.,

1969). A great deal of attention was given to the leadership of black college students, who shifted the emphasis of the movement from civil rights to individual dignity. *See* LOMAX, *supra* note 6, at 42–43 (referring to the psychological "dues" all Blacks pay for being black). For a detailed discussion of the history of the Civil Rights movement and the role of SNCC and Black college students, *see* SETH CAGIN & PHILIP DRAY, WE ARE NOT AFRAID (1988).

17. *See* Anthony E. Cook, *Reflections on Postmodernism*, 26 NEW. ENG. L. REV. 751, 766–82 (1992).

18. CLAYBORNE CARSON, IN STRUGGLE: SNCC AND THE BLACK AWAKENING OF THE 1960S (1981); HOWARD ZINN, SNCC: THE NEW ABOLITIONISTS (1965).

19. Black power was understood differently by different groups using the term. For helpful evaluations of the term, *see* STOKELY CARMICHAEL & CHARLES HAMILTON, BLACK POWER: THE POLITICS OF LIBERATION IN AMERICA (1967); EDWARD PEEKS, THE LONG STRUGGLE FOR BLACK POWER (1971); THE RHETORIC OF BLACK POWER (Robert Scott & Wayne Brockriede eds., 1969).

20. REPORT OF THE NATIONAL ADVISORY COMMISSION ON CIVIL DISORDERS (1968).

21. *Id.* at 236–50.

22. In a poll of whites who were asked what the term "Black Power" meant to them, the vast majority stated that it meant "Black rules white" while 65% of Blacks said the words meant "nothing" or "a fair share for Black people" or "racial unity." *See* Joel D. Aberbach & Jack L. Walker, *The Meanings of Black Power: A Comparison of White and Black Interpretations of a Political Slogan*, 64 AM. POL. SCI. REV. 367, 370 (1970).

For examples of the reaction to Black Power, *see* Martin Duberman, *Black Power in America*, 1968 PARTISAN REV., Winter, at 34 (contending that the dangers of Black racism in Black Power are real and not the frightened response of white liberals); Peter Feldman, *How the Cry for Black Power Began*, 13 DISSENT 472 (1966) (suggesting that those using the term Black Power were engaging in reverse racism and planned to engage in racial war).

23. *See* KING, *supra* chap. 4 note 11.

24. *See* JOHN MARTIN. THE DEEP SOUTH SAYS NEVER (1957); CARL ROWAN, GO SOUTH TO SORROW (1957); JAMES SILVER, MISSISSIPPI: THE CLOSED SOCIETY (1963); BOB SMITH, THEY CLOSED THEIR SCHOOLS: PRINCE EDWARD COUNTY, VIRGINIA, 1951–64 (1965).

25. *See* Numan Bartley, *The South and Sectionalism in American Politics*, 31 POL. 38, at 239–57 (1976) (arguing that the presence and struggles of blacks in the South have profoundly shaped Southern white identity).

26. To better understand these sensibilities, *see* CLEMENT EATON, A HISTORY OF THE SOUTHERN CONFEDERACY (1954); ESSAYS IN SOUTHERN HISTORY (Fletcher M. Green ed., 1949); I. A. NEWBY, THE SOUTH: A HISTORY (1978).

27. *See* Paul A. Beck, *Partisan Realignment in the Postwar South*, 71 AMER. POL. SCI. REV. 477 (1977) (attributing realignment to tendency of young native whites to bring partisan loyalties and racial attitudes in alignment under the national Republican banner); Bruce A. Campbell, *Patterns of Change in the Partisan Loyalties of Native Southerners: 1952–1972*, 3 J. POL. SCI. 39, at 730–61 (1977) (showing how Southern whites in the 1960s moved toward the Republican Party because that party more accurately reflected their attitudes on integration and the expanding power of the federal government in the area of race relations).

28. *See* Susan Welch & Buster Brown, *Correlates of Southern Republican Success at the Congressional District Level*, 59 SOC. SCI. Q. 732 (1979) (showing that Republican victories and other political developments in Mississippi were taking place throughout the South during the period, 1950–1976).

29. HAYNES JOHNSON, SLEEPWALKING THROUGH HISTORY: AMERICA IN THE REAGAN YEARS (1991).

30. HODGSON, *supra* note 11, at 423–24, contends:

> Nixon and Mitchell believed that . . . few average Americans would base their political choice on desire to improve their economic lot. Instead, they were betting that, for the majority of the voters, the highest priority was to save the nation from hippies and black power militants, from drug addicts and welfare mothers. . . . The Nixon administration made campaigning against those four categories of people its highest policy priority.

Chapter 8

1. *See infra* notes 2–6 and accompanying text.
2. *See generally* THOMAS JEFFERSON, NOTES ON THE STATE OF VIRGINIA (William Peden ed., 1972).
3. *Id.* at 138.
4. ABRAHAM LINCOLN, COMPLETE WORKS 457 (John G. Nicolay & John Hay eds., 1907).
5. *See, e.g.*, Washington v. Davis, 426 U.S. 229 (1976) (black applicants for positions as Washington, D.C. police officers brought suit alleging a disproportionate racial impact of the police department testing procedure); Shelley v. Kramer, 334 U.S. 1 (1948) (white homeowners sued to enforce a racially restrictive covenant prohibiting blacks from occupying homes in their neighborhood); *Brown*, 347 U.S. 483 (1954).
6. Sam McManis, *Campanis Says He Apologizes for Comments; Aaron and Dodger Players are Among Those Angered*, L.A. TIMES, Apr. 8, 1987, part 3, at 1.
7. JEROME H. SKOLNICK, THE POLITICS OF PROTEST 180 (1969).
8. "Racist effect" means that the effect of applying the institutional norm is to perpetuate an existing distribution of benefits and burdens that sustains perceptions of racial inferiority and realities of racial domination.
9. *See* Peller, *supra* chap. 7 note 9 (describing the psychodynamics of integra-

tionist philosophy); *see also* Richmond v J.A. Croson, Co., 488 U.S. 469 (1989) (race–based affirmative action plans are subject to strict scrutiny and must be necessary to achieve a compelling interest).

10. English explorers did not first land on the African west coast until after 1550. WINTHROP D. JORDAN, WHITE OVER BLACK: AMERICAN ATTITUDES TOWARD THE NEGRO, 1550– 1812, at 3 (1969). See *Id.* at 3–43, for further discussion of English exploration of Africa.

11. These differences consisted of physiological and cultural differences that related to the size of nose, lip, and texture of hair as well as forms of political, cultural and familial organizations.

12. JORDAN, *supra* note 10.

13. *Id.* at 6.

14. *Id.* at 4.

15. *Id.* at 9. Jordan explores the meaning and significance of the English encounter with Black people in greater detail:

> In England perhaps more than in southern Europe, the concept of blackness was loaded with intense meaning. Long before they found that some men were black, Englishmen found in the idea of blackness a way of expressing some of their most ingrained values. No other color except white conveyed so much emotional impact. As described by the Oxford English Dictionary, the meaning of "black" before the sixteenth century included, "Deeply stained with dirt; soiled, dirty, foul. . . . Having dark or deadly purposes, malignant; pertaining to or involving death, deadly; baneful, disastrous, sinister... Indicating disgrace, censure, liability to punishment, etc." Black was an emotionally partisan color, the handmaid and symbol of baseness and evil, a sign of danger and repulsion.

Id. at 7.

16. *Id.* at 8 (quoting ROBERT R. CAWLEY, THE VOYAGERS AND ELIZABETHAN DRAMA 86 [1938]). *See* WALTER CLYDE CURRY, THE MIDDLE ENGLISH IDEAL OF PERSONAL BEAUTY; AS FOUND IN THE METRICAL ROMANCES, CHRONICLES, AND LEGENDS OF THE XII, XIV, AND XV CENTURIES 64–67 & 310 (Baltimore 1916) (indirectly makes clear how very far African women were from matching prevalent English ideals of beautiful noses and lips).

17. *Id.* at 34.

18. *Id.* (quoting JEAN BODIN, METHOD FOR EASY COMPREHENSION OF HISTORY 103–06, 143 [Beatrice Reynolds trans., 1945]).

19. *Id.* (quoting JOHN OGILBY, AFRICA: BEING AN ACCURATE DESCRIPTION OF THE REGIONS OF AEGYPT, BARBARY, LYBIA, AND BILLEDULGERID, THE LAND OF NEGROES, GUINEE, AETHIOPIA, AND THE ABYSSINES . . . COLLECTED AND TRANSLATED FROM MOST AUTHENTICK AUTHORS, AND AUGMENTED WITH LATER OBSERVATIONS 451 [London, 1670]).

20. *Id.* (citing RICHARD JOBSON, GOLDEN TRADE: OR, A DISCOVERY OF THE RIVER GAMRRA, AND THE GOLDEN TRADE OF THE AETHIOPIANS 65–67 [Charles G. Kingsley ed., 1904]).

21. *See Id.* at 29 (citing H. W. Janson, Apes and Ape Lore in the Middle Ages and the Renaissance chap. 11 [1952]; Robert M. & Eda W. Yerkes, The Great Apes: A Study of Anthropoid Life 1–26 [1929]).
22. *Id.* at 35 (quoting William Smith, A New Voyage to Guinea . . . 146 [London, 1744]).
23. *Id.* (quoting John Barbot, *A Description of the Coasts of North and South–Guinea*, in V A Collection of Voyages and Travels 100 [John & Awsham Churchill compilers, London, 1704–32]).
24. James M. Jones, Prejudice and Racism (1972).
25. *Id.* at 150.
26. Jordan, *supra* note 10, at 11 (quoting Thomas Phillips, *A Journal of a Voyage Made in the Hannibal of London, Ann. 1693, 1694, from England to Cape Monseradoe, in Africa; and Thence Along the Coast of Guiney to Whidaw, the Island of St. Thomas, and So Forward to Barbadoes. With a Cursory Account of the Country, the People, Their Manners, Forts, Trade, etc.*, in VI A Collection of voyages and travels, *supra* note 23, at 219).
27. *Genesis* 9:21.
28. *Genesis* 9:22–23.
29. *Genesis* 9:24–25.
30. *See* Eugene Genovese, Roll Jordan Roll: The World the Slaves Made (1972) (discussing the legitimation and delegitimation function of Christianity in the era of American slavery).
31. *Genesis* 10:6–20.
32. Jordan, *supra* note 10, at 18 (quoting The Babylonian Talmud (I. Epstein et al. trans., 1935–60 (The Talmud consists of 35 vikynes)).
33. According to the Old Testament account of Genesis, when Adam and Eve disobeyed God's commandment and became aware of their nakedness and sexuality, they coverted themselves with the leaves of fig trees. *Genesis* 3:7.
34. Jordan notes that castration was a legislated punishment in many colonies, and in some, the punishment applied to both free and slave Black men.

> Castration of Negroes clearly indicated a desperate, generalized need in white men to persuade themselves that they were really masters and in all ways masterful, and it illustrated dramatically the ease with which white men slipped over into treating their Negroes like their bulls and stallions whose "spirit" could be subdued by emasculation. In some colonies, moreover, the specifically sexual aspect of castration was so obvious as to underline how much of the white man's insecurity vis–a–vis the Negro was fundamentally sexual.

Jordan, *supra* note 10, at 156.
35. *Id.* at 222.
36. Carolus Linnaeus, *Systema Naturae*, reprinted in Thomas Bendyshe, *The History of Anthropology*, in Anthropological Society of London, 1 Memoirs (1863–64).
37. Jordan, *supra* note 10, at 223.
38. *Id.*, at 220–21 (citing Linnaeus, *supra* note 36).
39. *Id.*, at 220–21.

40. *Id.* at 223 (citing to ANTHROPOLOGICAL TREATISES OF JOHANN FRIEDERICH BLUMENBACH 265–75 [Thomas Bendyshe trans. & ed., London 1865]).
41. ROBERT V. GUTHRIE, EVEN THE RAT WAS WHITE: A HISTORICAL VIEW OF PSYCHOLOGY 78 (1976) (quoting A. H. Hersh, *Eugenics, in* 10 THE ENCYCLOPEDIA AMERICANA 567 [1969]).
42. *Id.* (quoting FRANCIS GALTON, HEREDITARY GENIUS: ITS LAWS AND CONSEQUENCES [1869]).
43. *See, e.g.,* Joseph Berger, *Professors' Theories on Race Stir Turmoil at City College,* N.Y. TIMES, Apr. 20, 1990, at B1; *Milestones,* TIME, Aug. 28, 1989, at 61; *Missing Circuits,* DAILY TELEGRAPH, Aug. 24, 1989, at 17; *see also* Charlotte Allen, *Gray Matter, Black–and–White,* WASH. TIMES, Jan. 13, 1992, at 4.
44. *Id.,* at 220–21.

Chapter 9

1. STUDS TERKEL, RACE: HOW BLACKS & WHITES THINK AND FEEL ABOUT THE AMERICAN OBSESSION (New York: Doubleday, 1993).

Index

abolitionist movement, 160
abortion, women's rights to, 10
Adam and Eve, rebellion against God by,
    85, 200
affirmative action, 4, 64, 70, 155
    for African-American middle class, 220
    conservative assault on, 210–212
    definition of, 208
    progressive liberalism in debate on,
        207–230
African-Americans
    appropriation of Christian theology by,
        104
    castration of, 200, 204, 247(n34)
    cheap labor of, 216
    discrimination against, 62, 65, 66–67,
        69–71, 185, 208
    education of, 221
    Jefferson's comparison to whites, 179
    myth of inferiority of, 180, 182, 197,
        199, 216, 223
    myth of low intelligence of, 153, 182,
        189, 202
    nationalist movements of, 125, 127, 128
    physical attributes of, 179, 196–198,
        199–200, 245(n11), 246(n15)
    poverty of, 123, 153, 216, 218
    racism against.see under racism
    reaction to King trial, 174, 175
    school segregation of, 34, 44
    suggested genetic inferiority of, 202
African-American Church, 117, 135, 163,
    240(n16)
    role in slave experience, 98–110
Africans
    depiction in Old Testament accounts,
        199–200, 203
    early European contacts with, 196–198
    sexuality of, 197
    viewed as morally deficient, 102
Allen, Robert L., 3
American Democracy, egalitarian vision
    of, 3
American history, transitions in, 3
American politics, progressive vision of, 1
American Pragmatism, as variant of
    American liberalism, 19
antipoverty movements, 2, 3

antitrust laws, 49
antiwar movements, 2
Aristotle, 30, 31, 38, 39

Barth, Karl, 115
The Bell Curve (Murray), 153, 202
Beloved Community, 15, 29, 72, 75, 80, 82,
    97–110, 137–230, 144–145, 151, 154,
    157, 170, 178, 208, 212
    social conception of, 111, 117–125,
        215–222
    spiritual dimensions of, 111–116,
        212–214
    strategies for pursuit of, 111, 125–136,
        222–230
Berkeley, California, student anti-war
    protests at, 168
"best interest", of a constituency, 42
Bible
    Republican quotations from, 169
    slaves' interpretation of, 101
Bilbo, Bo, as overt racist, 178
Birmingham, Alabama, civil rights protests
    in (1963), 117, 118, 119, 167–168,
        241(n5)
"Black Consciousness", King's preference
    for term, 130, 133, 171
"Black Equality", King's preference for
    term, 130
black nationalism, 162, 217, 240(n16)
Black Power movement, 128, 163–164,
    165, 170, 171, 187, 242(n6)
    King's view of, 129, 130, 132, 133
    violent aspects of, 130–131, 132
"Black Power" slogan, 163, 165, 243(n19),
    244(n22)
blacks. *See* African-Americans
Blumenbach, Johann Friederich, 200
Bork, Robert, 63
Brown, H. Rap, 164
Brown, Henry B., 180
Brown v. Board of Education of Topeka, 34,
    36, 52, 58, 59, 60, 61, 159, 161, 170
    battle over meaning of decision in,
        61–72
Buchanan, John, 168, 169
Burke, Edmund, 42, 43
Bush, George W., 12

Manufactured by Amazon.ca
Bolton, ON

23172618R00146